Mastering
the Stock
Market

Founded in 1807, John Wiley & Sons is the oldest independent publishing company in the United States. With offices in North America, Europe, Australia, and Asia, Wiley is globally committed to developing and marketing print and electronic products and services for our customers' professional and personal knowledge and understanding.

The Wiley Trading series features books by traders who have survived the market's ever changing temperament and have prospered—some by reinventing systems, others by getting back to basics. Whether a novice trader, professional or somewhere in-between, these books will provide the advice and strategies needed to prosper today and well into the future.

For a list of available titles, visit our website at www.WileyFinance.com.

Mastering the Stock Market

High Probability Market
Timing & Stock
Selection Tools

JOHN L. PERSON

WILEY

John Wiley & Sons, Inc

Cover image: Paul McCarthy
Cover design: © iStockphoto/blackred

Published by John Wiley & Sons, Inc., Hoboken, New Jersey.

Published simultaneously in Canada.

For general information on our other products and services or for technical support, please
contact our Customer Care Department within the United States at (800) 762-2974, outside
the United States at (317) 572-3993 or fax (317) 572-4002.

Wiley publishes in a variety of print and electronic formats and by print-on-demand. Some
material included with standard print versions of this book may not be included in e-books
or in print-on-demand. If this book refers to media such as a CD or DVD that is not included
in the version you purchased, you may download this material at http://booksupport.wiley.
com. For more information about Wiley products, visit www.wiley.com.

Library of Congress Cataloging-in-Publication Data:
Person, John L.
  The master stock trader : timing techniques to profit from seasonal & sector analysis /
John L. Person.
      p. cm.
  Includes index.
  ISBN 978-1-118-34348-7 (cloth); ISBN 978-1-118-41659-4 (ebk);
  ISBN 978-1-118-43417-8 (ebk); ISBN 978-1-118-42054-6 (ebk)
  1. Stocks—Charts, diagrams, etc.   2. Investment analysis.   I. Title.
  HG4638.P474 2013
  332.63'2042—dc23
                                                            2012026739

10 9 8 7 6 5 4 3 2 1

To my loving wife Mary, my best friend and supporter.

Contents

Foreword

John Person has probably forgotten more about trading than most traders will ever learn. He has done it all in the industry—floor trader, broker, analyst, book author, and educator. Along the way, he has tested virtually every trading approach known to man. He knows what works, what doesn't, and what it takes to succeed as a trader.

I've known John for over 20 years. I've seen him after a good run in the market and seen him after he took a big hit. What I admire is his resiliency, tenacity, and his commitment to continuous learning. He is always increasing his knowledge and seeking to improve as a trader.

I think *Mastering the Stock Market* is John's best book yet. It brings together his extensive knowledge of sectors and seasonals with his deep understanding of technical analysis. It is the work of a market veteran who understands that your best bet to make money in the market is to have both technicals and fundamentals on your side.

Like John, I am optimistic that the financial and commodity markets will provide tremendous opportunities for investors in the years ahead. Technology, globalization, and entrepreneurship will drive economic growth and propel the U.S. stock market to new heights.

Many investors were chastened by the big stock market drop in 2008–2009. Four years later, a lot of these investors are still not back in the market. Instead, they may be earning just a few percentage points in bonds or CDs. That's not a recipe for growing a nest egg that will provide for a comfortable retirement or fund your children's education.

By studying the methods in *Mastering the Stock Market*, you will gain the knowledge to approach the markets with a high degree of confidence. You'll be able to identify opportunities and fine tune your entries and exits using technical analysis. You'll gain the discipline to cut your losses when a trade doesn't work and to maximize profits when everything works as planned. In short, *Mastering the Stock Market* will help you to make sound trades and build your wealth.

Jake Bernstein
Santa Cruz, California
October 2012

P.S.—I must also add that in my more than 44 years as a trader, investor, and market analyst, I have met and known many of the top people in the business. John is a "Person" who ranks at the top, top of my list in credibility, commitment, and a deep love for his work. When John talks, I LISTEN!

Introduction

I firmly believe the second decade of the new millennium will bring another wave of prosperity and a new level of educated traders and investors. I am longer-term bullish on stocks and have had that bullish outlook since the market bottomed in March of 2009.

The divergence between technology indexes such as the QQQ or the Nasdaq 100's posting a double bottom in March 2009 versus the prior low from November 2008 was one clue, and sentiment indicators such as the CFTC COT reports, volume studies, and the longer-term Person's Pivot support levels all helped me form that conclusion. Even into 2011, at PA Stock Alerts, we held steadfast to our bullish bias, and as we enter the 2012 presidential elections, I continue to remain on the longer-term buy side of the market. I will continue to do so, of course, expecting the normal corrections, or shakeouts or fadeouts, but I am more optimistic on investing in the stock market now than ever. That opinion could change if the conditions and indicators I use change as well. But let me add that the reasons why I am bullish is the advancement of technology, the globalization of markets, and, of course, the need for prosperity still thrives. With those factors in play, I am not betting against the obvious that almost every generation has seen an increase in the wealth effect.

The one concern I have is that when we start to see market performance improve, the vast majority of investors will either not participate in the market because they are disbelievers, or because they don't trust the markets due to past experience, such as the tech wreck from 2000 or the flash crash in 2010.

I also have a concern that many investors have become more short term in nature, since the extreme level of volatility that existed in our marketplace from 2005 throughout late 2011 has nurtured day and swing trading from buy-and-hold investment strategies.

I am sure you can relate to the fact that time is passing—every year seems to pass more quickly than the one before. You know the saying "time flies when you are having fun." There have been times in this life that it is not so much fun, but time still flies. Imagine buying a stock for 8.68 on the first week of March 2009, and after applying a buy-and-hold mentality, just

25 months later that stock was trading at 53.2. Not to brag, but this was a company I had shouted to everyone to get in on. I had traveled to Europe to speak at a conference in London and at the Technical Analysis Conference in Paris. I saw this company and the sales they were generating and said there is no way these guys are going to make a killing. The name of the company: Starbucks Coffee. Well, I know there are lots of success stories, such as Google, Wynn Hotels and Casinos, Apple, and the like. But here was a company whose product I actually used on a constant basis.

I believe buy-and-hold mentality for a period of time will pan out to be a stock picker's best friend in the next few years as this business cycle develops. An area of longer-term growth and opportunities will exist in the financial arena. Wealth management, real estate, energy, communication, technology, food, health care—these are all areas that will be in constant demand and as the global population grows and becomes more educated, I stand firm on the fact that there should be a place for investment dollars in these areas.

The key is choosing the right stocks, the right sectors, and the right time. I believe the chapters that follow will enlighten you to a logical approach for you to make better investment decisions.

CHAPTER 1

Stock Indexes and Sectors

For those picking up this book who have little to no experience in the markets, I'll start off by welcoming you to the world of trading and investing. One of the greatest achievements for the human mind and psyche is to identify a business opportunity and then profit by taking decisive action.

Let me start off by addressing the newcomer or novice investor. I am not going to scare you away with heavy technical stuff, at least not now because that will come later. For the advanced trader, there are quite a few golden nuggets of trading concepts packed in these pages.

I want to share with you a story about my next-door neighbors' experience. These are awesome people. The husband is retired; the wife works as a travel agent in a North Shore suburb of Chicago. As the world was facing the financial crisis back in early 2009, the wife came over to our yard while I was surveying the garden. She knew that I worked in the financial markets, but had no idea exactly what I did. In the past, she had seen me on CNBC commenting on gold or crude oil and wanted my opinion on what to do. She had a feeling that stocks were too cheap and that there might be something she should get in on. She was right; stocks were cheap in March and April 2009.

She explained that they hadn't invested in stocks since the tech wreck of 2000, but they had some money and wanted some advice. I had her come over the next week for a lesson. All we did was go over some companies and get her online to open a self-directed trading account. The online trading company at the time was Thinkorswim. Some of the stocks we started her off with were General Electric (GE), Starbucks (SBUX), and Bank of America (BAC), and then later she asked me about other names like McDonald's (MCD). I talked and she listened, and more importantly, took decisive action. I found it amusing when making comments like "here is where your stop should go." It was like I had just said something in a foreign language. But she learned. I am not saying she experienced enough success to start her own hedge fund, but she did experience success.

I wanted to start the book off with this story to show the beginner that good things can and do happen, but it takes the human mind and psyche's ability to identify an opportunity and then take decisive action.

Technology in the new millennium has given all of us a more equal playing field as far as pricing in regards to the cost of doing business, direct access to the markets by means of the Internet, and transparency by means of order execution platforms.

Many individuals exclude themselves from the markets for one reason or another. As it has been said, I believe more people plan for a family holiday than they do for their investments or financial futures. Perhaps others have a profound fear of loss and shy from making effective reasoning rationale.

Yet this is a business where it takes money to make money. There is no question about that. One has to be able to afford to lose once in a while and not let that hinder one's ability to make better educated and therefore more reasonable actions in the markets. My goal in this book is to help you to learn how to structure a formulated perspective in order to overcome all disputes that often lead to poor judgments or inaction.

Remember, the reason you are looking to trade is simple: to make money. Never forget this. Friedrich Nietzsche, the German philosopher, stated long ago, "The most fundamental form of human stupidity is forgetting what we were trying to do in the first place." Never forget that this is the bottom line, to make money. Yet many do, mostly as fear, doubt, and greed interfere with rational thinking.

In order to give you the edge, I want to take a comprehensive look at how we can use the information in this book and apply it to real-time trading. There are obviously volumes of different material we can look at, like macroeconomic effects and the business cycle. Or microeconomic events like earnings and other situations that will impact a stock or a sector and the overall market's performance. Quite frankly, we will most likely cover many of those subjects in this book.

My goal was to put together a sophisticated yet simplistic book in such an organized manner that any trader would be able to walk through the steps contained in these pages, which combine the most relevant tools we have at our disposal, to make better, lower-risk, and more profitable trades as a direct result of better educated investment decisions. I have what I consider some simple tools in a technically oriented and complex time.

In order of importance, here is my ideal checklist of noncorrelated, yet corroborating tools to use:

- Sector analysis
- Seasonal trend analysis
- Contrarian indicators
- Price patterns
- Momentum indicators
- Volume studies
- Breadth indicators
- Moving average tools
- Support and resistance

You can use fundamental analysis (study of current events), or you can take a pure technician's approach to studying the markets. I believe a trader needs to do both. The issue with fundamental analysis is that you need to receive information from the media and third parties, which can be unreliable. You can also look at the company's balance sheet, like the price-to-earnings growth rate (PEG) and the earnings per share (EPS) over multiple quarters. Most of this information is listed on your brokerage firm's trading platforms; if not, Yahoo! Finance works wonders.

The really fundamental question for traders and investors is not to seek answers to the questions of fact or finance, but rather the really deep question to seek an answer to is: What is value? What gives a stock value? When Netflix was at 304.79 back on July 13, 2011, many perceived this stock to be a good value, especially if one was long from a lower level. Fundamental news was released that they were going to charge more for their services, and that is what created a higher opening. We called it a "gap" higher open. The fundamental facts were released, and investors measured the mathematics of future earnings, but the real question that begged to be answered was: Is this stock at this point in time a good value or overvalued? As it turns out, the stock was more than overvalued, as it cratered to a low of 62.37 by November 30, just shy of four and a half months.

Were there ways to uncover the truth of whether this market was at a good or overvalued price over 300 per share? And, if so, were there avenues one could employ to take advantage of it? To be certain, there is a reasonable approach to investing that is unbiased, factual, and incorporates mathematic formulas, but best of all, uses what we all have at our disposal. It is the information provided to us in the form of prices such as the market's or stock's high, low, close, and opening levels, as well as the amount of volume traded and the volume detected in both the up and down directions. The information is what we can find in what is called technical analysis.

Technical analysis shows us what the market is or has done. Certain tools, based on past performance, give us a clue what might happen but not what will absolutely happen.

However, there are several indicators and methods we can use to effectively help us in formulating a market opinion that can improve our chances for success. There are hundreds of methods for picking stocks to buy. The key is to know when to fold. I am talking about an exit strategy. Most individual traders have a hard time taking a loss, mainly because they believe the company's stock price will turn back in their favor. More importantly, most traders don't know when to take a profit either. Thus, the phrase "cut your losses and let your winners ride" might not be a complete truth. While it is important to cut losers, it is also just as important to establish profitable exit levels. This concept of setting an exit plan is imperative for overall success in trading. A pretty good analogy on this point can be summed up by a friend of mine, who once asked, "When flying a plane, what's more important—take-off or landing?" That's a profound question, as they are both important, but once you are in the air—just like once you are in a trade—landing is like your exit strategy. You need to have a profit objective in order to land the investment plane safely. That is why the subject on profit objectives will be covered in this book.

STOCK-PICKING QUANDARY

Picking stocks from a large universe can be overwhelming. So let's look at what I consider a systematic approach for picking stocks to trade. Rarely does one look at one method in what I call the top-down approach. Let's look at the Standard & Poor's (S&P) 500. It is compiled of 10 sectors. Jeffrey Hirsch, my co-editor in the *Commodity Trader's Almanac*, along with his father Yale, put together a seasonal guide from a study done long ago by Merrill Lynch. Yet I believe most traders are not aware of this, or at the least, it is most often ignored.

Many of the reasons we see seasonal strength or weakness in markets are very logical. We will we cover many of these reasons when we delve into seasonal analysis in the next chapter.

Many individual retail investors and traders start off their careers by looking at stocks that are brought to their attention by either the company they work for or by some means of communication, either in an e-mail or the news media—print, online, cable TV, and so on—or, the best way of all, a hot tip from a family member or friend.

Others who are invested in the stock market indirectly, either in a 401(k) or through mutual funds, rely on the professionals who run those funds. The fund manager's sole responsibility is to beat the benchmark, what is considered the S&P 500 Index. Here is the listing of these sectors:

1. Consumer Discretionary
2. Consumer Staples
3. Energy
4. Financials
5. Health Care
6. Industrials
7. Materials
8. Technology
9. Telecom Services
10. Utilities

The iShares U.S. sector and exchange-traded fund symbols are:

1. Technology (IYW)
2. Consumer Goods (IYK)
3. Consumer Services (IYC)
4. Energy (IYE)
5. Health Care (IYH)
6. Financial (IYF)
7. Industrial (IYJ)
8. Basic Materials (IYM)
9. Utilities (IDU)
10. Telecommunications (IYZ)

Next, there are the subsectors and then the stocks listed in those subsectors we can look at for investing and trading opportunities.

First, let's examine the Energy sector as a whole, not the actual commodities like Brent Crude Oil or West Texas Intermediate. I will cover these, including natural gas, in the next chapter.

We can break down this space into:

a. Oil & Gas Exploration & Production
b. Oil & Gas Storage & Transportation
c. Oil & Gas Equipment & Services
d. Oil & Gas Refining & Marketing
e. Oil & Gas Drilling

EXCHANGE-TRADED FUNDS

In this section, we will cover the exchange-traded fund (ETF), including inverse ETFs, leveraged ETFs, and inverse leveraged ETFs. We will also cover the features, benefits, and risks of trading leveraged ETFs, good risk-to-reward opportunities, and a comparative market analysis that dissects a leveraged ETF and a sector ETF strategy.

ETFs are investment instruments that have their own symbol and are traded on stock exchanges. An ETF includes assets such as stocks, commodities, and futures. The easiest way to understand an ETF is to think of it as a mix between a mutual fund and a group of stocks in the same industry sector or futures contract . ETFs trade on an exchange just like an equity or futures contract, but contain bundles of the underlying asset like a mutual fund. Investors and traders are attracted to ETFs primarily because they have the ability to diversify risk like a mutual fund but have the flexibility of equities and contracts, which can be traded throughout the day and can be sold short. Since ETFs trade like stocks, a commission rate will apply just like a stock trade. Prices on an ETF change throughout the day as they are bought and sold, just like a stock. ETFs typically have lower marketing, distribution, and accounting expenses, and most ETFs do not have 12b-1 fees.

Investors look to ETFs to provide easy diversification, low expense ratios, and tax efficiency, while still maintaining all the features of ordinary stock, such as limit orders, short-selling, and options. ETFs are very versatile and can be included in an investment portfolio or trading plan as a long-term investment for asset allocation purposes, or to trade frequently to implement market timing investment strategies. The advantages of investing or trading in ETFs are:

- *Lower costs.* ETFs generally have lower costs than other investment products because most ETFs have lower management fees due to the fact that they are passively managed versus an index mutual fund or an active mutual fund that incurs higher fees due to increased trading and research expenses.
- *Buying and selling flexibility.* ETFs can be bought and sold at current market prices at any time during the trading day, unlike mutual funds and unit investment trusts, which can only be traded at the end of the trading day. As publicly traded securities, their shares can be purchased on margin and sold short (enabling the use of hedging strategies) and traded using stop orders and limit orders, which allow investors to specify the price points at which they are willing to trade.
- *Tax efficiency.* In most cases, ETFs generate relatively low capital gains because they typically have low turnover of portfolio securities.

While this is an advantage they share with other index funds, their tax efficiency is further enhanced because they do not have to sell securities to meet investor redemptions.

- *Market exposure and diversification.* ETFs provide an economical way to rebalance portfolio allocations. ETFs are designed to track the underlying assets, which may contain hundreds or even thousands of securities. This offers the trader or investor the diversification of an index mutual fund with the trading flexibility of a stock. ETFs offer exposure to a diverse variety of markets, including broad-based indices, international and country-specific indices, industry sector-specific indices, bond indices, and commodities.
- *Transparency.* Most investment vehicles provide quarterly disclosure of their holdings. ETFs, whether index funds or actively managed, publish their exact holdings on a daily basis (transparent portfolios) and are priced at frequent intervals throughout the trading day. Investors are able to see exactly what is included in the ETF, from fees to the basket of assets.

There are many types of ETFs, ranging from stock indices like the S&P 500 (SPY) to commodities that relate to precious metals like gold (GLD), energies such as crude oil (USO), and agricultural markets like grains (DBA) and livestock (COW). In addition, there are ETFs that correlate to the financial markets such as bonds (TLT), and those that reflect changes in the yield (TBT). In December 2005, Rydex launched currency ETFs, with the first being FXE, which tracks the euro currency.

Inverse ETFs

Inverse ETFs are structured to perform in the opposite direction of the underlying or benchmark asset. These funds short-sell derivatives and other leveraged investments as the basis for the inverse relationship. Over a short time frame, the inverse ETF should provide performance, which is opposite the benchmark vehicle. For example, if the established benchmark is the S&P 500, the inverse ETF should move in the opposite direction by a similar amount. If the S&P 500 declines by 1 percent, the inverse ETF should rise by 1 percent (not including fees and costs). Because short-selling stocks is extremely risky, inverse ETFs can provide trade opportunities for stock traders in bearish market conditions, since bear ETFs should rise during a declining market.

Leveraged ETFs

Leveraged ETFs are designed to take advantage of short-term market swings by using debt to amplify the returns of the underlying asset.

The goal of the ETF fund manager is to maintain the debt ratio at 2:1 or 3:1 depending on the fund. In the case of a 2:1 debt ratio, the ETF is matched with twice the amount of debt to investor capital, while a 3:1 debt ratio is matched with three times the amount of debt to investor capital. With this leverage, the ETF is expected to gain a return of 200 percent or two times (2×), or 300 percent or three times (3×) the average return of an underlying index or other benchmark over a specific period of time. For example, if the S&P 500 goes up 2 percent, a 2× S&P 500 ETF is expected to return 4 percent.

Leverage is two-sided. While leverage applied to a winning trade compounds the size of the return, leverage applied to a losing trade compounds the size of the loss. If a trader wishes to profit from uptrends in an index, sector, commodity, or currency move with less cash outlay than traditional ETFs, they will take advantage of the increased compounding effect that is found with leveraged ETFs. The opposite is also true. If the market moves against the direction of the fund, the losses will be compounded as well.

Another important consideration in trading leveraged ETFs is to understand that fund managers work to maintain the leverage balance and produce returns over one trading day. If the fund is out of balance, the manager will incur trading losses because they need to keep the debt ratio intact. This means that in a bear fund, they must buy when the index goes up and sell when the index goes down in order to maintain a fixed leverage ratio. For example, if an ETF is a −2× bear fund, a 2.5 percent daily change in the index will reduce the value by about 0.18 percent per day, which means that about a third of the fund may be wasted in trading losses within a year ($0.9982^{252} = 0.63$).

Inverse Leveraged ETFs

When a trader wishes to trade the inverse, or opposite, of the daily performance of the benchmark asset in a single day and wishes to use leverage, he or she would look to trade an inverse leveraged ETF. Using a combination of leverage and the inverse relationship to the benchmark, the inverse leveraged ETF will seek a return of −2× (−200 percent), positioning itself in the opposite direction of the benchmark.

Detailed information regarding leveraged ETFs can be found at the following web sites:

ProShares: www.ProShares.com
Direxion Funds: www.direxionfunds.com
Rydex-SGI: www.rydex-sgi.com
Deutsche Bank: www.dbfunds.db.com

Following are some of the most well-known ETFs, as well as specific examples of several ETFs and their application:

- *SPY ETF.* One of the first ETFs developed was SPY. Known as the SPDR, the benchmark is the S&P 500.
- *QQQ ETF.* Known as the "Q's," this ETF uses the Nasdaq 100 as the benchmark. In 2011, the name was changed from QQQQ.
- *DIA.* Dow "Diamonds" uses the Dow Jones Industrial Index as the benchmark.
- *XLF.* The financial select sector SPDR is produced to match the returns of the financial select sector.
- *SSO.* The SSO is a leveraged ETF that uses the S&P 500 as the benchmark and seeks investment results of 200 percent utilizing leverage of 2:1.

The SPY ETF is a product that could provide a good trading vehicle for a trader that is looking at an investment option that provides good liquidity and volume and does not wish to utilize more leveraged products such as futures.

One of the most important disclaimers or warnings on a leveraged ETF is to advise you to do your due diligence, as these instruments employ constant leveraging and compounding, which can skew the average returns. Make certain you clearly understand how this investment vehicle works before entering a trade.

If we use a chart on the ETF index XLE that represents the energy complex, based on past historic price data we can draw a seasonal chart, which I have included in the lower quadrant of the graph as shown in Figure 1.1. You will see that the seasonal trend history shows the typical annual high is established in the May through June time frame. The market then typically bottoms in October, with a strong move upward starting in early February. With this chart one can conclude that by buying in late October and holding through late May, one may capture the best upside trend of the year for this sector.

Now let's look at the subsector Refining & Marketing as shown in Figure 1.2 from 2011. Notice that the seasonal peak was around late April and bottomed in early October. This is a very similar pattern to the overall sector as shown in Figure 1.1 with the XLE.

Now let's look a bit further and dissect this energy sector to examine one of the companies listed under that subsector. I started with Sunoco (SUN), as shown in Figure 1.3. The seasonal chart on this stock itself resembles the seasonal chart on the subsector it is listed under and as was just explained the seasonal price movement of that sector formed a peak in May and bottomed in October. Now we can conclude not only is it highly

FIGURE 1.1   XLE: Energy Select Sector SPDR Fund (Weekly Bars)

correlated to the subsector and the subsector, but Sunoco is highly correlated to the Energy complex itself as represented by the XLE. Armed with that information, one can now start looking for buying opportunities in October and start looking for a profit target by the late April through early May time frame.

Let's examine another sector, Telecommunication or Telecoms. In the chart in Figure 1.4, the seasonal study shows where we typically have a strong buying opportunity from late August through early October that can last into the first part of January. Once we scan and look for the top stocks in that space, we can then apply a seasonal study to if the individual stock has a similar seasonal price pattern compared to the sector itself.

Now let's look at one component in this sector, Verizon (VZ), as shown in Figure 1.5. Notice that a seasonal low is established in the July time period and then makes an annual low in early October. We then see a peak or deceleration in price gains by mid-January. Not every year is created equally, meaning we cannot expect the same performance year after year.

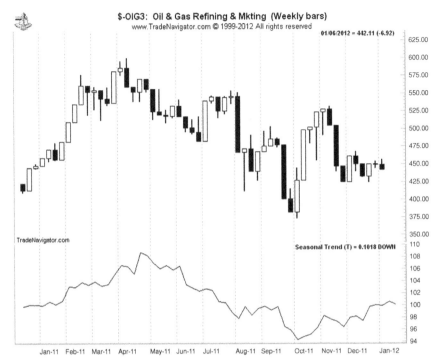

FIGURE 1.2 $-OLG3: Oil & Gas Refining & Marketing (Weekly Bars)
www.TradeNavigator.com © 1999–2012. All rights reserved.

Some years, as we experienced in 2010, will see magnified moves and others, like 2011, will have a muted or less price appreciation than in prior or past years. The point is, we have a method for setting up selected stocks during certain times of the year.

Now let's examine one more sector, the Pharmaceuticals, as shown in Figure 1.6 represented by DRG. Notice that it, too, sees a seasonal low in July that lasts through until January. Then it makes a seasonal decline and starts the bullish cycle again from early March through May. Since 2009, as the chart shows, there have been five cycle periods of seasonal and annual lows, so this trade has worked four times for an 80 percent win for this small sample back-testing period. As the chart reveals, we have made a progression of higher peaks and higher lows almost like a rising staircase. This leads to another interesting concept: nothing moves up in a straight line. Now, armed with this idea that if this sector, which is comprised of specific drug companies, moves up and down with considerable consistency, then I can surmise one of two things. Pay attention to buy a stock that is contained in this sector when it is near the seasonal low and look to take

FIGURE 1.3 SUN: Sunoco, Inc. (Weekly Bars)
www.TradeNavigator.com © 1999–2012. All rights reserved.

a profit no matter how big or small when the seasonal highs are due. This way you can rotate your working capital in and out of the market when the timing is right. Famed trader Jesse Livermore was quoted as saying, "It isn't as important to buy as cheap as possible as it is to buy at the right time." So, timing must be important.

What determined this timing was simply the historical study of past price action applied to a mathematical ratio calculation. Once again, the overall price action is dictated by value from supply-and-demand functions every single year. Oh, the wisdom gained from learning history! Another famous piece of wisdom to live by in this industry is to learn from history or be doomed to repeat it.

Now let's take this simple top-down approach again and look at one drug company, Bristol-Meyers Squibb (BMY; see Figure 1.7). It's a very popular and heavily-traded company. On an individual traded basis, this stock looks like it has had a much healthier price gain than the overall sector it is in. But comparing an apple to an apple here buying at or near the seasonal low, which occurs in July and lasts through until January, see how you have

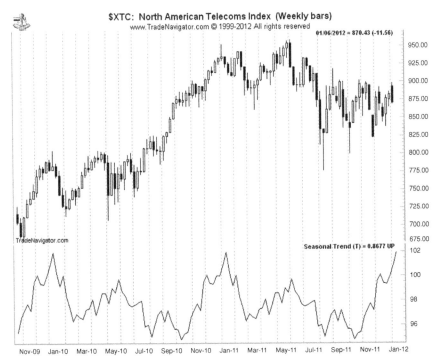

FIGURE 1.4 $XTC North American Telecoms Index (Weekly bars)
www.TradeNavigator.com © 1999–2012. All rights reserved.

been able to pick the right stock and time the market direction for a profitable move consistently?

By just looking at specific stocks in specific sectors year after year, one can capture an edge and literally keeping the number one fundamental idea of trading engrained in your thinking, which is making money for yourself.

There are many styles and numerous ways to invest or trade and pick stocks; in fact, we have more stock indexes such as the Dow Jones Industrial Average, which is compiled of 30 large-capitalized stocks, all of which are in the S&P 500. Next we have the Technology weighted sector, the Nasdaq, and the Nasdaq 100. Then the Russell 2000, which represents the small-capitalized stocks in that sector. And don't forget about the Transportation and Utility sectors. Next, we can look at the world of ETFs, of which we now have a whole universe to explore, including inverse as well as leveraged ETFs. Then, we can look at specific commodity-based stocks and commodity futures. As you can see, picking stocks from this wide variety of market indexes can be exhausting and can create an extensive workload if you are not a specialist or veteran analyst. So how do we look

FIGURE 1.5 VZ: Verizon Communications Inc. (Weekly Bars)
www.TradeNavigator.com © 1999–2012. All rights reserved.

for opportunities as to where and when we should look at specific sectors and stocks in those sectors? That's what we are here to do—learn what form of market and the best possible combinations of confirming technical analysis tools can give us a higher degree of probable success. After all, if we can determine a market or stock's direction, the next phase is to determine an entry level, a risk or loss amount we are willing to lay out, and then an exit strategy or profit objective. So, figuring out and determining market direction or value is paramount to making money, and that is our fundamental idea.

THE OPTIONS MARKET

For those readers who are veteran traders, it would not be fair for me not to mention the "O" word: options. The options market is another derivative product where one can optimize strategies to protect a stock position as

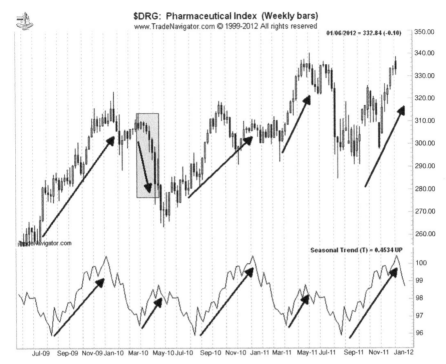

FIGURE 1.6 $DRG: Pharmaceutical Index (Weekly Bars)
www.TradeNavigator.com © 1999–2012. All rights reserved.

well as simply implement a stock replacement strategy. To start with, you may see a risk disclosure stating, "Using options is risky"; no doubt it is a true statement. However, buying Google (GOOG) before earnings, or Netflicks back in July 2012, or tens of thousands of other long stock purchase examples was even more risky.

I believe options have been given a bad rap due to the lack of ability for the masses to time entries. It is a terrible feeling to be correct on your investment idea but lose money because you were wrong on the timing.

Many investors will never use options to implement their investment ideas simply for this reason. Investors have an outlook on "value," as we have discussed, meaning they buy a company because they believe that the company's share price can move higher in time. What can happen is that they are right, but find out only after their option has expired, meaning the stock price moved up after their option expired worthless or slightly in the money, which would leave them without a profit. Then, at that point in time, they are at the same decision point as in the first place, which was whether to buy another option or get long the stock.

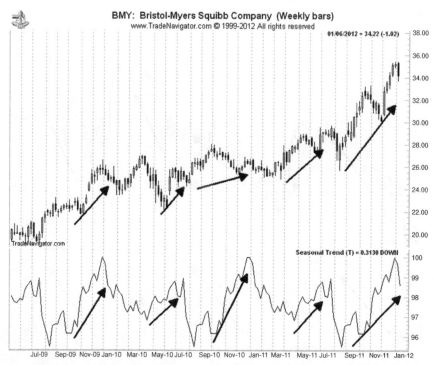

FIGURE 1.7 BMY: Bristol-Myers Squibb Company (Weekly bars)
www.TradeNavigator.com © 1999–2012. All rights reserved.

So what about options around earnings season? This is a more useful concept because the timing is known, meaning the earnings report date is a known event that will generally prompt a market reaction. Using options for a short-term trade makes sense in this aspect. One reason is that many times, one can put down little money and see a 3, 4, 5, or even a 10 percent move in the underlying stock overnight. In this instance, investors can utilize weekly options and not pay as much premium due to a longer maturity dated option such as the monthly or quarterly expiration.

So whether you want to trade a stock into earnings or protect your capital on a long stock that will be exposed to an earnings event, options strategies are a smart choice for traders and investors in the new millennium.

Take a look at Figure 1.8, the daily chart on Google before earnings that came out after the closing bell on January 19, 2012. The market fell 8.25 percent on the opening the next day. If an investor who was long this company had the knowledge to use options, then he or she would have been

FIGURE 1.8 GOOG: Google Inc. (Daily Bars)

www.TradeNavigator.com © 1999–2012. All rights reserved.

able to buy a put option for protection. To take it one step further, one would not need to buy much in a far-out time value as the earnings event was known. The trader would simply be looking for protection with limited outlay of capital. So, in this case, buying a weekly option would have done the trick.

Now let's explore this a bit further. No doubt this is what we would consider (if long) a very ugly opening, correct? It would almost serve you better to get a root canal—you might have more fun, and it would most likely be cheaper. But what about a trader who was bearish and had some good, solid technical analysis that may have indicated a market decline? What about the trader who didn't have $64,357 to sell this company short— that's right, sell short first and buy back later. It's a trader's right to do so. In this situation, put options or a bearish option strategy would have been a great day indeed.

Here are the tools that we will cover in this book that actually helped give an indication that Google was, in fact, in a bearish market condition. These are just a few techniques and technical analysis indicators that I will spell out for you in detail in order for you to help determine a stock, a commodity, or ETF's value. With that information, you will be able to aptly make better informed trading decisions. Remember what Nietzsche said: "The most fundamental form of human stupidity is forgetting what we were trying to do in the first place." As traders, we are here to make money.

I know from past experience that many readers will pick up a book, read the first chapter, and skim through the rest to find what appeals to them, especially books on trading. At the Traders Expo New York back in 2007, after I completed a workshop, a man approached me in front of a small audience wanting to ask questions, and stated that the material I went over was not in my book that he read twice over, cover to cover. The subject, incidentally, was the basis of Person's Pivot Indicator and the moving average formula used to filter the support and resistance targets. I said, "Really?" I mean, I wrote the book and I knew it was in there at least three times, so I pulled out a copy of the book, *Candlestick and Pivot Point Trading Triggers*, and said, "It's in Chapter 5, on page 135; again in Chapter 6, on pages 161, 170, and 175; and in Chapter 11, on page 284." His response was priceless. In front of 40 or so people, he said, "Oh, perhaps I should read your book again." The crowd laughed and he went on his way. So, believe me, I know some will not make it through the entire book. But I beg you to try. The methods have and, I believe, will continue to stand the test of time. But for those who will flip through these pages like a leaf in a windstorm, here is a small sampling of what will be covered in coming chapters. Examine Figure 1.9. This is a weekly chart; the very peak was formed by a bearish candle formation called a shooting star. In addition, overlaid on top of the price chart are the monthly "Person's Pivots" price targets projecting the January high right near where the actual high was created. Next, and just as important, we have an old indicator least used by the masses, the on-balance volume indicator, created by financial writer and speaker Joe Granville. Notice on the chart at point A where prices made the high, at point B the on-balance volume indicator made a lower high from the first major price peak from July. This condition is called bearish divergence. Simply stated, this means that the price of the stock rallied on weaker volume.

WHY USE SEASONAL ANALYSIS?

Here is one more bit of information that was missing from the last two charts that really sealed the deal that this market may move lower. We talked about seasonal analysis at the beginning of the chapter. Aren't you the least bit curious what typically happens to Google at this time of the

FIGURE 1.9   GOOG: Google Inc. (Weekly Bars)

www.TradeNavigator.com © 1999–2012. All rights reserved.

year? Figure 1.10 is the same daily chart, but this time with the seasonal trend study in the lower quadrant. Typically, Google peaks on or around January 4 and continues its decline into the first week of March. So, once again in order of importance, check the seasonal trend of the market on a sector or an individual stock, look what candle price patterns are showing, then look to see if the market is overvalued or trading near a resistance level, and look at the volume analysis to help confirm the market condition, either bullish or bearish. Once that is done, formulate a game plan, and then take action. As with any trade, if the risk does not look like it's worth the reward, take a pass on the trade. However, during earnings season on individual stocks, this is a great methodology for short-term traders looking to capitalize on a directional option strategy.

Okay, if I can teach you to look for a particular candlestick pattern at a Pivot Point resistance level using other indicators like seasonal analysis to help give confirmation of a weakened uptrend, then you will have a great start on making better trading decisions. Fair warning: The steps, indicators, tactics, and real trade examples that will be covered in this book all

FIGURE 1.10 GOOG: Google Inc. (Daily Bars)

www.TradeNavigator.com © 1999–2012. All rights reserved.

have one thing in common: each outcome is different. That's right, we will never know what the exact outcome will be in the future. Just like with Google, who knew the market would trade 8 percent lower? Most were willing to take 3 percent; that's my point—it is up to us to make logical and systematical decisions based on a series of defined rules and a great set of criteria and then act on them. If the trade has merit, then we will be rewarded.

CHAPTER 2

Seasonal Analysis

I n the previous chapter, we scratched the surface on what is called a top-down approach. This entails identifying opportunities in the overall stock market as either represented by the trends made in the Standard & Poor's (S&P) 500, the Russell 2000, the Nasdaq 100, or the Dow Jones Industrial Average, breaking it down into the subsectors, and then looking at the individual stocks and these companies' competitors listed in those subsectors.

If you ever wondered what stocks perform during which months or wanted to know why Wall Street professionals switch money around, which is referred to as "asset reallocation" or sector rotation, then this chapter may answer those questions. In the following pages, I will show you how to start planning what stocks to buy and when to start looking at trading opportunities in each of the top sectors in the S&P 500—as well as specific commodity and currency markets—by using seasonal analysis. Included will be the charts and graphs of the seasonal trends, plus a performance table showing the percentage of returns for each of the top 10 sectors in the S&P 500 during their respective seasonally strong periods.

So what is seasonal analysis? From a technician's point of view, it is the study of past price action averaged over the course of time. This gives us an idea of what the price trend is during the year from a historic price perspective.

Creating your own seasonal analysis is not complicated. To create it, you simply need to acquire the data and enter them into a spreadsheet. If you are looking at weekly prices, you input the prices for each week, average the prices for that time period, and then tabulate the results. However, prices increase over time, such as a stock like Apple (AAPL) that in 2002 traded under $7 per share. When you input the stock price from February 2012 at $495 per share, the 10-year study might be skewed. Therefore, the more accepted and viable method is to look at percentage changes.

There are many software programs that calculate the seasonal trend using percentage changes. In the following chapter, the charts I provide are from Genesis software. Their definition for the seasonal trend indicator is: the average price move for every Nth day/week of the year over the data history (futures use Close – Close.1, stocks and indices use Close/Close.1). We take the closing price and display it on the chart as a line, which accumulates the average price moves.

A few words of warning when using seasonal analysis—one needs to take into account that not all years are created equally. Generally speaking, in periods of economic expansive times, we might see prices in a seasonally strong period undertake a more magnified move, and in periods of economic contraction or recessions, prices have a tendency of experiencing muted moves. A few key points to consider are:

Pros
- Guides traders to typical changes in price direction.
- Enables traders to give better price forecasting models.
- Aids in establishing leverage and risk and reward targets.
- All traders can benefit.

Cons
- Does not give exact time and price of each move.
- Not reliable to anticipate supply/demand imbalances.
- Simplicity of this tool enables the user to forget using confirming indicators.
- Traders will typically abandon this analysis the first year it fails to work.

Keep in mind the number one lesson learned from Economics 101 is that price is dictated by supply and demand. It is a fact that, throughout the course of history, supply-and-demand changes have occurred. Thanks in part to technology and innovations in industry, we no longer travel by wagon trains pulled by the trusty steed, but have evolved into traveling in cars fueled by gasoline, and now by liquid natural gas, battery, and electricity. Look at specific products like a camera, once a mighty product. Kodak, one of the original bellwether stocks, filed bankruptcy in early 2012. Technology changes to digital cameras and smartphones, like the Apple iPhone, allow users to take a photo, print it from a home computer, or simply upload it to a web site or social media site such as Facebook. As Kodak was unable to compete or shift products (supply) according to consumer demands, there was only one avenue of resolution: bankruptcy.

So, we need to have an understanding of what a company does in order to measure the supply-and-demand functions. In a competitive business world, and a world of constantly changing technologies and innovations, plus changes in government rules and regulations, this can be difficult over a long period of time.

However, basic human functions will never change. We sleep, eat, and pay taxes; we spend on products; and what is left over we save. Moreover, we do have repetitive cycles in two real basic events—weather and political elections—don't we? There are specific patterns of consumer buying habits, for example, the holiday shopping season. In winter, more people tend to catch a cold, not to mention "flu season." You may have experienced or perhaps you will experience it, but in August there tends to be a heightened volume in travelers, either from last-minute summer vacations or young adults making the annual exodus from parents homes to college. Now think here for a minute. If a majority or large part of the global population is getting ready to travel nearly at the same time, one would assume that fuel may be in higher demand and that this event may cause a spike in prices. As an investor or trader, I would be looking for the opportunity to be a buyer in gasoline or refinery stocks before demand picks up in order to get in at lower prices.

That is a very interesting thought! What about the department store sector? Take, for example, Nordstrom (JWN), Macy's (M), JCPenney (JCP), or Kohl's (KSS). Traders know that studious young adults will be returning to college and that all children will be returning to elementary and high school. Is it not customary for retail apparel stores to launch a "back to school sale" event?

So, if you were watching a basket of stocks in the retail store sector and saw that share prices were moving up in the summer, you might want to check to see if there is indeed a seasonal trend for that sector during that time period. Then you would ask yourself what events take place that might create a demand for clothes, shoes, and accessories during that time of year.

There are, in fact, seasonal events that occur in the spring—such as graduations and weddings—right? Therefore, there are approximately three big events during that time of year that may affect demand in the retail apparel sector. These events generally drive consumers to purchase clothes, accessories like belts and ties, or shoes. As an investor or trader, I would be looking for the opportunity to be a buyer in retail apparel stocks during this time since there is a forced event that increases demand for these goods. But with so many choices and a fierce competitive business environment, how is one to choose the right company or stock?

That's where a trader might find the advantages of exchange-traded funds (ETFs). Choosing this kind of product will allow an investor to select the right sector of performance, rather than pinpoint it down to an individual stock. As we discussed in Chapter 1, the benefits of trading ETFs compared to a mutual fund are enormous. Some of the main benefits of the funds are that they allow diversification through more effective transaction costs, there is pricing transparency, and they are tax efficient. After all, it is almost impossible for an individual trader with limited trading resources to effectively track and trade every stock in all sectors of the market.

The advantage here is that the trader can mix the benefits of applying technical analysis and fundamental analysis to a combined hybrid of stock and index trading. Instead of agonizing over which stock will outperform in a certain sector, an ETF is an investment vehicle that has certain stocks in a basket as one unit, listed as a sector fund.

This allows individual investors to invest in a group of stocks in a sector, rather than rely on a mutual fund to do it for you. Moreover, many mutual funds charge management fees, and at times do not fully invest all your cash in the market. Because ETFs trade like a stock whose price fluctuates daily, an ETF does not have its net asset value (NAV) calculated every day like a mutual fund. By owning an ETF, you get the diversification of an index fund as well as the ability to sell short, buy on margin, and purchase as little as one share.

Another advantage is that the expense ratios for most ETFs are lower than the average mutual fund. When buying and selling ETFs, you have to pay the same commission to your broker that you'd pay on any regular order. ETFs allow you to sell without the uptick rule, so you can short right away even after the market is in a strong downtrend. You do not have to wait until the close-of-the-day settlement price as with a mutual fund. Another benefit is the avoidance of tax consequences because of the potential shielding from capital gains, thanks to the fact that ETFs do not change holdings or actively trade in the underlying stock like an actively managed mutual fund does. So purchasing shares of ETFs is a viable alternative to investing in mutual funds for individual investors. Keep in mind that many of the ETFs available today have access to trading options around the ETF. Therefore, one can develop a simple or more complex hedge or spreading strategy tied around an ETF. There are some negatives such as the three-day settlement restriction and you have a bid/ask spread just like any other market, but the benefits certainly outweigh the negatives, especially for longer-term swing and position traders.

PONDERING THE PERKS

It is estimated that, on average, mutual funds charge approximately 1.34 percent in annual fees, according to mutual fund tracking company Morningstar. That compares to ETFs averaging around 0.59 percent. One consideration is that a mutual fund manager may actually trade throughout the year, which can expose you to taxable capital gains distributions, even if you buy and hold the mutual fund and the fund does nothing. When trading the ETF, your tax bill is delayed until you sell the instrument. ETFs that have been around for a while have transparency, just like a stock, whereas mutual funds do not. We can see the open, the high, the low, and the closing price for an ETF, but that is not the case with a mutual fund. Mutual fund holdings' values are reported at the close of the day, week, and quarter, and most of the holdings are typically not revealed until the end of the month or on a quarterly basis.

One more perk that ETFs offer traders is the ability to apply seasonal analysis due to this transparency of prices. After all, it is almost impossible for an individual trader with limited trading resources to effectively track and trade every stock in all sectors of the market. ETFs can help solve this problem.

Trader's Tip

When using seasonal analysis for stocks, first take a look at the sector as a whole, and look at an older, more established sector that has a longer trading price history. Then look at the top holdings of that sector to see if the stock you want to trade is contained in that sector. If it is, then it has a high probability that it will have a strong correlation to the ETF that you are tracking. Just to be sure, you can also do a seasonal study on the individual stock.

In the upper section of Figure 2.1, we have a weekly candle chart of the exchange-traded fund XRT going back to October 2009. In the lower quadrant is the seasonal trend. With the exception of 2010 during the weak period from September through November, as marked in the gray shaded box, the price trend adhered to the longer-term seasonal trend for this sector. But here is the important aspect: Notice that there is a minor low that starts in July and lasts through September, and then we see that the annual low point or bottom of this sector begins in November and moves up through April. That's the key right there. If you have this information now, what you need to do is look for stocks within that sector that are moving in tandem or conjunction with the overall trend of the sector as a whole.

As of January 2012, the top 10 stocks in this sector were Winn-Dixie (WINN), SuperValu (SVU), CVS Caremark (CVS), Ruddick Corp. (RDK),

FIGURE 2.1   XRT: SPDR S&P Retail ETF (Weekly Bars)

www.TradeNavigator.com © 1999–2012. All rights reserved.

Urban Outfitters (URBN), Casey's General Stores (CASY), JCPenney (JCP), GNC Holdings (GNC), PetSmart Inc. (PETM), and PriceSmart, Inc. (PSMT). For male readers, if you are or were married, you have likely been shopping at the malls and know who J.C. Penney is. You should also know that Macy's (M) is a competitor, as are Nordstrom and Bloomingdale's. You will notice that Macy's stock price moves in tandem or mirrors the S&P's retail exchange-traded fund (XRT). It should, because Macy's is a direct competitor of one of the companies that is a top 10 holder in that sector.

I find the top-down analysis approach a more reliable technique because when the sector is moving up it shows there is money flowing toward these stocks as a whole. Let's say you notice an individual stock moving up; this could be due to a special announcement that is limited and specific to that individual company, which means the price of the stock may have already priced in this event. It might be "after the fact" information. However, if you look at the retail sector (XRT) and see that this index, which is composed of a group of stocks, is moving up in tandem with an individual stock, then you may be looking at a buying surge in the sector as a whole rather than a company-specific news event. This is a strong confirmation that money is being committed to this space, which can mean a higher probability that you will make money. Technicians and analysts have been using this technique for years. Most trading firms illustrate industry groups or sectors as "heat maps." Even financial television networks like CNBC show where the percentage gains or losses are in the top S&P sectors, as do Bloomberg and Fox.

This is one of the methods I use for trading opportunities throughout the year. In fact, this is a trade that was taken for the past few years. Examine the chart in Figure 2.2; it is a weekly chart for Macy's. This company's stock price has seen a continuous trend higher, and, of course, it has had its share of pullbacks along the way. Just focus on the moves from late September through May for each of the last three years. Notice that the more aggressive price appreciations or upswings have occurred in this time frame. This is one company with which we did very nicely back in 2010, and again in 2011, simply by using seasonal analysis in conjunction with other criteria, which I cover in the next few chapters. The later entry on this stock was at 26.34 on September 30, 2011; our initial exit stop loss was 23.62, with the initial profit target of 29.50.

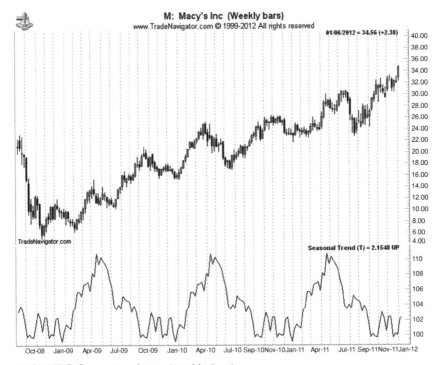

FIGURE 2.2 M: Macy's Inc. (Weekly Bars)

www.TradeNavigator.com © 1999–2012. All rights reserved.

Many traders will not think too much of this trade, as it's not a high-flying or sexy stock like Google or Apple, but it is sexy in its predictability and the fact it has a low risk profile. That is what matters most to me, and it should for you as well. This was a short-term trade that lasted several weeks. In hindsight, I look back and say I wish I had held on to that one just a bit longer, but that's a good problem to have, and I want you have those same problems. Besides, this stock demonstrates a strong seasonal tendency to give buying opportunities consistently year after year. I know I will be looking at it again in 2012 and beyond. Let's call it the back-to-school trade.

We will look at the various sectors, but also keep in mind that the mantra "Sell in May and go away" refers to the best time to be in the overall market is from October through May. With that said, if money flows and transactions are increasing in this period, then the brokerage stocks should be performing, as more traders are, well, trading. Even as commission charges are the lowest in history, they still profit from more transaction. In addition, if the overall stock market is in a bull phase, this group tends to make more profits. There is usually more trading activity and certainly more initial public offering in prosperous trading times. Furthermore, brokerage firms lend money to those traders using margin, as well as financing short-sellers who need to borrow the shares they are selling short to buy back at a later date. This is done when one expects the stock to move lower. The bottom line is that this business activity translates to more profits from revenue generated from commissions and underwriting fees for the brokerage firm.

Another obvious seasonal event is the cold and flu season. When would you be looking to stock up on cold and flu medicines or flu shots: after you get sick or before? If you are like me, it's usually during the peak of the cold or flu season, so one might draw a conclusion that buying drug stocks could be a reasonable trade idea. There are more considerations to take into account before implementing a buy program for stocks in this sector. As a trader, I would look into what each specific drug company specializes in. If you decide to buy Nyquil nighttime cough syrup, you will find it is manufactured by Procter & Gamble.

Pure pharmaceutical companies like Merck (MRK) and Pfizer (PFE), as well as others, have medicines that treat diseases of an aging population such as Alzheimer's disease and arthritis. These companies also develop medicines in areas like cardiovascular and metabolic diseases, immunology, neuroscience and pain, and oncology, plus vaccines both for humans and animals.

In a situation where you are looking at individual drug companies, this is when I would want to look at the seasonal trend history of the individual stock company. After all, I do not know what each drug company has on patents and which drugs come off patents and what drugs they are working on or have in the "pipeline" ready for release. But, using seasonal analysis,

I can see if there is a tendency of price increases or decreases at certain times of the year.

Let's examine Figure 2.3, which is a weekly chart on Pfizer dating back to June 2009. Notice that the company's stock price tends to go up in value from September through the first of January, and then from March through the late-June time period. Again, if I match this company with its respective sector, then I can narrow down my search and start to pick price levels on where to go long and where to get out. As was covered earlier, remember that when using seasonal analysis, one needs to consider that not all years are created equally. With individual companies, especially ones that are overseen by government agencies such as the Food and Drug Administration (FDA), news releases of accepted or rejected drugs in testing phases can impact a company share price regardless of its seasonal trend, as can lawsuits and expiring patents. But, over time, if you can identify when a stock in a seasonally weak or strong period, it can certainly improve your odds of success.

The next section includes a list of top sector ETFs that track the various sectors, which are derived from the S&P 500. These products have been around since the early 1990s. Perhaps you are trading them already.

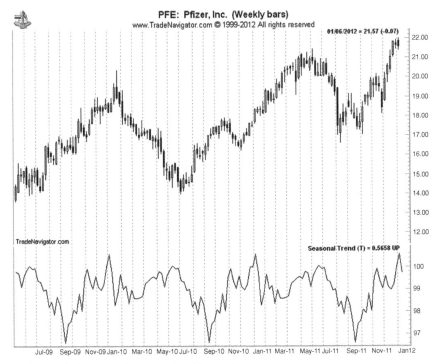

FIGURE 2.3 PFE: Pfizer Inc. (Weekly Bars)

NOT ALL ETFS ARE MEASURED EQUALLY

There are competitors of companies and, of course, there are subsectors to look at. In addition, some companies are in more than one sector ETF. For example, Verizon (VZ) is listed as a top 10 holding of the Telecommunication sector (VOX), and this stock is also listed in the Technology sector ETF (XLK).

Keep in mind that there is an enormous universe of stocks; many are not even listed in their respective sectors. In fact, some of these ETFs do not list pure sector plays. Look at the homebuilder ETF XHB and you will see that the top 10 holdings are missing actual home building stocks such as PulteGroup (PHM), Toll Brothers (TOLL), KB Homes (KBH), Hovnanian Enterprises (HOV), Beazer Homes USA, Inc. (BZH), and D. R. Horton, Inc. (DHI). In fact, the XHB has what I call a peripheral company basket of stocks, such as Home Depot, Mohawk Industries, and Pier 1 Imports. It makes sense to consider what occurs when a new home is sold: Carpet is installed, so Mohawk Industries will benefit; homeowners will purchase furniture and accessories, so perhaps Pier 1 Imports will sell more home good items. It is the ripple effect concept, or in a micro-sense, a top-down approach. When housing sales begin to pick up, we see an increase in demand for appliances, furnishings, linens, and kitchenware, so stocks from Tupperware Brands (TUP) to mattress giant Tempur-Pedic International (TPX) might see an increase in sales.

The key is to check to see, in good times or bad, on average, if there is a time of the year when this sector goes up or down in value on a consistent basis. That is why you want to focus on seasonal analysis. Think of using seasonal analysis as your own shopping list of when to buy and sell stocks. Instead of acting after a market has moved, using this information will prepare you to get in before it has moved. Consider this the playbook for your own NFL team. You decide what to trade and when to trade it. In Table 2.1, you will see there is a sector to enter a long position in 10 of the 12 calendar months. The two months that have no beginning long entry positions are May and August. Call this a coincidence, but May is a month where we have the peak in planting season for farmers, as well as graduations and weddings. Business can see downturns due to a shift to personal and family events. August is traditionally the peak for summer vacationers from a global perspective, so we normally see volume levels taper off as well as stock market declines in these two months, hence the phrase "Sell in May and go away," as said by Yale Hirsch, the creator of the *Stock Trader's Almanac* (now edited by his son Jeffrey).

TABLE 2.1 Sector Performances

Symbol	Buy	Sell	3 year	5 year	10 year
XLY	September 8	May 27	7	9	52
XLP	October 14	May 3	0	−1	47
XLE	February 3	August 22	−3	28	95
XLF	November 8	May 17	2	−19	7
XLV	March 9	June 12	20	19	22
XLI	October 7	May 1	3	28	95
XLB	October 15	May 1	−10	29	90
XLK	April 3	July 12	16	25	−20
XTC	Sept 12	January 3	21	−37	−10
XLU	July 15	January 2	22	−19	50
XLK	April 3	July 12	16	25	−20

Furthermore, Table 2.1 shows you the listed performance in the past 3, 5, and 10 years picking these sectors as buying opportunities. Considering the benchmark stock index, the S&P 500 has been relatively flat as far as a buyer for the last 10 years. I thought this may shed light on the sector's overall performance.

Now look at Table 2.2. This table shows 2011's performance by quarter for each respective sector and the S&P 500 as a whole. Notice that the energy sector's (XLE) performance in the first quarter reflects the seasonal buying strength we showed in Table 2.1 for this time period. It was a staggering 16.8 percent. Considering the year-end performance for the S&P 500 as a whole was unchanged, an investor would have been better off investing in the energy sector for just that one quarter. However, longer-term investing in one sector in one quarter and calling it quits would be a big mistake; it is advisable to be aware that certain sectors perform best at certain times of the year.

TABLE 2.2 Select Spyder Sector Review

Select Spyder Sector Review	1st Quarter	2nd Quarter	3rd Quarter	4th Quarter	2012 Change	2012 Close
Financial Select Spyder (XLF)	2.9%	-6.3%	-23.1%	10.1%	-18.5%	13.00
Technology Select Spyder (XLK)	3.5%	-1.4%	-8.2%	10.3%	1.0%	25.45
Industrial Select Spyder (XLI)	8.0%	-1.1%	-21.5%	16.6%	-3.2%	33.75
Materials Select Spyder (XLB)	4.2%	-1.6%	-25.5%	17.2%	-12.8%	33.50
Energy Select Spyder (XLE)	16.8%	-5.5%	-22.3%	21.8%	1.3%	69.13
Consumer Staples Select Spyder (XLP)	2.1%	4.4%	-5.0%	7.7%	10.8%	32.49
Health Care Select Spyder (XLV)	5.1%	7.3%	-10.7%	5.8%	10.1%	34.69
Utilities Select Spyder (XLU)	1.7%	5.1%	0.4%	4.2%	14.8%	35.98
Consumer Discretionary (XLY)	4.4%	3.0%	-13.4%	13.2%	4.3%	39.02
S&P500 Cash	5.4%	-0.4%	-14.3%	11.1%	0.0%	1257.60

Agricultural sector (MOO)—buy November–June (Figure 2.4).

History: August 2007–January 2012 (4 years) Holdings as of January
2012: Monsanto (MON); Potash Corp. (POT); Deere & Co. (DE);
Syngenta (SYENF); Wilmar (F34.SI); Archer-Daniels Midland
(ADM); Mosaic Co. (MOS); BRF Brasil Foods (BRFS.SA); Yara
International (YAR); Agrium (AGU).

FIGURE 2.4　MOO: Market Vectors Agribusiness ET (Weekly Bars)
www.TradeNavigator.com © 1999–2012. All rights reserved.

Broker/Dealer sector (RKH) [(XBD)]—buy November–May (Figure 2.5).
History: April 1994–January 2012 (17 years). Holdings as of January
    2012:
Wells Fargo & Company (WFC); HSBC Holdings (HBC.L); JP Morgan
    Chase & Co (JPM); Citigroup, Inc. (C); Royal Bank of Canada (RY.
    TO); TD US Small-Cap (TD.TO); Banco Santander SA ADR (STD.
    BC); Bank of America Corporation (BAC); Bank of Nova Scotia
    (BNS.TO); Mitsubishi UFJ Financial Group (MTU).

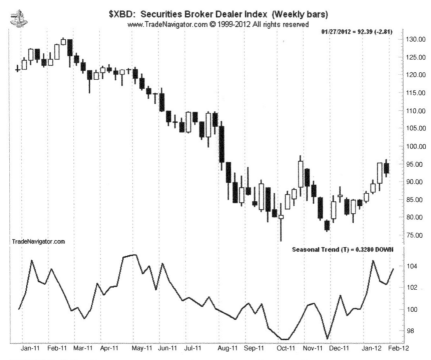

FIGURE 2.5 $XBD: Securities Broker Dealer Index (Weekly Bars)
www.TradeNavigator.com © 1999–2012. All rights reserved.

Biotechnology sector (IBB; BBH)—buy August–February (Figure 2.6). History: February 2001–January 2012 (10 years). Holdings as of January 2012: Pharmasset, Inc. (VRUS); Amgen (AMGN); Alexon Pharmaceuticals (ALXN); Celgene Corporation (CELG); Gilead Sciences, Inc. (GILD); Biogen Idec Inc. (BIIB); Teva Pharmaceutical Industries (TEVA); Perrigo Company (PRGO); Regeneron Pharmaceuticals, Inc. (REGN); Vertex Pharmaceuticals Inc. (VRTX).

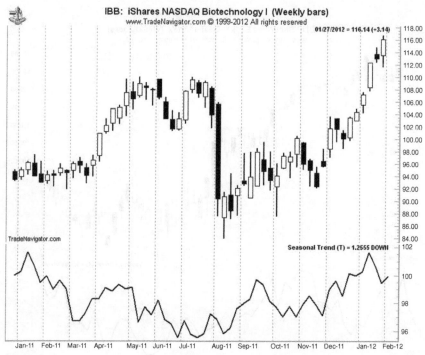

FIGURE 2.6   IBB: iShares NASDAQ Biotechnology I (Weekly Bars)

www.TradeNavigator.com © 1999–2012. All rights reserved.

Consumer Discretionary sector (XLY)—buy September–May (Figure 2.7). History: December 1998–January 2012 (13 years). Holdings as of January 2012:

McDonald's Corporation (MCD); Walt Disney Company (DIS); Home Depot, Inc. (HD); Comcast Corporation (CMCSA); Amazon. com, Inc. (AMZN); Ford Motor Company (F); News Corporation (NWSA); Time Warner Inc. (TWX); Nike (NKE); Target Corporation (TGT).

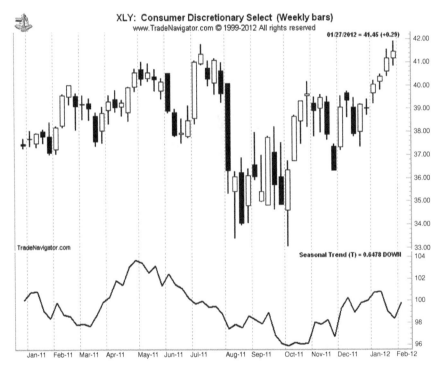

FIGURE 2.7 XLY: Consumer Discretionary Select (Weekly Bars)

Consumer Staple sector (XLP)—buy during recessions and yearly in
October–May (Figure 2.8).

History: December 1998–January 2012 (13 years). Holdings as of
January 2012: Procter & Gamble (PG); Philip Morris Internation-
al Inc. (PM); Wal-Mart Stores, Inc. (WMT); Coca-Cola Company
(KO); Kraft Foods Inc. (KFT); Altria Group, Inc. (MO); CVS Care-
mark (CVS); PepsiCo Inc. (PEP); Colgate-Palmolive (CL); Costco
(COST).

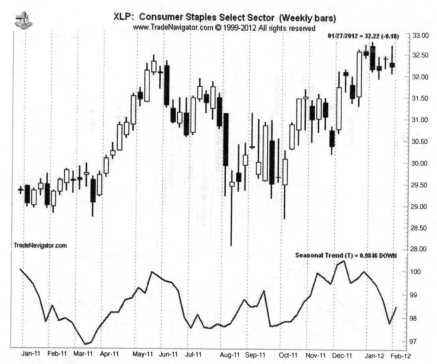

FIGURE 2.8   XLP: Consumer Staples Select Sector (Weekly Bars)

Energy sector (XLE; OIH)—buy February–August (Figure 2.9).

History: December 1998–January 2012 (13 years). Holdings as of January 2012: Exxon (XOM); Chevron (CVX); Schlumberger (SLB); Conoco Philips (COP); Occidental Petroleum (OXY); Anadarko Petroleum (APC); Apache Corporation (APA); Halliburton (HAL); National Oilwell Varco (NOV); El Paso (EP).

FIGURE 2.9   XLE: Energy Select Sector SPDR Fund (Weekly bars)

www.TradeNavigator.com © 1999–2012. All rights reserved.

Financial Sector (XLF; RKH)—buy November–May (Figure 2.10).

History: December 1998–January 2012 (13 years). Holdings as of January 2012: Wells Fargo & Company (WFC); Berkshire Hathaway Inc. B (BRK.B); JP Morgan Chase & Co. (JPM); Citigroup, Inc. (C); Bank of America Corporation (BAC); U.S. Bancorp (USB); American Express Company (AXP); Goldman Sachs Group, Inc. (GS); Simon Property Group, Inc. (SPG); MetLife, Inc. (MET).

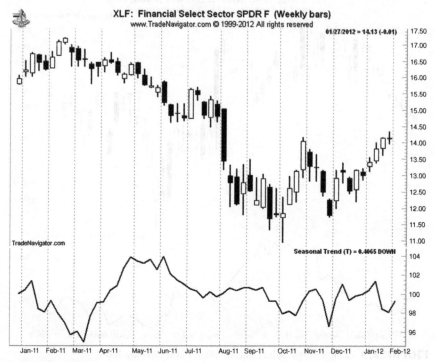

FIGURE 2.10   XLF: Financial Select Sector SPDR F (Weekly Bars)

Health Care sector (XLV)—buy March–June (Figure 2.11).

History: December 1998–January 2012 (13 years). Holdings as of January 2012: Johnson & Johnson (JNJ); Pfizer, Inc. (PFE); Merck & Company, Inc. (MRK); Abbott Laboratories (ABT); Bristol-Myers Squibb Company (BMY); UnitedHealth Group Inc. (UNH); Amgen Inc. (AMGN); Eli Lilly and Company (LLY); Medtronic Inc. (MDT); Gilead Sciences, Inc. (GILD).

FIGURE 2.11 XLV: Health Care Select Sector SPDR (Weekly Bars)

www.TradeNavigator.com © 1999–2012. All rights reserved.

Homebuilders sector (XHB)—buy November–May (Figure 2.12).

History: January 2006–January 2012 (6 years). Holdings as of January
2012: Masco Corporation (MAS); Mohawk Industries, Inc. (MHK);
Select Comfort Corporation (SCSS); Home Depot, Inc. (HD);
Owens Corning Inc. (OC); Lowe's Companies, Inc. (LOW); NVR,
Inc. (NVR); Pier 1 Imports, Inc. (PIR); Lennar Corporation (LEN);
A. O. Smith Corporation (AOS).

FIGURE 2.12   XHB: SPDR S&P Homebuilders ETF (Weekly Bars)

Industrial sector (XLI)—buy October–May (Figure 2.13).

History: December 1998–January 2012 (13 years). Holdings as of January 2012: General Electric (GE); United Parcel Service, Inc. (UPS); United Technologies Corporation (UTX); Caterpillar, Inc. (CAT); 3M Company (MMM); Boeing Company (BA); Union Pacific Corporation (UNP); Honeywell International Inc. (HON); Emerson Electric Company (EMR); Deere & Company (DE).

FIGURE 2.13   XLI: Industrial Select Sector SPDR (Weekly Bars)

Materials sector (XLB)—buy October–May (Figure 2.14).

History: December 1998–January 2012 (13 years). Holdings as of January 2012: E. I. du Pont de Nemours (DD); Monsanto Company (MON); Freeport-McMoRan (FCX); Praxair, Inc. (PX); Newmont Mining Corporation (NEM); Dow Chemical Company (DOW); Ecolab Inc. (ECL); Air Products and Chemicals (APD); Mosaic Company (MOS); International Paper Company (IP).

FIGURE 2.14   XLB: Materials Select Sector SPDR F (Weekly Bars)
www.TradeNavigator.com © 1999–2012. All rights reserved.

Pharmaceutical sector (XPH; PPH)—buy September–May (Figure 2.15).
History: June 2006–January 2012 (5 years). Holdings as of January
2012: Hospira Inc. (HSP); Mylan Inc. (MYL); Salix Pharmaceuti-
cals (SLXP); Eli Lilly and Company (LLY); Merck (MRK); Pfizer
(PFE); Jazz Pharmaceuticals (JAZZ); Bristol-Myers Squibb (BMY);
Allergan, Inc. (AGN); Abbott Laboratories (ABT).

FIGURE 2.15   XPH: SPDR S&P Pharmaceuticals ETF (Weekly Bars)
www.TradeNavigator.com © 1999–2012. All rights reserved.

Retail sector (RTH; XRT)—buy July–August and November–April (Figure 2.16).

History: June 2006–January 2012 (5 years). Holdings as of January 2012: Wal-Mart (WMT); Home Depot (HD); Amazon.com (AMZN); CVS Caremark (CVS); Lowe's Companies (LOW); Costco (COST); Walgreen Co. (WAG); Target Corporation (TGT); TJX Companies (TJX); Sysco Corporation (SYY).

FIGURE 2.16 XRT: SPDR S&P Retail ETF (Weekly Bars)

Technology sector (XLK)—buy April–July and October–January (Figure 2.17).

History: December 1998–January 2012 (13 years). Holdings as of January 2012: Apple (AAPL); International Business Machines (IBM); Microsoft (MSFT); AT&T Inc. (T); Google Inc. (GOOG); Verizon Communications Inc. (VZ); Intel Corporation (INTC); Oracle Corporation (ORCL); Cisco Systems, Inc. (CSCO); QUALCOMM Incorporated (QCOM).

FIGURE 2.17 XLK: Technology Select Sector SPDR (Weekly Bars)
www.TradeNavigator.com © 1999–2012. All rights reserved.

Telecommunication sector (VOX; XTC)—buy September–January (Figure 2.18).

History: December 1998–January 2012 (13 years). Holdings as of January 2012: Verizon Communications Inc. (VZ); AT&T Inc. (T); American Tower Corporation (AMT); CenturyLink, Inc. (CTL); Crown Castle International Corporation (CCI); Sprint Nextel Corporation (S); Windstream Corporation (WIN); Frontier Communications Company (FTR); SBA Communications Corporation (SBAC); NII Holdings, Inc. NIHD).

FIGURE 2.18 $XTC: North American Telecoms Index (Weekly Bars)

Utility Sector (XLU)—buy July–January (Figure 2.19).

History: December 1998– January 2012 (13 years). Holdings as of January 2012: Southern Company (SO); Dominion Resources, Inc. (D); Exelon Corporation (EXC); Duke Energy Corporation (DUK); NextEra Energy, Inc. (NEE); American Electric Power (AEP); FirstEnergy Corporation (FE); Consolidated Edison, Inc. (ED); PP&L Corporation (PPL); Pacific Gas & Electric Co. (PCG).

FIGURE 2.19 XLU: Utilities Select Sector SPDR F (Weekly Bars)

www.TradeNavigator.com © 1999–2012. All rights reserved.

Commodity ETFs

Agricultural sector (DBA)—buy January–June (Figure 2.20).
History: January 2005–January 2012 (5 years). Holdings as of January 2012: Live Cattle, Sugar, Coffee, Cocoa, Corn, Soybeans (new crop), Lean Hogs, Wheat, Feeder Cattle, Soybeans (year out).

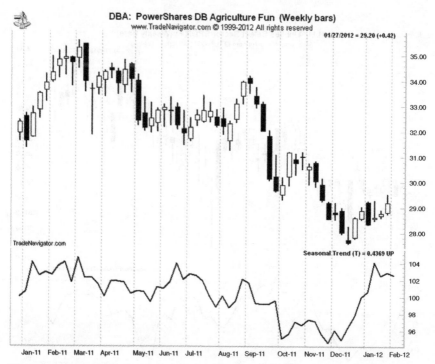

FIGURE 2.20   DBA: PowerShares DB Agriculture Fun (Weekly Bars)

Livestock sector (COW)—buy January–June (Figure 2.21).
History: October 2007–January 2012 (4 years). Holdings as of January 2012: Live Cattle and Lean Hogs.

FIGURE 2.21 COW: iPath Dow Jones—UBS Livestock (Weekly Bars)

Precious Metals

Gold (Figure 2.22).

FIGURE 2.22   GC2-057: Gold Comex (Comb) Cont Liq. (Weekly Bars)
www.TradeNavigator.com © 1999–2012. All rights reserved.

Silver (Figure 2.23).

FIGURE 2.23 SI2-057: Silver Comex (Comb) Cont Liq. (Weekly Bars)
www.TradeNavigator.com © 1999–2012. All Rights reserved.

Commodity Markets

Treasury bonds (T-bonds; Figure 2.24).

FIGURE 2.24   ZB-067: T-Bonds 30-Yr. CBT Elec Cadj Liq. (Weekly Bars)
www.TradeNavigator.com © 1999–2012. All rights reserved.

Crude oil (Figure 2.25).

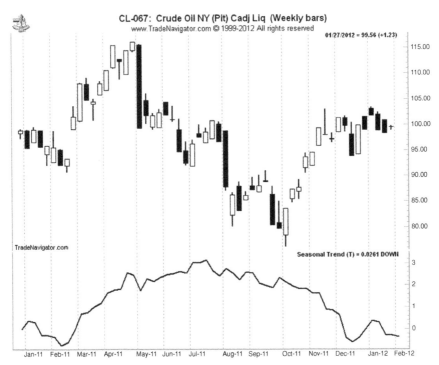

FIGURE 2.25 CL-067: Crude Oil NY (Pit) Cadj Liq. (Weekly Bars)
www.TradeNavigator.com © 1999–2012. All rights reserved.

Currencies

Euro (Figure 2.26).

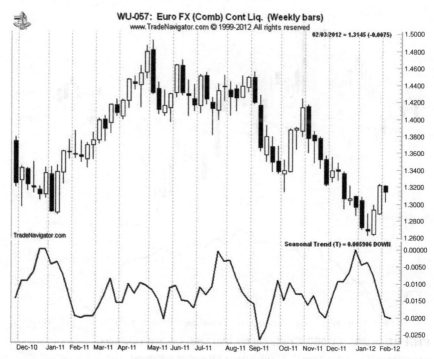

FIGURE 2.26   WU-057: Euro FX (Comb) Cont Liq. (Weekly Bars)
www.TradeNavigator.com © 1999–2012. All rights reserved.

Australian dollar (Figure 2.27).

FIGURE 2.27 WD-057: Australian $ (Comb) Cont Liq. (Weekly Bars)
www.TradeNavigator.com © 1999–2012. All rights reserved.

Japanese yen (Figure 2.28).

FIGURE 2.28   WY-067: Japanese Yen (Comb) Cont Liq. (Weekly Bars)
www.TradeNavigator.com © 1999–2012. All rights reserved.

Canadian dollar (Figure 2.29).

FIGURE 2.29 WC-057: Canadian $ (Comb) Cont Liq. (Weekly Bars)
www.TradeNavigator.com © 1999–2012. All rights reserved.

CONCLUSION

This chapter covered the seasonal price tendencies on major industry sectors, commodities, and foreign currencies. In the beginning of my trading career back in the early 1980s, this was an important discovery. In the past decade, as more and more ETFs have been created, using seasonal analysis on the underlying commodity or in fact looking at individual stocks has been a very useful technique.

Moreover, as we have had more businesses and industries go public, many of these companies, which do not have a lengthy history to allow us to examine a seasonal trend, are in sectors in which we can do a comparable analysis.

An example would be exchanges like the Nasdaq OMX Group Inc. (NDAQ), the NYSE Euronext (NYX), and the Chicago Board Options Exchange (CBOE). These are the exchanges through which traders' stock and options orders are cleared. Since these companies directly correlate with the broker dealers sector but do not have historical data to run a seasonal analysis study, we can track the seasonal trends using the XBD, the Securities Broker Dealer Index.

Whether you are a futures trader or a stock trader, or if you are a day, swing, or position trader, the material presented here is designed to help introduce you to how to make more informed investment decisions based on a past market action and factual information rather than market opinions. Another technique to incorporate is to compare the typical price move from recent history to a longer-term history to see if a market's recent history still reacts similar to its overall historic seasonal price move.

To this day I am still amazed that markets continue to adhere to their seasonal price trends, but not every year does a market make an exact bottom or top at the precise time or at previous price levels. Therefore, we need to examine other forms of technical analysis. In the next few chapters, we will go over many different techniques that professionals use to help uncover buy signals and which technical tools work best to uncover support and resistance value areas for entry and exit strategies.

CHAPTER 3

Sentiment Analysis

T he first two chapters covered sector and seasonal analysis. Now let's look at one more important form of analysis: sentiment or consensus studies. I am sure you have heard the term *contrary opinion.* As a trader, whenever there is a strong consensus, especially output from the media as the market has remained or been in a strong trend, I become interested in looking at taking an opposite position from what the media are projecting. In other words, after a market or stock sector has had a long up move with a sharp price appreciation over a sustained time, this is when it gains the attention of the media. The paradox is that most people receive this information and want to buy to join an already established trend; thus, perhaps this is why many people tend to buy high or buy near an all-time high of the market. We follow market sentiment indicators because they do help identify market tops and bottoms.

The sum of a market participant's expectations as a whole is what helps derive market sentiment or a consensus of the market. A contrarian takes the opposite side of the masses. To be truly successful is to time the peak of an extreme opinion of a market's value.

As such, examining contrary opinion is part of an integral approach of investing and trading in the stock, exchange-traded fund (ETF), or commodity market. After all, everybody can't be right. A good analogy is, if everybody on a ship switches to the port side of the vessel, a strong chance exists for that vessel to capsize. If everybody is long the market and no one is left to buy or there are no more resources to add to longs (demand drops the market to make it go higher), then it's only a matter of time before the first individual decides to start liquidating longs before the market starts to correct or move lower. The last man standing with long positions generally tends to lose money. There are two reporting services I have relied on for years. One is a private, nonprofit organization and the other is a release of the U.S. government.

THE AAII SENTIMENT SURVEY

The American Association of Individual Investors (AAII), a nonprofit education group, has been conducting weekly surveys since July 1987 and polls or asks their members whether they think stock prices will rise, remain essentially flat, or fall over the next six months. Results of the survey are compiled on a weekly basis (Thursdays) at the AAII website and are also published weekly in *Barron's*. The survey period runs from Thursday (12:01 a.m.) to Wednesday (11:59 p.m.).

The average AAII member is a male in his late 50s with a graduate degree. In addition, over half of AAII members have an investment portfolio of at least $500,000. Taking this into account, the AAII Sentiment Survey is unique among sentiment surveys in that it represents the upper echelon of active individual investors, as we say, with "skin in the game" or money on the line backing their opinions.

Here are the definitions for their outlooks:

- *Bullish sentiment.* Expectations that stock prices will rise over next six months.
- *Neutral sentiment.* Expectations that stock prices will essentially stay flat in the next six months.
- *Bearish sentiment.* Expectations that stock prices will decline in the next six months.

Historical averages are:

- Bullish: 39 percent
- Neutral: 31 percent
- Bearish: 30 percent

For example, the AAII bearish sentiment reading reached a record high of 70.3 percent when the stock market (as measured by the S&P 500) reached its low on March 5, 2009. One sampling of data does not prove to be an end-all indicator, and these all-time extreme levels of bearishness and bullishness could take years to develop, and the possibility exists that one may not see such an extreme sentiment reading ever again. Instead, this report suggests looking for extreme levels that happen with greater frequency to use as your indicator for excessive bullishness or bearishness. In order to establish a more frequently occurring extreme level, they calculate those values by using two or three standard deviations from the mean for both bullish and bearish sentiment.

The survey and its results are available online at www.aaii.com/sentimentsurvey.

COT DATA

Another way of looking at sentiment data is to remember that for every winner, there is a loser, specifically in the commodity markets, which are what we call a zero-sum game. For every long, there was an equal short position. So if we had a measurement guide that showed us a consensus that 80 percent of the traders were bullish, it would mean, for example, that there were four bullish traders for every one bearish trader. Since the rules of a zero-sum game are applied, that would mean the average bear would hold a position four times larger than the average bull. Typically, it's the large, well-funded or big money traders, which we call the *smart money*, who would be on the short side of the market within 80 percent bullish consensus. Now the question begs: How do we detect and look for this extreme level of optimism or pessimism, or what we call the *sentiment in the markets* or *crowd extremes?*

The most reliable form of information comes from the realm of commodities, the Commitment of Traders (COT) report. This is a weekly report released by the Commodity Futures Trading Commission (CFTC). Many books and studies have been written about this report, including my own books *Candlesticks and Pivot Point Trading Triggers* (2006) and *Forex Conquered* (2007), both by John Wiley & Sons. However, I want to include it in this book since it relates to the commodity-based stocks and ETFs that are aligned with bonds, commodities, and foreign currencies.

Whether you trade individual stocks, sector ETFs, or commodity-based ETFs, this is an incredible source of information, and best of all, it's free. Let's face facts—if everyone is bullish or bearish on the market and if the old adage is correct that more than 80 percent of traders lose in the markets, then why in the world would I want to be on the same side of a trade as everyone else?

First, let me explain how to get the report and understand the components of the report so you can use this information to your advantage in order to make money. As a veteran futures trader for over 30 years, I have used this information to capture many significant moves in the markets as well. We all have equal access to this data. Some just know how to apply it better than others. So let's look at one of the best ways to dissect and use this information to our advantage.

INSIDER TRADING INFORMATION

The primary purpose for the Weekly Commodity Futures Trading Commission's COT report is to monitor and have a tight surveillance program in order to identify situations that might pose a threat of a market or price manipulation, and therefore be capable to take appropriate action. The CFTC market surveillance staff closely monitors trading activity in the futures markets in order to detect and prevent instances of potential price manipulation. Some consider this "insider trading" information because every week we get to take a look at which investor group is taking which side of a trade.

Just to give you an idea of what kind of buying or selling power you need to be a reportable position limit trader, as of February 15, 2012, any trading entity or individual that controls a position in size, above a specific amount for each commodity, is classified in a specific category; for instance, the reportable position limit for the Standard & Poor's (S&P) 500 futures contract was 100 contracts. However, the total aggregate amount for all contracts and months in the S&P 500 is 20,000 contracts. The aggregate position limit in the S&P 500 Stock Price Index (S&P 500) futures and options, S&P 500 Growth futures, S&P 500 Value futures, and E-mini S&P 500 futures and options, and is the specified number of S&P 500 futures or futures equivalent contracts net long or net short in all contract months combined. For purposes of aggregation, one S&P 500 futures contract shall be deemed equivalent to one S&P 500 Growth futures contract plus one S&P 500 Value futures contract. One S&P 500 futures contract shall be deemed equivalent to five E-mini S&P 500 futures contracts.

The reportable position for the currencies like the euro, the yen, the Swiss franc, and British pound was 200 contracts. Cattle, hogs, and feeder cattle were 25 contracts. The aggregate position limit for cattle is 6,300, for hogs that number is 4,150 positions, and for feeder cattle the amount is 1,950 contracts. For the 30-year Treasury bond, the reportable futures level is 1,500 contracts. However, the position accountability for futures is 10,000, and for options is 25,000. Option levels refer to option contracts for all months and all strike prices combined in each option category (long call, long put, short call, and short put). For more information, visit the exchange's web site at www.cme.com.

COT DATA COMPONENTS

Figure 3.1 shows that there are several categories and components. First, let's discuss the categories, otherwise known as the *players*. We have the noncommercials, which are all large professional speculator traders or entities such as a hedge funds, commodity trading advisers, commodity pool operators, and locals on and off the exchange floors, or just about anyone who has a reportable size position on. The next category of importance is the commercials: banks and institutions or multinational conglomerate corporations looking to hedge a cash position. Next, we have the nonreportable positions category; this is considered the small speculators.

How the positions are figured out for these categories is by subtracting total long and short positions from the commercials and the large speculators from the total open interest, and the balance of positions is assigned to the small speculators. The main component to breaking down the positions is the open interest, which is listed on each commodity. In this example, as you can see, open interest as of February 7, 2012 was 3,025,509.

When I use this report, I like to look at the short format using both futures and options. The main reason is that hedge fund commercials and small speculators who place a bet on the market direction can and do use options. A long or short synthetic position can be created by using options without placing a trade on the underlying futures market. Furthermore, even if one were to place a bet that the market price was to decline, and then bought a deep out-of-the-money put option (buying out-of-the-money options has a low-probability success rate), despite the low probability that the option will make money, that individual has put money in the market

E-MINI S&P 500 STOCK INDEX – CHICAGO MERCANTILE EXCHANGE   Code–13874A
OPTION AND FUTURES COMBINED POSITIONS AS OF 02/07/12

| | | | | | | | | NONREPORTABLE | |
| NON–COMMERCIAL | | | COMMERCIAL | | TOTAL | | | POSITIONS | |
Long	Short	Spreads	Long	Short	Long	Short		Long	Short
($50 X S&P 500 INDEX)						OPEN INTEREST:			3,025,509
COMMITMENTS									
368,586	446,949	167,218	2245104	2081346	2780908	2695513		244,601	329,996
CHANGES FROM 01/31/12 (CHANGE IN OPEN INTEREST:					54,923)				
−7,893	−36,509	23,043	56,129	57,264	71,279	43,798		−16,356	−11,125
PERCENT OF OPEN INTEREST FOR EACH CATEGORY OF TRADER									
12.2	14.8	5.5	74.2	68.8	91.9	89.1		8.1	10.9
NUMBER OF TRADERS IN EACH CATEGORY (TOTAL TRADERS:					522)				
105	109	85	216	212	361	366			

FIGURE 3.1 COT Report

backing his or her bearish opinion. More and more individuals are becoming familiar and using options strategies; the fact that one places a "bet" using these derivative products does give us a good contrarian indicator on what the majority of traders are doing in each respective category. That is why I encourage you to use the combined futures and options data.

The other components of this report are long versus short positions. If you look at the first column under noncommercials, it shows the breakdown of how many long positions versus short positions are held.

The next component shows the changes from the prior week. This is important information because you will be able to see if these players unloaded some of their positions or added to them from one week to the next.

The next component is very important and the basis of creating a tracking method for alerting you to big changes in the specific category of traders' positions. It is the percentage of longs and shorts held, and the last line shows how many traders there are that control longs or shorts. This is important, as size of positions as measured in terms of percentage to open interest gives a better consensus gauge.

One of several key concepts to understand is that the information is gathered as of the close of business every Tuesday by each of the clearing brokerage firms and turned over to exchange officials, who then report the information over to the regulatory body known as the CFTC. This information is released on Friday afternoons at 3:30 p.m. (ET). This means there is a lag time of almost three trading days to when the information is released. It is critical before acting on a decision based on this information if there was a major price swing from Tuesday's close to the time the information was released because positions may have changed hands.

Remember, you need to look at several key points in this report:

- Total open interest.
- Percentage of long versus short positions held compared to overall open interest.
- Net change of positions from one week to the next week.
- Historic data.
- Moving average of those data, to compare past highs and lows of positions, both long and short.

CAN TRADERS BENEFIT AND MAKE MONEY FROM THIS INFORMATION?

The answer is that there is always a chance to make money; the key is to be able to afford to not be too heavily leveraged if the market moves further than anticipated. This report is like an insider information report. It acts like a true consensus of who literally "owns" the market. A trader can use these data to determine in a long-term trend run if market participants are too heavily positioned on one side of the market. It is generally the small speculator who is left holding the bag.

Let's face it; money moves the market and the banks, and large professional traders are a bit savvier when it comes to their business, apart from the occasional rogue trader (like what happened to UBS Bank in 2011). As far as overall business conditions are concerned, one would think a bank has a good idea of what direction interest rates are going to go once a central bank meeting occurs, right?

If a company's board of directors were to issue stock to a new CEO and that stock's price moved in tight correlation to the S&P 500, or if a pension fund was seeking to lock in a profit or cost, these two groups would be considered commercials. They are looking to hedge or protect against risk against their cash position. They might not necessarily know the overall market is going down or up, but they do want to lock in a price, and they do know that they will be issuing or taking delivery of a cash position. This is their business—they want to "fix" their cost of doing business. If the commercials are on the long side of the market, considering they have a good handle on their business, we certainly want to focus on this group's net long or short position. Here are some observations I look for to give me a better idea if the market is bullish or bearish.

When the small speculators are showing a nice short position of, say, at least two longs for every one short. If the noncommercials are net long and the commercials are net long, chances are the small speculators will be wrong.

I am looking for imbalances in markets that have been in a trending market condition for quite some time, so I can therefore develop a game plan and start looking for timing clues to enter trades accordingly. Keep in mind that the commercials are sometimes—not always—right. They are not in the market to time market turns; they are hedging their risk exposure in a cash position. Therefore, the noncommercials, or professional speculators, in the short term, are considered the smart money. Here are some general guidelines to follow:

- If noncommercials are net long, commercials are net long, and the nonreportable positions are net short by at least a two-to-one margin, look at buying opportunities. In other words, go with the professional speculators and the commercials. They typically know more than the average small speculator as a whole.
- If noncommercials are net short, commercials are net short, and the nonreportable positions are net long by at least a two-to-one margin, look at selling opportunities.

- If noncommercials are net long, commercials are net short, and the nonreportable positions are neutral, meaning not heavily net long or short, look at selling opportunities. Stick with the in-the-know smart money—the commercials. After all, not all speculative professional hedge funds are always right either.

Typically, I do not make trade decisions by tracking the small speculators (nonreportable traders) category except in certain cases. I do so in markets in which the small speculator is heavily involved. For example, with the S&P 500 contracts, I look at the E-mini contracts rather than the big S&P contracts. Think of the logic here: Most small speculators do not trade in the big contract. Normally, small speculators tend to hold positions overnight in the smaller contract, as the margin requirement is one-fifth of the big S&P 500 futures contract. If they are in the E-minis, then I am looking for a lopsided holding of these contracts versus the professional traders against the commercials.

As they say, a picture paints a thousand words. One of the most compelling pieces of evidence that reveals small speculators tend to be on the wrong side of the market or tend to get out of winning trades too early is in black and white.

Figure 3.2 shows a weekly chart using the E-mini S&P 500 futures contract in the upper quadrant, with a graphical depiction of the COT report showing the three categories of traders level of net shorts versus net longs in the lower quadrant. This is a zero line graph. When you see the line's above the zero line, that shows a net long position. When you see line's below the zero line, that reflects a net short position.

Look at point A marked on the chart. The dark gray line represents the large speculator, namely, hedge funds or large private investors. The black line represents the commercials, the group that is looking to lock in a price or cost structure, which is known as a hedge against their cash position. The light gray line represents the small speculators' holdings; as you can see, they had amassed one of the largest net short positions, while the hedge funds or large speculators had amassed one of the largest net long positions at the exact time when the lows were posted in March 2009. The commercials, who were hedged by being short the overall market, started to buy back their short futures positions, being at a more neutral stance by the time the market hit that low. So commercials were getting out of their hedges, professional speculators were going along, and small speculators were adding to their shorts at the worst possible time.

When we see the COT report showing small speculators net short and the hedge funds are net long, with a bias for the commercials to be reducing shorts or net long, this typically leads us to believe that prices will move higher. And that is what occurred in March 2009.

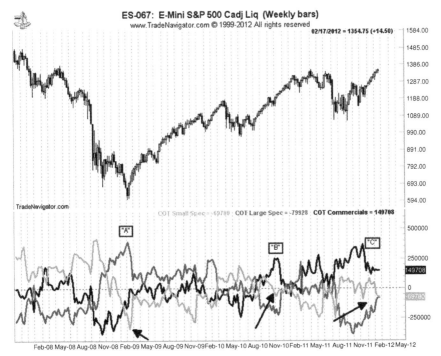

FIGURE 3.2 ES-067: E-mini S&P 500 Cadj Liq. (Weekly Bars)
www.TradeNavigator.com © 1999–2012. All rights reserved.

If you follow the progression of the gray line, which represents the small speculators, you will see that this group stayed on the short side of the market for much of the entire move to the upside until approximately April 2010. At that time, notice the dark line at the crossover, which revealed that the commercials were adding to their short positions. This was just four weeks prior to the flash crash in May 2010. From a seasonal perspective, this is the worst time of the year to be long stocks, thus the phrase "Sell in May and go away." As the data show, the commercials were taking on protection from an impending market crash, while speculators, near the end of a two-year bull market, decided to bail on their short positions and go long near the top.

The small speculators took the beating, and toward the end of summer finally got the courage to get long the market in late August 2010. However, notice that in early October small speculators switched to a net short position in the market and remained short until approximately May 2011. So while the stock market enjoyed nearly a two-year rally for the majority of time, small speculators were on the wrong side of that move as well. Then, when they finally threw in the towel and joined the bulls, they went long just prior to the historic flash crash. Once the markets recovered, the small speculators continued selling the rally.

Now examine point C on the chart. It shows the stock market's move from December 2011 through February 2012 as the S&P 500 rallied over 9 percent. Notice that the small speculators were once again on the wrong side of the market.

This is compelling evidence that shows when the stock market is either at a major turning point or in a strong trend condition, one can get a better consensus by examining the COT data. This form of contrarian opinion on the market is based on a set of facts based on people's opinion on the market with "skin in the game," or money on the line. This is a much better form of a market opinion than asking a cab driver on the way to an airport—that's for sure. But remember, it is the E-mini S&Ps that I look at to determine the small speculators' position.

HOW CAN THIS INFORMATION POSSIBLY BE OF ANY HELP TO US?

The next market example you will see is that the commercials are usually on one side and the large speculators are typically on the exact opposite side. In fact, this is what you need to watch out for, when both these groups are on the same side of the market from a net position perspective. It is rare but can occur, especially for a short period of time, as occurs when these groups are changing sides in the market. A good example of this was at the lows in March 2009.

Figure 3.3 shows the weekly chart on crude oil. You will notice that the commercials had neutral on their positions from that time period and then began building a massive short position until April 2010. So simply judging which side of the market they are on does not help us out much at all in our decision-making process deciding to buy or sell crude oil-related securities. But if we track their changes by the use of a moving average, we can gain some valuable insights.

This concept of using a moving average to smooth data, combined with the data of the percentage of net position of open interest, can be extremely useful. Signals are generated when moving average crossovers occur. Examine Figure 3.4; this is a 12-period simple moving average laid over the net commercial position line. At point A, we see the commercials adding more shorts as the price is nearing a bottom. Then, as you can see by point B on the chart in Figure 3.5, they start to unload these shorts right near the top. Then, as point C shows in Figure 3.6, they start to accumulate or add to their short position as the line crosses beneath their 12-week or 12-period moving averages.

The one market where I strictly follow the small speculators is the E-mini S&P 500. If 80 percent of traders are suspected of losing in the

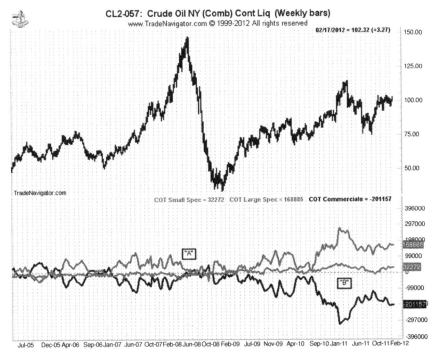

FIGURE 3.3 CL2-057: Crude Oil NY (Comb) Cont Liq. (Weekly Bars)
www.TradeNavigator.com © 1999–2012. All rights reserved.

markets, this is the one single market that represents a large pool of individual speculators. Therefore, I like to use the information on the net positions of the small speculator or nonreportable position category of trader for this market as my contrarian indicator rather than follow the commercials as I do for other markets. The logic behind this could be the fact that the small speculator will more than likely trade the smaller contract size E-mini S&P 500 contract rather than the full-size contract. While the full-size contract has a nonreportable category, it tends to be a small fund or smaller lot size professional traders, whereas the E-mini contract seems to attract the lower-capitalized speculator, as the margin requirement is one fifth the size of the big S&P futures contract.

Here are my observations I want to share with you:

- Watch for a switch of positions after a long trend move.
- Wait at least three weeks of participation and accumulation of positions.
- Watch for the percentage of open interest to rise between 12 percent and 14 percent of net position.

FIGURE 3.4   CL-067: Crude Oil NY (Pit) Cadj Liq. (Weekly Bars)

    I look at the short format combining futures and options, since traders can place a synthetic net long or short position using options. So I believe a stronger or better contrarian indicator is from taking the "temperature" of the market from the opinion from a pool of all investors with money on the line, whether it is from a futures contract or a combination of option positions.

    The table in Figure 3.7 is from the report that was released on Friday, March 6, 2009. This shows the data collected from the close of business on Tuesday, March 3. As you can see, the open interest was 3,519,460 contracts, and the small speculators held 13.9 percent of the short interest, as indicated by point "A." The change from the prior week shows that they liquidated 27,138 longs and added 29,189 new shorts from the prior week.

    On the other side of the table, the noncommercial or large speculators held nearly 20.6 of the net long open interest, nearly double of the net short side. See at the bottom there were a total of only 96 traders? This means 96 account holders were long a total of 724,270 contracts. The commercials were almost neutral, with 69 percent of net long versus

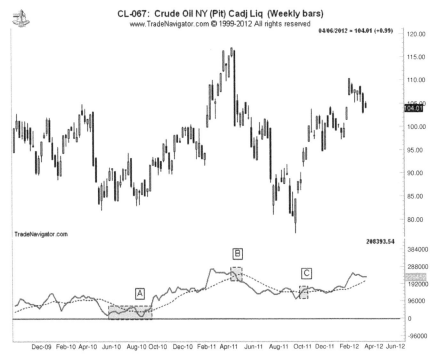

FIGURE 3.5 CL-067: Crude Oil NY (Pit) Cadj Liq. (Weekly Bars)
www.TradeNavigator.com © 1999–2012. All rights reserved.

73 percent of net short open interest. Now when I see a report like this where the small speculators hold between 12 percent and 14 percent of one side of the market against the large speculators, typically you will want to trade with the large speculators. I also like to see how long the small speculators have been accumulating a large one-sided position. Remember, a chart is composed of two axes, time and price. The longer the time a market stays at a price, the more time a trader has to develop an opinion of the market. That is why we refer to this as being "married to a position." The condition I consider to be a trader's emotional defect is ego, as it is an emotion that interferes with logic.. This can play a part in the inability of traders to admit they are wrong. Most often, people form opinions rather than look at the facts. It is these opinions that are formed by news and in the markets when a stock or overall market is in a prolonged trend. The small speculator finally builds the confidence to enter trades toward the end of a trend as the market has proved itself. As you study this rationale, look at Figure 3.8, which is the E-mini S&P with the commitment of traders' net position graphed using a zero line histogram

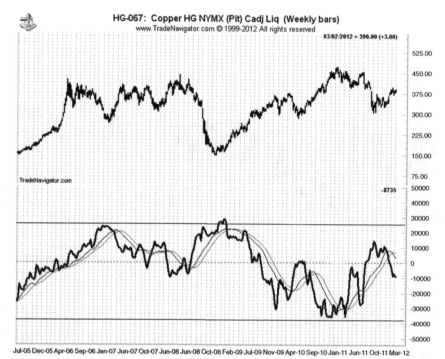

FIGURE 3.6 HG-067: Copper HG NYMX (Pit) Cadj Liq. (Weekly Bars)
www.TradeNavigator.com © 1999–2012. All rights reserved.

E–MINI S&P 500 STOCK INDEX – CHICAGO MERCANTILE EXCHANGE   Code–13874A
OPTION AND FUTURES COMBINED POSITIONS AS OF 03/03/09

	NON–COMMERCIAL			COMMERCIAL		TOTAL		NONREPORTABLE POSITIONS	
Long	Short	Spreads	Long	Short	Long	Short	Long	Short

($50 X S&P 500 INDEX)   OPEN INTEREST: 3, 519, 460
COMMITMENTS

Long	Short	Spreads	Long	Short	Long	Short	Long	Short
724, 270	330, 826	129, 225	2427047	2569516	3280542	3029567	238, 919	489, 893

CHANGES FROM 02/24/09 (CHANGE IN OPEN INTEREST: 271, 661)

54, 431	17, 747	29, 648	214, 719	195, 076	298, 798	242, 471	−27, 138	29, 189

PERCENT OF OPEN INTEREST FOR EACH CATEGORY OF TRADER

20.6	9.4	3.7	69.0	73.0	93.2	86.1	6.8	13.9

NUMBER OF TRADERS IN EACH CATEGORY (TOTAL TRADERS: 431)   "A"

96	110	70	157	152	287	298		

FIGURE 3.7 COT Report (March 6, 2009)

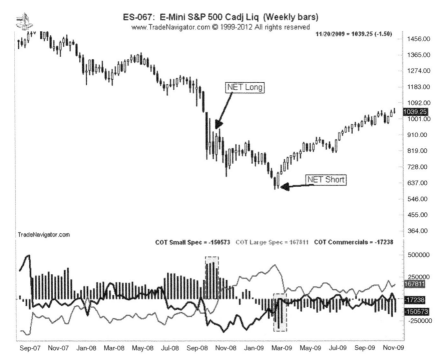

FIGURE 3.8 ES-067: E-mini S&P 500 Cadj Liq. (Weekly Bars)
www.TradeNavigator.com © 1999–2012. All rights reserved.

at the lower section of the chart. Above the zero line shows a net long position for each category, and anything below the zero line reflects a net short position. Due to this book's being printed in black and white, I have separated the three categories of traders, with the dark line representing the commercial category, the light gray line representing the large speculators, and the bar histogram representing the small speculator. As the graph shows, small speculators stayed long from the peak in late August 2007 and, as the market continued to decline, added to their losers and increased their net long position until approximately seven weeks prior to the absolute lows. It was this week that they added to their short position, obviously convinced the stock market would go down even further. It was this switch in opinion after a long-term trend that made them add to the largest net short position at the exact low. From the highs of August 2007 until the low of March 2009 was posted, the news was bombarding

investors with bad news on the economy. There was an obvious disconnect between what was on the news and how the markets were reacting.
As a result, the net positions held by small speculators revealed that this
group was convinced the stock market was headed lower. As the graph
shows, they certainly became married to that opinion as they held on to
their shorts as the price of the overall stock market recovered into the
year's end.

At the beginning of this chapter, the COT report table from Figure 3.1
showed that small speculators were net short as of February 2. As the
charts will show, the stock market was in an uptrend from the first of the
year. Now I am going to fast-forward to April 2012. Look at the table in
Figure 3.9. This shows that as the market continued to move higher, the
small speculators switched to a net long position. After a prolonged trend,
they not only held this net long position after three weeks, but added to
their positions to the tune of 13 percent of the net long open interest as
indicated at point A. Again, the large professional traders were next short
by a whopping 17.6 percent and the commercials were pretty neutral with
70.2 percent of net longs against 68.8 percent of net shorts—almost the
exact setup, just the opposition of positions.

The chart in Figure 3.10 shows that the small speculators not only went
from being short for the six weeks, missing a substantial move, but as a
group, reversed positions—and a hefty one at that, with 13 percent on the
short open interest, as the histogram shows. This means something must
have thoroughly convinced them to amass a large net long position at the
highs of a three-year rally.

E–MINI S&P 500 STOCK INDEX – CHICAGO MERCANTILE EXCHANGE   Code–13874A
OPTION AND FUTURES COMBINED POSITIONS AS OF 03/27/12

NON–COMMERCIAL			COMMERCIAL		TOTAL		NONREPORTABLE POSITIONS	
Long	Short	Spreads	Long	Short	Long	Short	Long	Short

($50 X S&P 500 INDEX)   OPEN INTEREST: 3, 064, 087
COMMITMENTS

| 361, 425 | 537, 923 | 152, 265 | 2150617 | 2108708 | 2664308 | 2798896 | 399, 779 | 265, 191 |

CHANGES FROM 03/20/12 (CHANGE IN OPEN INTEREST: 62, 560)

| 21, 301 | 1, 672 | –2, 537 | 20, 405 | 59, 480 | 39, 169 | 58, 615 | 23, 391 | 3, 945 |

PERCENT OF OPEN INTEREST FOR EACH CATEGORY OF TRADER

| 11.8 | 17.6 | 5.0 | 70.2 | 68.8 | 87.0 | 91.3 | 13.0 | 8.7 |

NUMBER OF TRADERS IN EACH CATEGORY (TOTAL TRADERS: 533)

| 102 | 121 | 86 | 218 | 212 | 372 | 367 | "A" | |

FIGURE 3.9 COT Report (April 2012)

FIGURE 3.10   ES-067: E-mini S&P 500 Cadj Liq. (Weekly Bars)
www.TradeNavigator.com © 1999–2012. All rights reserved.

COMPELLING EVIDENCE

This certainly is compelling evidence of how this report can help individual
traders potentially avoid chasing markets. The best part is that the information is free. The key to remember is that this report is better used as a
temperature gauge of the overall stock market. Certainly, if you are in a
high-beta stock that is correlated to the S&P stock index, then this report
should be followed, especially when the markets demonstrates prolonged
trends and significant price change. Looking solely at net positions is not
as important as the percentage of net position to open interest. Once again,
the E-mini S&P is one of the few markets in which I track the small speculator category. As these charts and graphs have shown, as long as small
speculators continue to trade and as long as this report is released, it will
pay off big time for you in the future.

CONCLUSION: COT OPTION STRATEGY

I know we have not delved into the intricacies of options, such as implied versus historic volatility and the theoretical pricing variables such as the "greeks," but for readers who are either learning or currently trading options, the COT data can act as a great confirming tool, especially when combined with seasonal analysis. Traders can employ an option credit spread strategy that can be applied to either individual high-beta stocks or sector ETFs or the broad market indexes like the SPY, DIA, IWM, or QQQ.

Bullish

When these instruments and/or the broad stock market are in a seasonally strong period, and if the COT data suggest that small speculators are net short more than 12 percent of the open interest in the E-mini S&Ps, then once you have a bullish trigger such as the Person's Pivot Study (PPS) to generate a weekly buy signal, then sell an at-the-money put (credit) spread with an option expiration of less than 35 days but more than 15 days. For added confirmation, look for the 9-day simple moving average (SMA) to cross above the 18-day SMA. If the market moves up, you profit by keeping the premium collected. If the premium erodes by more than 75 percent before expiration, exit the trade so you do not have to wait until expiration to realize the profit. Your loss is limited to the difference between the two strikes of the spread minus the premium collected. However, to reduce losses further, exit the strategy if the PPS indicator generates a weekly sell signal and/or the 9-day SMA crosses back below the 18-day SMA.

In the event of a free-falling market due to an unexpected catastrophic event, if the short put is assigned a long underlying position, remember that the credit spread has a long put for protection. To help further reduce damage control, if an assigned long position is made, then sell an out-of-the-money call option to take in premium to offset some of the predetermined losses. This will then effectively place you in what is referred to as a "collar strategy" (long a put, long an outright instrument, and short a call) for further damage control.

Bearish

The bearish strategy is the exact opposite of the bullish strategy. When these instruments and/or the broad stock market are in a seasonally weak period (e.g., as they are in late April into early May), and if the COT data suggest that small speculators are net long more than 12 percent of the open interest in the E-mini S&Ps, then sell an at-the-money call (credit) spread with an option expiration of less than 35 days but more than

15 days. For added confirmation you can look at a trigger such as the PPS to generate a weekly sell signal and/or look for the 9-day SMA to cross below the 18-day SMA. If the market moves lower, you profit by keeping the premium collected. If the premium erodes by more than 75 percent before expiration, exit the trade so you do not have to wait until expiration to realize the profit. Your loss is limited to the difference between the two strikes of the spread minus the premium collected. However, to reduce losses further, exit the strategy if the PPS indicator generates a weekly buy signal and/or the 9-day SMA crosses back above the 18-day SMA.

In the event of a strong bullish counter seasonal rally due to an unexpected positive earnings or monetary stimulus by the Fed or fiscal policy change by the government, if the short call is assigned a short underlying position, remember that the credit spread has a long call for protection. To help further reduce damage, if an assigned long position is made, then sell an out-of-the-money put option to take in premium to offset some of the predetermined losses. This will then effectively place you in the "collar strategy" (short a put, short an outright instrument, and long a call) for further damage control.

CHAPTER 4

Comparative Relative Strength

This chapter will share insights on a valuable lesser known form of market analysis referred to as *comparative relative strength* (CRS). This is the study of one stock or sector in relationship to other sectors or the overall market. This technical study can give a better look at where the money may or may not be flowing. Comparative relative strength is not to be confused with Welles Wilder's relative strength index or Williams Percent "R" indicators. Both of these technical tools are considered oscillators and give an indication if the stock or security is overbought or oversold relative to its past price action over a specific period in time.

WHAT IS IT USED FOR?

In using CRS, we take one market and divide by another, and the result is a continuous close line graph. Typically, the numerator is the product that we are comparing against the denominator, or benchmark. This technique is used to uncover or detect any hidden weakness or strength when analyzing one company against another in the same sector or comparing an individual stock against its related industry sector. We can also use this technique to compare individual stocks or sectors to the benchmark stock index like the Standard & Poor's (S&P) 500, the Dow Jones Industrial Average, the Russell 200, the Nasdaq 100, or the Nasdaq Composite.

Why do traders use this analysis method?

- To see where the money is flowing to help confirm a trade bias.
- To see if a stock or sector is outperforming compared to its benchmark.
- To see which are the weakest sectors compared to the benchmark.
- As an early warning signal.

With the graphic representation of where money is flowing or which asset is outperforming other assets, we can focus our attention and trading capital on that area.

Another way to use this information is in what is called *pairs trading.* A pair trade simply consists of buying one company and simultaneously selling short another similar or "like" company with the expected results to see the company one bought outperforming the company that was sold. Keep in mind that the key word here is *performance.* As you will see, markets can move higher or lower, but one product may not move up or down as far or fast compared to the like market. This is why a spread or relative strength chart may show an increase or decrease in the trend.

CREATING THE CHARTS

Setting up your charting platform is relatively easy. A basic relative chart is created as a spread chart. Here are a few reasons why you want to look at a comparative difference chart. Comparative analysis or pairs-trading charts are easy to create. Again, we're only looking at the price relationship of one product against another. Logically, since price is dictated by the laws of supply and demand, you can anticipate that when one market outperforms another, it will do so over a period of time, which lends itself to a trending condition. Therefore, we can simply analyze the spread chart by itself just as we would a typical price chart using simple trend-line analysis. We can even apply specific price pattern analysis to the spread chart such as a head-and-shoulders top, inverted head and shoulders bottom, double-top or "M", and double-bottom or "W" formations. Thanks to computers and sophisticated software that most brokerage firms have, traders can construct a trading system built by applying moving average crossover techniques to the relative strength chart rather than the absolute price of the individual products; I will demonstrate how you can construct these and why they are beneficial. For example, if you are looking at investing in the beverage sector, you may look at a chart comparing Coca-Cola (KO) and Pepsi (PEP). Examine the chart in Figure 4.1. The very top section has a bar chart on Coca-Cola (KO). The middle section is a chart on Pepsi (PEP). The bottom

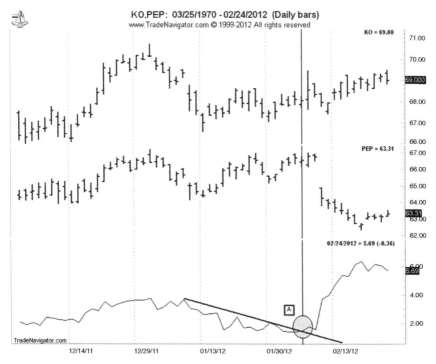

FIGURE 4.1 KO, PEP: 03/25/1970–02/24/2012 (Daily Bars)
www.TradeNavigator.com © 1999–2012. All rights reserved.

quadrant is the close line chart between KO and PEP, with an overlay of a moving average.

Using simple trend-line analysis techniques, drawing a resistance line from the peak made on January 10 to the peak formed on January 30 and extending it out, you will see that by February 6 prices broke out to the upside, as illustrated at point A on the graph. This suggests that Coca-Cola was starting to outperform Pepsi. In fact, on February 6, Coca-Cola closed at 68.03 and Pepsi closed at 66.52. In a little less than three weeks, by February 24, Coca-Cola closed at 69.00, showing a gain of $0.97, while Pepsi closed at 63.31 reflecting a loss of $3.21 per share. What's interesting is that the relative strength performance graph reflected a trend change in Pepsi two days prior to a significant decline. So the relative strength performance gave us an earlier warning sign that there was an impending price directional change in one or both of the markets we were analyzing. In this case it was Pepsi that underperformed Coca-Cola. I find this a fascinating tool, especially in the use of derivative products like options, where instead of spending $68,000 or so on 1,000 shares of Coca-Cola, and spending another $66,520 on 1,000 shares of Pepsi, one can put together an option strategy, spending roughly $1,500 on 10 out-of-the-money Pepsi puts and another $1,500 buying 10 out-of-the-money calls on Coca-Cola. In less than three weeks, the Coca-Cola call options would not have made a significant amount, but the Pepsi put options would have certainly picked up a decent profit, or outperformed the calls in Coke.

Let's take another example in this space looking at Dr. Pepper Snapple (DPS), which has a strong lineup of leading brands, including Snapple A&W Root Beer, 7UP, Hawaiian Punch, Sunkist, Country Time Lemonade, and Yoo-hoo chocolate beverage against Monster Beverage Corporation (MNST), the high-caffeine energy drink maker. Look at Figure 4.2. Here, we have Monster Beverage in the top section of the chart with Dr. Pepper Snapple in the middle of the chart, and in the lower quadrant is the relative strength (RS) chart. Notice that at point A on the RS chart, the price line as shown in the line graph broke below the uptrend line, which was the week ending April 3, 2009. At that time, MNST closed at $1,859 and DPS closed at $1,850. The RS chart trended lower, indicating that Dr. Pepper was outperforming

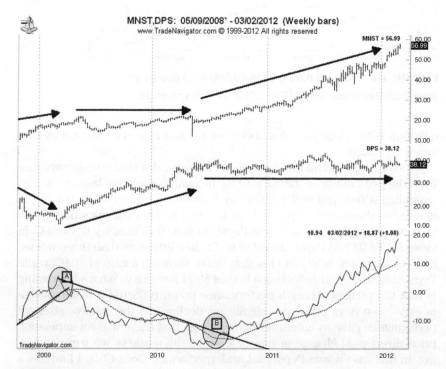

FIGURE 4.2   MNST, DPS: 05/09/2008–03/02/2012 (Weekly Bars)
www.TradeNavigator.com © 1999–2012. All rights reserved.

Monster. The charts show DPS stock moved up while MNST moved sideways. Over time, until mid-2010, this relationship continued as indicated by drawing in a downtrend or resistance line. Then as point B on the charts shows that performance changed, and significantly, I might add. Notice that the RS line broke out above the resistance line. The stock MNST moved up as DPS moved sideways. On September 3, 2010, Monster closed at $23.64 and Dr. Pepper Snapple closed at $38.30. While both companies enjoyed a profitable ride, Dr. Pepper Snapple significantly outperformed Monster Beverage. However, the breakout of the RS line at point B revealed that the relationship was changing. Clearly, you can see from that point forward Dr. Pepper Snapple had not managed to really appreciate in value, as the end of the chart shows its value at $38.14, while Monster was valued at $57.45 a share.

The moral of the story is that while DPS was a solid company, it was dead money compared to its sector competitor. By monitoring these relationships with RS charts, you may be able to better identify which stocks to be in.

Let's examine one more example of a "like" company or pairs trade situation. Examine Figure 4.3; here we have Home Depot (HD) in the upper

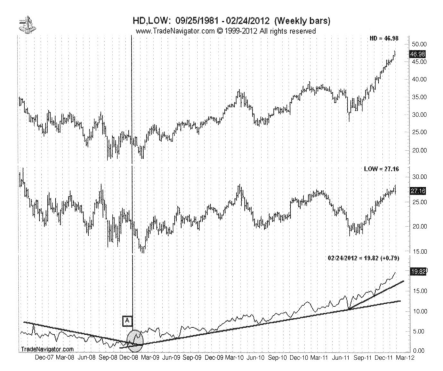

FIGURE 4.3   HD, LOW: 09/25/1981–02/24/2012 (Weekly Bars)
www.TradeNavigator.com © 1999–2012. All rights reserved.

quadrant and Lowe's (LOW) in the middle quadrant with our RS chart in the lower quadrant. After the market's substantial decline from 2007 into 2009, we see the spread chart between the two competitors, HD and LOW, reveals that HD was weaker than LOW as the trend was down. Then, by January 2009, as indicated at point A on the graph, the RS chart broke out above the trend line. This indicates a shift in performance and tells traders to buy Home Depot rather than Lowe's. When the RS chart broke above the resistance line on the week ending January 30, 2009, the close of HD was $21.53 and the close on LOW was $18.27. As of the time of the writing of this book, Home Depot continued to outperform Lowe's: at the close on February 29, 2012, HD was $47.57, which reaped a gain of $26.04 or 120 percent, and on the same date comparing the close of LOW at 28.38 was a gain of $10.11 or 55 percent.

Both stocks moved up, but the RS chart would have had you stay with Home Depot for a substantially greater return on investment dollars.

Now let's examine a sector against the benchmark index in Figure 4.4. We have the financial group sector (XLF) versus the S&P 500 in the top

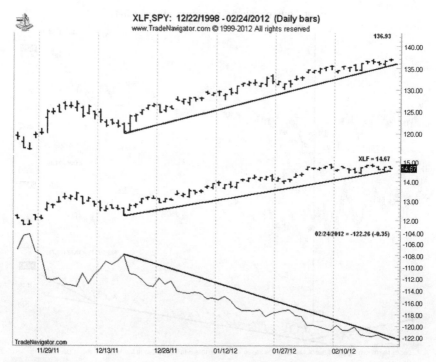

FIGURE 4.4   XLF, SPY: 12/22/1998–02/24/2012 (Daily Bars)

www.TradeNavigator.com © 1999–2012. All rights reserved.

section, we have the S&P 500 in the middle section in the graph of the XLF, and the lower quadrant is the RS chart. Using simple trend-line analysis techniques, we can clearly see that both markets are in an uptrend, but the RS chart is in a significant downtrend, which suggests that the financial sector is not corresponding to the similar performance as the benchmark stock index. Even though investing in the financial sector would've reaped a profit, the RS chart shows us that there were obviously other sectors where our investment dollars could have performed better for us.

Since we are looking at the difference between the financials to the benchmark S&P 500 Index, let's take a look at a stock that relates to the industry sector in Figure 4.5 comparing Wells Fargo (WFC) to the financial sector exchange-traded fund (ETF) XLF using a weekly chart. The RS graph does indeed lend itself to give good indications using simple trend-line breakouts, or violations as we call them. This is when the line breaks out above a resistance trend line. It generally tells us that there is a shift of positive momentum or that the stock or the numerator is outperforming the denominator. I have placed the vertical lines intersecting the

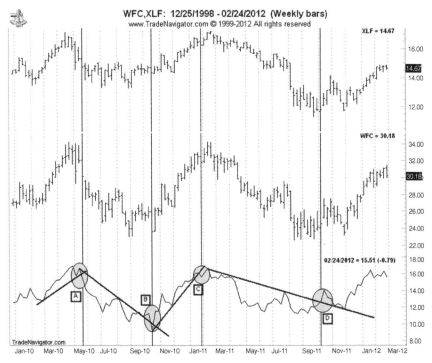

FIGURE 4.5   WFC, XLF: 12/25/1998–02/24/2012 (Weekly Bars)

points of price crossover on the RS chart to illustrate the under- or over-performance of the stock to the underlying sector. Point A on the chart represents the week ending May 21, 2010. Notice the price breakdown on the RS chart, which signifies that Wells Fargo may underperform or outperform to the downside its industry sector XLF. Comparing the two markets, the XLF closed at 14.75 and Wells Fargo closed at 30.11. On the week ending October 22, as point B on the chart shows, Wells Fargo was at $26.11 and the XLF was at $14.60. From point A to point B, the difference in prices was a loss of $0.15 or 1.1 percent on the XLF, while WFC lost $4 or 15 percent.

Then, from point B when the RS chart broke above the downtrend line, to point C, the XLF closed at $16.46, and WFC closed at $32.51 on the week ending January 21, 2011. From point B to point C the results showed a gain of $1.65 in the XLF or 12.7 percent and a gain of $6.40 per share or 24.5 percent in WFC.

Once again following the trend break from point C to point D on October 7, 2011, Wells Fargo was priced at $24.54, and the XLF was at $11.83. When the RS line broke below uptrend line at point C, this signaled that Wells Fargo should underperform the XLF. Indeed, it did in price: WFC lost $7.97 or 32 percent. The sector group lost $4.42 or 37 percent. Once the RS line broke back above the resistance line from point D to the last data on the chart, you can see one more trade signal generated to buy WFC compared to the XLF. As of the time of witting this book, XLF was at $14.67, while Wells Fargo was at $30.18, as the chart shows on the right-hand side. I believe this makes a good case for using an RS chart with trend-line analysis to help aid in the direction of prices when comparing which is the stronger of like and/or similar markets. While I must disclose that using a simple trend line is not the holy grail of market analytical tools, it does help in identifying potential shifts in trends when using relative strength performance charts.

In the commodity markets, pairs trading is called *spread trading*. A popular spread among energy traders is buying light sweet crude oil at the New York Mercantile Exchange and selling Brent Crude Oil futures on the Intercontinental Exchange (ICE). Another typical spread trade is the petroleum crack spread, which involves purchasing crude oil futures and selling in a ratio proportion of heating oil and gasoline futures. Examine Figure 4.6. This is a daily chart with crude oil in the upper section, gasoline in the second section, heating oil in the third section, and the "crack" spread chart in the lower section.

If the products (gasoline and heating oil) are more expensive relative to crude oil, the spread or RS line chart will rise as it did from point A on the charts. As the products begin to decline in value in relation to crude oil, the spread chart will decline, as shown at point B. This tool is very helpful

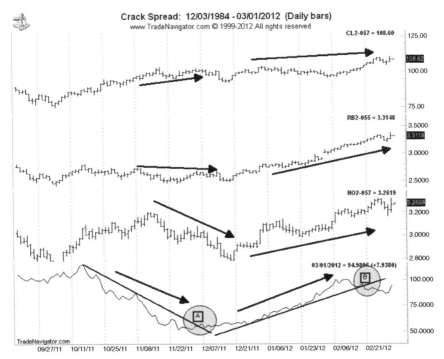

Crack Spread: 12/03/1984 - 03/01/2012 (Daily bars)

FIGURE 4.6   Crack Spread: 12/30/1998–03/01/2012 (Daily Bars)

for those trading energy stocks, as once the RS line break up above the trend line, it suggests that the refinery stocks sector should improve.

SPREAD TERMINOLOGY

There are intermarket and intramarket spreads, which are both recognized by the futures exchanges. That means a spread trade that is recognized by the commodity exchange is granted a relief in margin requirements, meaning traders receive a discount from a normal margin requirement for a trade.

The definition of an intermarket spread is a simultaneous purchase and sale of the similar futures contract on two different exchanges within the same delivery month. An example would be buying a May Wheat contract on the Chicago Mercantile Exchange (CME) and simultaneously selling a May Wheat contract on the Kansas City Board of Trade.

The definition of an intramarket spread is the simultaneous purchase of one commodity against a short position of the same commodity in a farther-out contract month, also known as the *time spread*. As a stock trader, you may not wish to trade in the physical commodity market; however, that does not mean you cannot use the information from the futures arena to help in your decision-making process of stocks or commodity-related ETFs.

Two examples of a spread trade in the precious metals area are gold versus silver and gold versus platinum. In Figure 4.7, we have a weekly chart with gold in the upper section, platinum in the middle, and the spread or RS chart in the lower quadrant. As the RS trend line shows, throughout much of 2011, gold outperformed platinum. As you can see from point A, it wasn't until the RS line crossed below the trend line that gold could start to underperform platinum. Not that gold would move down, just that it would underperform platinum's performance. Comparing the markets, for the week ending December 16, 2011, gold closed at 1,601.50, while platinum closed at 1,421.90. At the time that I was writing the book and as the chart

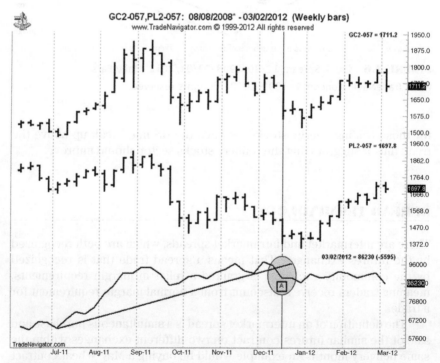

FIGURE 4.7 GC2-057, PL2-057: 08/08/2008–03/02/2012 (Weekly Bars)

shows, gold was trading at 1,711.2, while Platinum was trading at 1,697.80. That's a gain in gold of 109.7 or 6.8 percent; meanwhile, platinum gained 276.80 or 19.5 percent.

In equities, other popular spread trades are the S&P 500 futures versus the Nasdaq 100 (large-cap blue chips versus large-cap technology). Or there is the S&P 500 versus the Russell 2000. This spread is sometimes referred to as the *January effect trade* since the small-cap sector tends to outperform the large-cap from late December into late February. If that is the case, then applying a spread or RS chart should help to confirm such performance moves. Examine Figure 4.8. In the top quadrant we have the S&P 500 (SPY), and the middle section is the Russell 2000 (IWM), representing the small-cap sector. In the lower quadrant is the spread chart or RS line. Notice the downtrend coming to point A; this reflects weakness in the S&Ps versus the IWM. As the RS line breaks out above the resistance trend line at point A, this reflects that the S&Ps should outperform the IWM. This was December 21, 2011; the SPY closed at 124.17 and the IWM closed at 74.16 until the line break intersecting

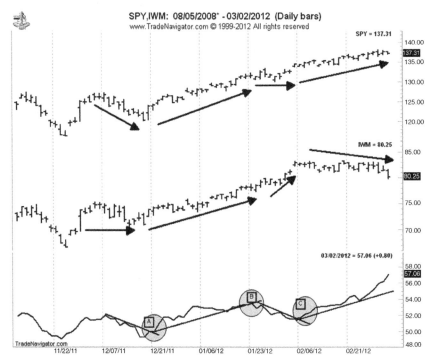

FIGURE 4.8 SPY, IWM: 08/05/2008–03/02/2012 (Daily Bars)
www.TradeNavigator.com © 1999–2012. All rights reserved.

at point B on the chart. This was January 23, where the SPY closed at 131.61 and the IWM closed at 78.15. From that time until February 6, the RS line trended lower and then reversed, breaking back above a resistance trend line. As you can see, from February 6 through March 2, the SPY outperformed the IWM as the SPY traded at 137.31 and the IWM traded at 80.25, as indicated on the chart. The conclusion here is that the overall January effect did not materialize in the sense that the small-cap sector as represented by the IWM did not outperform the large-cap sector as represented by the SPY. From point A on January 1, 2011, the SPY gained 13.14 points or 10.75 percent; while the Russell did move up, it gained only 6.09 points or 8.2 percent. Again, using the spread or RS chart would have helped investors to switch to the large-cap sector rather than the small-cap sector. As we discussed in the chapter on seasonality, remember that not all years are created equal. Some years the January effect works, and other years such as 2011 it doesn't work as well, as the RS chart showed in Figure 4.8.

More and more stock traders are taking advantage of the currency ETFs. As such, as a spread chart shows we can spot strength or weakness of one currency—such as the euro, the British pound, and the Japanese yen—against the U.S. dollar. Since these markets are priced in terms against the dollar, we can look at spreads between these currencies. A very popular spread trade among Forex traders is the euro/yen cross, or pairs trade. Remember, traders use spread positions when they see prices of one or more products under- or overperforming in relation to the other. As you can see in Figure 4.9, what makes this a very interesting spread relationship is that throughout the fourth quarter of 2011 the Japanese yen moved sideways, while the euro currency struggled amidst the European debt crisis. But notice the spread chart at point A; we see that the relationship starts to change as the euro currency starts to outperform the Japanese yen. The reason this is so interesting is that not only did the yen decline in value, but at the same time the euro appreciated in value. The RS spread chart identified a great trading opportunity. Equity option traders could have taken advantage of this by buying calls in the euro via the FXE and put options in the yen via the FXY. At the very least, by examining the relationship between two currencies, spread or RS charts help in identifying shifts in performance and, as this example shows, an early warning sign of an impending change in market direction.

Now let's return to looking at individual stocks against the industry sector. Since my origins as a trader began in the commodity arena, and being the co-editor of the *Commodity Trader's Almanac*, I look for trading opportunities in the agricultural sector using seasonal analysis. When we are in a strong period, I like to see confirmation using the spread or

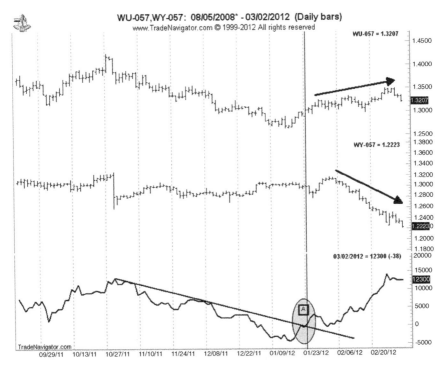

FIGURE 4.9 WU-057, WY-057: 08/05/2008–03/02/21012 (Daily Bars)
www.TradeNavigator.com © 1999–2012. All rights reserved.

RS charts. One stock in particular I like in the agricultural sector space on which to do comparative analysis is Monsanto (MON) versus the ETF MOO. For added confirmation, if we are in a seasonally strong period of time, then we should see the industry sector and corresponding stocks trade in sync, meaning they should both be trending higher. Using RS or spread charts can help us detect not just buying opportunities, but situations where hidden dangers lie. As I stated earlier, RS will help us uncover where money might be flowing, as well as where money might not be flowing. As you can see in Figure 4.10, the weakness between MON and the agricultural ETF MOO was evident not only in a simple trend-line analysis on the price chart, but it also showed up at point A on the spread or RS chart line. In fact, if you examine this closely, you will see the RS spread chart detected a day earlier an impending decrease in Monsanto versus the underlying industry sector ETF. This helps keep us out of a bad trade. Instead of looking to go long Monsanto, the RS charts help to show us that there was a disconnect between the stock and the underlying market.

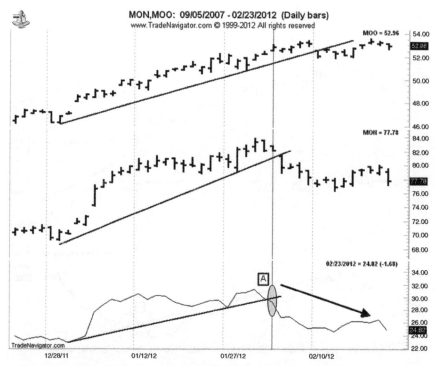

FIGURE 4.10 MON, MOO: 09/05/2007–02/23/2012 (Daily Bars)
www.TradeNavigator.com © 1999–2012. All rights reserved.

As you will discover, the RS charts can in fact give early warning signals, as you can see in Figure 4.11. We had the Dow Jones transportation average compared to Federal Express (FDX). Both the stock and the industry sector were in a strong uptrend. But notice it was the RS chart that revealed an impending market direction change, again illustrating the fact that the RS charts can give an earlier warning sign of trend changes in the markets.

Now let's take a look at what many call the lifeblood of the global economy, crude oil versus the stock market, as represented by the S&P 500. This is another interesting example in Figure 4.12, where we take a look at a commodity versus the overall market. It has been stated that as does crude oil prices, so does the stock market, but we do not always see that relationship exist. There comes a point in time when crude oil prices are relatively cheap and may reflect a poor economic environment. On the other side of the coin, if crude oil prices are relatively too expensive, it may reflect an overheating economy or a supply disruption. Either

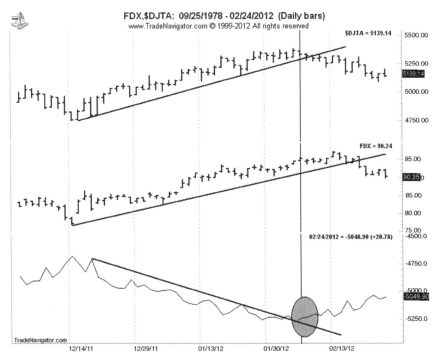

FIGURE 4.11   FDX, $DJTA: 09/25/1978–02/24/2012 (Daily Bars)

Trader's Tip

When placing a spread trade, one should remember to enter the size of each side of the trade basis, the notional value of each side of the spread. Spread trades are not necessarily placed on a "one-to-one" basis, such as selling 100 shares and buying 100 shares. In commodity spreads, for example, one platinum contract is 50 ounces and one gold contract is 100 ounces. Therefore, as a correct spread trade, a ratio of two contracts of platinum versus one contract of gold would be the correct trade per spread order. As for the S&P 500 (ES) versus the Nasdaq 100 (NQ), if the E-mini S&P is valued at 1,340 and the index is priced at $50 times the index, then the notional contract value is $67,000. At the same time, if the E-Mini Nasdaq 100 contract is valued at 2605 and the index is priced at $20 times the index, then the notional contract value is $52,100. Therefore, a correct ratio for a spread trade between the ES and the NQ would be four contracts of the S&P versus five contracts of the Nasdaq.

FIGURE 4.12   CL2-057, SPY: 02/11/1988–02/24/2012 (Daily Bars)
www.TradeNavigator.com © 1999–2012. All rights reserved.

way, when energy prices start to escalate, it does act as a taxing effect on consumers, which is bad for the economy and, more importantly, the stock market. Notice the S&Ps are in a strong uptrend, where the crude oil market was in a strong downtrend that relationship changed at point A, as indicated in the RS line chart. But notice that the line chart broke its resistance for days prior to crude oil breaking above its downtrend resistance line. As it shows, the rise in crude oil prices put a ceiling of resistance in the S&P 500 rally.

If I see a sector outperform others by more than two to one on a percentage basis, especially in a short period of time, generally I can look for the balance of sectors to either catch up or look for the strongest sector to pause or correct. Imagine if a sector were outperforming others by a large margin, say two to one, and we were entering a weak period or a seasonal peak for that sector. I could start to form a more educated trading strategy by looking to sell that sector or look at stocks in that sector to sell.

Now I can look at stocks to the sector and compare sector to sector and sectors to the benchmark index and the S&P 500. We can also look at commodity and currency markets in this light, such as gold, grains, meats, and the euro currency.

Let's call this true trading metrics. Two definitions of *metrics* found in *Webster's* dictionary are

1. The art of metrical composition, which is pertaining to measurement.
2. Combining form meaning the science of measuring that specified by the initial element.

Thus, using comparative RS is by definition trading metrics. Once again, the question begs: How we can make money using this form of analysis? Spread charts or RS comparisons graphs can give you an idea of the best place to put your money, but perhaps it may help you decide where not to put your money. Using trend-line breaks in the RS charts helps us to uncover what we call *divergence* between the spread chart and absolute prices. Therefore, make sure you set up your trading platform so that you look at the two different markets that you want to compare against, as well as the spread or the RS chart.

AUTOMATING SIGNALS

Most traders and technicians ask themselves what they can do to improve their indicators so they can respond more quickly to changes in market condition. The obvious answer is speed at which the data is received. But for end-of-day analysis, speed is not an issue. With thousands of markets to analyze, it would be nearly impossible to detect signals in all the market combinations, a requirement of using RS analysis. Therefore, it is best to take advantage of computer technology and create an automated scanning feature. How do we create this? By using moving averages on the RS charts themselves. As a rule of thumb, when using moving averages, the shorter the time frame, the more sensitive it is to price changes. I find that using a simple moving average for shorter time periods is effective for using longer time frames. Using a weighted moving average to the nearest close is more effective. For instance, if I'm using a 3-period moving average, I would use a simple moving average. If I'm using 12 or more time periods, I would use a weighted close moving average. In the following examples, I am using a 15-period weighted moving average.

Examine Figure 4.13, which is a daily chart on the S&P 500 (SPY) versus the Russell 2000 (IWM). In early January 2011, notice how the Russell, which is listed in the middle quadrant, significantly outperforms the S&Ps. The RS chart has an overlay of a moving average (dashed line)

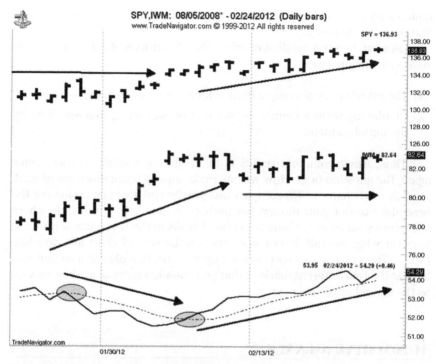

FIGURE 4.13 SPY, IWM: 08/05/2008*–02/24/2012 (Daily Bars)

to help smooth out price but also to help generate a sell signal. When the RS line crosses and closes below the moving average line, this signifies that the Russell is outperforming the S&Ps. As we have discussed, due to market conditions in their nature to trend, this relationship exists until early February. If you can learn to scan for a moving average crossover to the RS chart, it will alert you to potential trend or market direction changes. At the very least, with the scan using the moving average features, you will then be able to make a decision on how to act on a particular trade. More importantly, the number of markets that you're able to analyze will be greatly enhanced. As they say, the trend is your friend until it ends. Using the moving average to the RS approach rather than trend-line analysis, which is mechanical, moving averages are automated, and this automation will help you identify when a trend change is occurring.

Now examine Figure 4.14, which is the weekly bar chart on an RS comparison between IBM and the S&P 500 index. As you can see at point A on the chart, IBM breaks out above the moving average (dashed line),

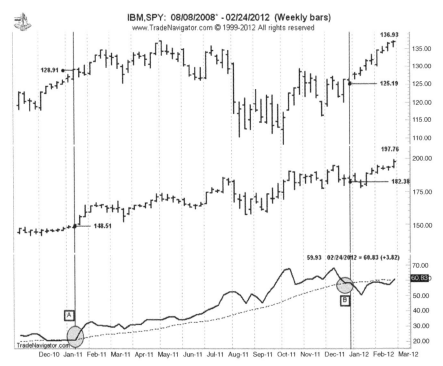

FIGURE 4.14 IBM, SPY: 08/08/2008*–02/24/2012 (Weekly Bars)
www.TradeNavigator.com © 1999–2012. All rights reserved.

generating a signal that IBM is outperforming the benchmark index. On the chart we have marked the prices so that you can see both markets' price at the intersection of point A and point B, with IBM from a trend trader's perspective to go along at 148.51 and then to exit at 182.38 in feed showing that it was better to be in an individual stock than the overall index. And at the same time the S&Ps traded at 128.91, and point B on the chart shows it closed at 125.19. Easily one could automate a trading system to scan for this change in relationship to identify when the trend was ending.

Automating the signals should not be confused with designing a trading system. A trading system does incorporate the use of moving averages in most cases. When using RS comparison spread charts, we're only looking for changes in performance of one market in relationship to the other. As shown in Figure 4.14, the relationship where IBM was outperforming the index changed at point B even though IBM continued to move higher; the S&Ps outperformed IBM as both markets continued to experience price gains. The key here to remember is that

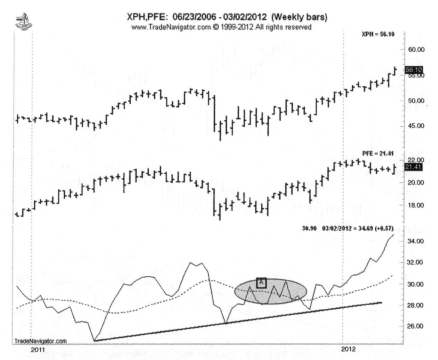

FIGURE 4.15   XPH, PFE: 06/23/2006–03/02/2012 (Weekly Bars)
www.TradeNavigator.com © 1999–2012. All rights reserved.

we automate the signals to allow us to do further examination to help us make better trade decisions. There will be times where we will get whipsaws, meaning the price or the index will flip-flop above and below the moving average, thus generating false signals. In fact, look at Figure 4.15, where we have a weekly chart between the pharmaceutical sector (XPH) and Pfizer (PFE).

The spread chart has an overlay of a 15-period weighted moving average; as you can see at point A, there are seven crossovers of the RS line in relationship to the moving average, beginning on September 16 and lasting through November 18. However, notice that the uptrend line connected from the lows continued to hold. If you apply trend-line analysis to the RS chart but use a scanning feature to alert you to trend changes, you may improve upon cleaner setups or trend changes. Automating the signals to alert you of impending trend changes is one thing, but using this method as a trading system to generate buy and sell signals on its own is another. It's most likely wiser to use the moving average to RS line as an indicator in of itself rather than as an automated trading system.

COMPARING MARKET PERFORMANCE

With the graph in Figure 4.16, as you will see, one can grasp a better understanding of the relative value of one asset or product versus another. This is not a spread chart or an RS chart. This is a performance graph, which can be changed from any starting point. Most brokerage firms' trading platforms show what are called *heat maps*, which reflect only the current market environment's money flow. This performance chart shows the relationship of the market trends and the percentage move over time for each respective market or sector.

This is important to me, because I can see if a certain sector is underperforming the overall market and look for buying opportunities, and I look for markets that have outperformed all the others and keep my indicators on alert for selling opportunities. In addition, it keeps me grounded by showing what the performance of the market is over a specific period of time.

The beginning of this chart is January 2006, which shows the performance of gold crude oil bonds, the Nasdaq composite index, the euro

FIGURE 4.16 FXE: Currency Shares Euro Trust (Weekly Bars)
www.TradeNavigator.com © 1999–2012. All rights reserved.

currency, and the S&P 500. It clearly shows that in 2008, as crude oil spiked sharply higher, most assets, including gold, declined. As the stock markets continued to struggle, crude oil moved higher as did gold, which outperformed all assets through this time. So as a trader and investor, I will be looking at a performance chart like this to see if there is a shift in value in the best performer and in the worst performer. During this time, gold was the best performer and the S&P 500 was the worst performer, so it would stand to reason that if gold starts to decline, we may see the equity market start to appreciate further in value. I will be looking for clues using a comparison performance chart to show the relationship of the markets. This, combined with other forms of analysis that we cover in this book, will help you make concrete investment decisions that will hopefully improve your performance.

Now let's look at specific markets and sectors to see where the money was going and not going, as shown in Figure 4.17.

Since the beginning of 2006, the worst sector of all has been the financials, and the best performer has been consumer staples. Typically, in

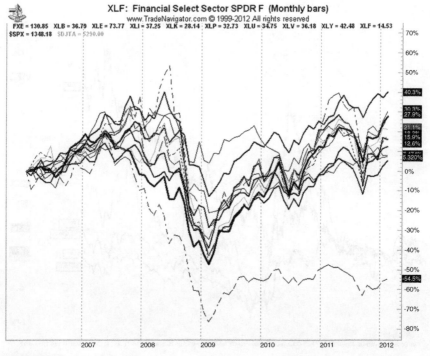

FIGURE 4.17   XLF: Financial Select Sector SPDR F (Monthly Bars)

periods of strong economic times, one would see the financials. The technology sector in transportation picks up, but certainly this chart may fully explain why the economy has been in a recession or a nongrowth period. Because this book is in black and white, it's hard to see the different performances and percentage figures, so I have them listed in Table 4.1. The two worst performing sectors during this time frame, as shown in bold are consumer staples and the financials. This, in essence, is another form of comparative market analysis in the sense that I'm able to gauge that money is in consumer staples; we're seeing a pickup in investment in technology and in the consumer discretionary sector. Notice that the euro currency outperformed the overall S&P 500 through this time frame.

In order to succeed in the markets, it's imperative to have solid analysis, which includes using multiple noncorrelated indicators and measurements of the market. Your analysis should include relative strength and comparative market interpretations. That way, you will know, based on a set of facts, where the money is flowing, and sometimes, more importantly, where the money's not flowing. Remember, money follows money. That's why momentum traders chase markets that are breaking out and making newer highs. An RS chart using trend lines is an effective way to see when a price relationship is changing, most times earlier than looking at the actual price of the individual market itself. This may help give you an inside edge in detecting money flows. Remember to use strategic and time-tested relationships, specifically looking at a stock to its industry group or a like market, as is the case when following commodity or commodity-based ETFs. An exception to this is when you use an inverse relationship like stocks to bonds. In Figure 4.18, we have a weekly chart between the S&P and the TLT, the ETF that tracks bond prices.

TABLE 4.1 Sector Performance and Percentage Figures

Sector	Symbol	% Change	Dec. 2005	2/14/2012
Consumer Disc.	XLY	27.60	33.23	42.41
Financial	XLF	**−54.7**	31.67	14.48
Energy	XLE	27.4	57.66	73.58
Material	XLB	15.7	31.74	36.72
Industrials	XLI	18.1	31.51	37.21
Technology	XLK	30.2	21.6	28.11
Consumer Staples	XLP	**40.2**	23.33	32.7
Utilities	XLU	7.84	32.15	34.67
Health care	XLV	12.5	32.13	36.13
DJ Trans.	DJTA	21.1	4367	52.9
S&P 500	SPY	5.2	1,280	1,346
Euro FX	FXE	7.4	121.75	130.81

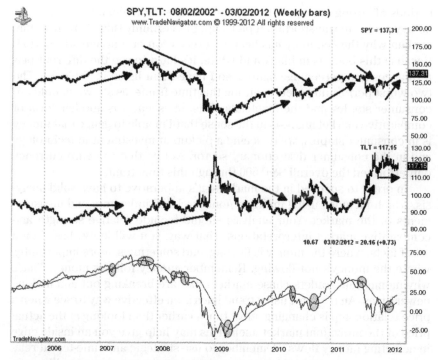

FIGURE 4.18   SPY, TLT: 08/02/2002*–03/02/2012 (Weekly Bars)
www.TradeNavigator.com © 1999–2012. All rights reserved.

Usually when stocks go down, bond prices will rise and vice versa. However, this is not a perfect market relationship, as there are times when stock and bond prices move in tandem, but over the long term we see that this inverse relationship has a strong correlation. The RS line has the 15-period weighted close moving average overlaid with highlights showing when the SPY under- and outperformed the TLT. In using the RS line chart, one can determine as the SPY starts to outperform bonds, equities are more bullish or in a friendlier environment, so we can now start to look at buying opportunities in various sectors. At this point, we can start to look for sectors that are entering or in their respective strongest seasonal time frames in order to enhance our performance for greater returns.

CONCLUSION

Comparative RS analysis demonstrates the concept of sticking with stocks in the strongest-performing groups—that's not to say that you can't make money in an overall rising stock market, but your best rate of return or performance will be with the stocks that are tied to strong industry groups. It also helps identify the weaker sectors, so you may figure out what to avoid. That way you are not putting good money to use on a less productive market. I don't want to make this out to be the end-all form of analysis. As I will discuss, there is no one single holy grail of market analysis tools or techniques; that's why we look for corroborating analysis, such as trying to fine-tune our indicators and finding the need for using a moving average of the spread or RS line in addition to trend-line analysis. The coming chapters will show how we can apply other tools and techniques to help pinpoint our price entries as well as exit strategies.

CHAPTER 5

Breadth Studies

This chapter is dedicated to explaining indicators that measure what is referred to as the *breadth of the market*. Namely, we will look at the measurement of advancing shares versus declining shares of a stock index. There are several indicators that we can use; I will focus on the most useful indicators and more aptly how to apply them in your market analysis. What I am attempting to do here with market data using breath indicators is simply gathering and organizing facts about the market.

Market breadth indicators will not give indications on a single stock but rather the market as a whole. And if the overall market is experiencing an undertone of strength or weakness, then it most likely will have an effect on individual stocks that are correlated in price movement based on the company's capitalized weighting to the overall stock index. Therefore, it's imperative to look at the health of the overall market before you select an entry or an exit on individual stock.

When it comes right down to it, there are many indicators out there that have been created with only six pieces of information: the number of advancing versus declining issues, the number of new 52-week highs and new 52-week lows, and the amount of volume on the advancing versus declining stocks.

Many of the pioneers in this field who deserve credit include Sherman McClellan, who created the McClellan Oscillator and Summation Index; Joe Granville, who is credited with structuring the on-balance volume indicator; and Richard Arms, of the popular Arms Index or the Trading Index (TRIN). Credit also goes out John McGinley, Martin Pring, John Murphy, Greg Morris, and Tom Aspray. These technicians mentioned here have either helped create or popularize, and certainly all of them have excelled in writing and teaching the correct mechanics of using breadth indicators. I recognize that there are more technicians and authors who have covered market breadth studies; however, these are the individuals I know or have had the pleasure of meeting in the past.

I want to cover some of the best indicators on measuring the breadth of the market and differentiate how it applies for both longer-term and short-term traders.

Market breadth analysis is an area in the field of technical analysis that concentrates on the performance of stocks, those that are moving up within an index versus those that are moving down. This way, we are looking at the overall health of the price action of the stocks within the index itself.

Volume, breadth, and momentum indicators all help us to evaluate price action. Think of these values like an X-ray or, better yet, as an MRI that reveals developments hidden from pure price analysis.

Slowing momentum and the decline in the pace of price change, combined with a weakening breadth, are often harbingers of a market top.

Here's another way to take the temperature of the market's strength or weakness, go through a list of stocks within an index, and then chart the percentage of stocks above their 10-, 20-, or 50-day simple moving average (SMA). You'll see that when there are more stocks that are trading below these short-term moving averages, even as the prices of broad indexes move up, eventually we see a market meltdown.

Why this is important to study is simple. Let's say you are looking to enter the market on a really good stock trade. If this measure of breadth is negative, you might want to wait on your purchase or, in fact, look for a deeper correction to buy that stock. In essence, this will help you price in a trade with less risk, thus giving you an edge in the timing of your trade.

This is exactly why discretionary traders use market breadth indicators as a tool to help signal when to buy and sell a security, especially a stock that might be weighted toward the overall index.

In addition, these tools help traders identify changes within an overall index so that they can trade the exchange-traded fund (ETF) based off of that index such as the S&Ps (SPY), the Nasdaq 100 (QQQ), the Russell 2000 (RUT or IWM), or the Dow Jones Industrial Average (DJIA).

The reason we want to look at advancing versus declining stocks within an index is simple: Most stock market indexes are created based on the formula of a market capitalization weighted model. In simple terms, this means that the market capitalization of an individual company can affect that company's impact on the overall index. Take, for example, the S&P 500; it is used as a benchmark for the overall U.S. stock market, and it is a market value weighted index, which means each stock's weight is proportionate to its market value.

The DJIA uses a price weighted index calculation. The detriment of the price weighted index is that a higher-price stock will have a larger impact on the overall index than the lower-price stock for the same percentage return. On the other side of the coin, a market capitalization index is more affected by a stock with a larger market capitalization than a stock with a smaller market capitalization. Therefore, companies that have a greater number of shares will have a larger influence on the index price movement for the same percentage change of their stock price. Due to this, we look at the market internals to help interpret potential bullishness or bearishness of a stock index.

You may have heard of the advance-decline (AD) line. This indicator is calculated as the cumulative value of the dancing issues of the stock index, minus the declining issues of the same index. There is no weighting or preference to a large- or a small-cap stock. Many stock advisory services' trading platforms typically refer to the New York Stock Exchange (NYSE) index.

This chapter will explain the importance of studying market internals and how to create your own AD lines for other popular indexes, including the S&P 500, the Nasdaq 100, the Russell 2000, and the DJIA. The reason I find it important to break down these four indexes is due to the weighting between technology; large-cap, dividend-yielding stocks; and small-capitalization stocks. By looking at market internals on these four indexes, we may also get an idea of whether money flows are going from one area to another, or we may see if there is an asset allocation movement occurring in the marketplace. In addition, it is also a good idea to see confirmation that a market move is not just isolated to one index. It is important to make sure that it is not just one stock index showing signs of weakness or strength, but rather all of the major stock indexes are moving in the same relative direction.

TREND-LINE ANALYSIS

Examine Figure 5.1. Here we have a short-term daily chart on the S&P 500 as represented by the SPY with the advance-decline comparative ratio line on the S&Ps. As you can see, stock prices were rising, making newer highs in late February, and the AD line was not rising in tandem, suggesting that perhaps more stocks were not participating in the rise in price as the index was showing. Just like we did in the preceding chapter with relative strength charts, here too, we apply a simple trend line to the AD line connecting the lows and extending upward. You can see where the AD line broke below the uptrend support, signifying an early-warning weakness or that market correction was eminent. As a result, nearly five trading days later, the market did experience a setback.

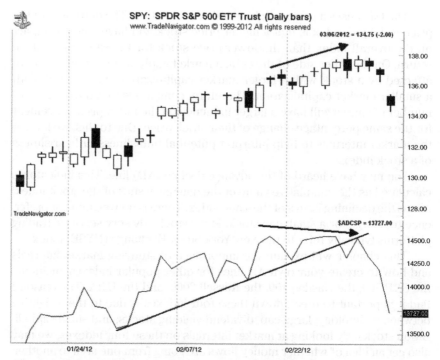

FIGURE 5.1 SPY: SPDR S&P 500 ETF Trust (Daily Bars)
www.TradeNavigator.com © 1999–2012. All rights reserved.

This event, where prices were rising but the indicator was declining, shows divergence, and that is when the most boring aspects of drawing a simple trend line will can help identify if the stock market has the necessary ingredients to move higher. When there exists a trend of rising stocks, there should be an accompanying event of advancing number of stocks moving higher with the overall market index. It should serve as a warning signal when the index moves up but is not followed by more stocks making positive gains in conjunction with the market.

When the comparative AD line starts to move lower as the broad-based market index moves higher, this forms a divergence, and that in itself is a true signal and the setup that we are looking to learn how to identify and then act on.

Now let's take a longer-term look at the S&Ps in relationship with the cumulative AD line. At almost every turn in the market, if you connect a trend line against prior lows and extending upward, when the AD breaks below that trend line, it is associated with a decline in price, as shown in the chart in Figure 5.2.

FIGURE 5.2 SPY: SPDR S&P 500 ETF Trust (Weekly Bars)
www.TradeNavigator.com © 1999–2012. All rights reserved.

Starting with point A, when the AD line broke below the trend line, see how prices were associated with a sharp decline in relationship with the AD line. At point B, when prices broke out above that resistance trend line, we saw price rise in connection with the AD line. At point C, when the AD line broke its upward trend line, notice how it came back and tested the old support line, which then acted as a new resistance line. This is a common occurrence when using the technique of drawing support and resistance trend lines. In addition, these breaks of the trend support and resistance often occurred prior to price reversals. As you can see, there are times when this form of analysis will uncover potential trend reversals in the market well in advance.

The area of concern became what is known as the Apple (AAPL) effect on stock indexes, of which it is a component. Just to name a few, there are the S&P 500 (SPX or SPY), the S&P 100 (OEX), the Nasdaq 100 (NDX) and the exchange-traded fund (ETF) QQQ, and there is also the technology SPDR Select Exchange Traded Fund (XLK). Those are just the most popular ones off the top of my head. All of these are examples of capitalization-weighted indexes, and as the price of Apple soared beyond 500 and traded

FIGURE 5.3   QQQ: PowerShares QQQ Trust, Series (Weekly Bars)
www.TradeNavigator.com © 1999–2012. All rights reserved.

over 600, it had such a large market capitalization, it impacted the perform-ance of these index values. For example, look at Figure 5.3; as a result of Apple's price move, the technology ETF QQQ has moved about 11 percent above its July 2011 high, as the resistance line shows at point A on the chart. Notice that it is almost at the same time Apple's stock price broke out above its July high as well, as shown at point B. Apple's stock price in-creased by more than 42 percent from that breakout level; you can see the impact it had on a "weighted index."

There is an equal weighted tradable ETF version of the (NDX), is the First Trust NASDAQ 100 (QQEW), as shown in Figure 5.4. I have Apple and the cumulative advance decline line on the Nasdaq in the lower quadrant. Notice that the equal weighted index more closely resembles the AD line. That is because the other 99 stocks in the index have the same weight as Apple's stock. This chart also suggests that while the QQEW has trended higher and finally broken out above its July high, the AD line has not con-firmed a broad-based rally in the technology sector—at least not until the AD line crosses above its July high as well. The AD line signals that not all stocks

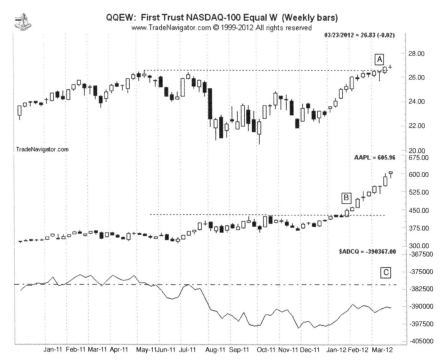

QQEW: First Trust NASDAQ-100 Equal W (Weekly bars)

FIGURE 5.4 QQEW: First Trust Nasdaq-100 Equal W (Weekly Bars)

in the Nasdaq are following through, making newer highs. If Apple does indeed decline, imagine the impact it will have on the capitalization weighted indexes? This combination of market data surely paints a different picture.

Now let's take this one step further. We discussed market capitalized weighting on stock indices. With its recent surge in share price, Apple became the second company to be valued just north of a half trillion dollars. That means Apple's stock price is about 4.07 percent of the S&P weighting. That compares to ExxonMobil, which in July 2007 became the first company to be valued above a half trillion dollars. By comparison, ExxonMobil is now (as of February 2012) valued at around $390 billion. Exxon has about a 3.35 percent weighting on the S&Ps. Microsoft's market cap is around $250 billion and has about a 1.92 percent weight. IBM's market capitalization is around $220 billion, with a 1.87 percent weight on the S&P. So let's say the S&P 500 is moving higher due to three stocks: Apple (AAPL), Microsoft (MSFT), and IBM (IBM). On the surface, it would appear that the stock market is moving higher, but looking at all the components that are built into the index may show a different story.

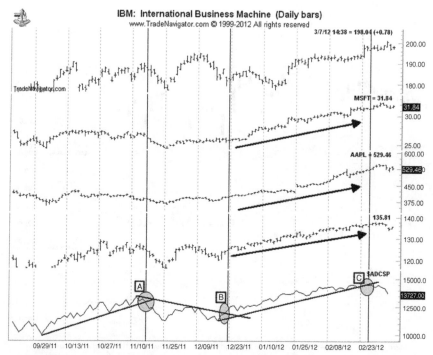

FIGURE 5.5   IBM: International Business Machine (Daily Bars)
www.TradeNavigator.com © 1999–2012. All rights reserved.

Look at Figure 5.5 and you'll see the top section has IBM. Underneath is Microsoft, then Apple, then the S&P 500, and finally, the AD line on the S&P 500 Index. Notice the trend from point B to point C. In fact, everything was moving higher initially except for IBM. Then, as the AD line broke the uptrend line, you continue to see higher prices in these three top stocks. This suggests that as the AD line was breaking its support versus these large caps, weighted stocks were moving higher. Most of the components within the S&P 500 were moving lower, so the AD line really did help alert us to a short-term decline in market price within the S&P 500 Index.

Now let's highlight sector weighting on the overall market. Figure 5.6 shows the 10 sectors in the S&P, starting with the lowest weighted sector, Telecommunications, with a weight of 3.07 percent. Next is Utilities with a 3.59 percent weighting, then Materials with 3.58 percent, Consumer Discretionary at 10.57 percent, Consumer Staples with 11.19 percent, Industrials with 10.48 percent, Health Care with 11.57 percent, Energy with 12.62 percent, Financials with 14.28 percent, and finally, Technology with a 19.06 percent weighting factor. So you see where just a few stocks in specific sectors can artificially give a false sense of market strength or weakness.

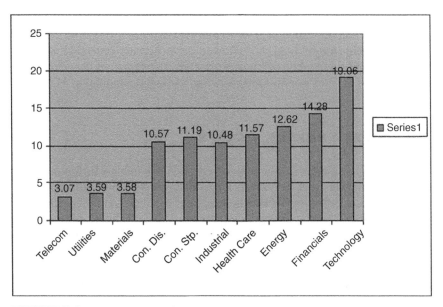

FIGURE 5.6 S&P Sector Weight

If, for example, several technology stocks move up but the telecoms and utilities move lower, there is more weight to the Technology sector, which means the overall index might not reflect the majority of stocks that were lower versus the few stocks that traded higher.

As you can see, the Energy, Financials, and Technology sectors comprise the bulk of the S&P 500 weighting. Therefore, it's understandable why most traders focus their attention on the top holdings in these sectors and may ignore the others, as they have low weighting or effect on the overall stock market performance. However, I argue that it's important to look at the complete picture, and that's what AD work will do for you. Examine the complete picture to see if there is a substantial rally in all stocks of all sectors.

Before we go on, we need to discuss some of the necessary information on breadth measurements. I prefer to look at the cumulative indicator, which simply adds the daily results to the previous total. When compiling day-to-day information, it may look different than AD for the week because we're looking at the difference between the prior Friday's close to the close of the current week.

So, you look at its daily chart and see that the AD line is moving lower, but when compared to a weekly chart at the end of the week, it shows that the AD line was rising. That's because the week should be based on the price change from the private previous Friday's close to the close of the current week. It has nothing to do with the daily data.

That is why the weekly trend changes on the AD line have a much higher significance than the daily line. Due to market volatility throughout 2010 and 2011, by the time a weekly AD line showed a convergence or trend-line break the market had succumbed to a horrific decline; therefore, you need to incorporate both daily and weekly analysis when using the cumulative AD lines.

BEARISH DIVERGENCE SIGNALS

As touched on in Figure 5.1, bearish divergence will help us formulate early signals on market tops; inversely, it's bullish convergence that will help identify market bottoms. Trend-line breaks can allude to short-term trend changes, but I consider divergence patterns a more reliable setup than a trend-line break. Bearish divergence patterns occur when the price of the security moves higher as the indicator or, in this case, the AD cumulative line trends lower. Price and indicator detach from a tandem price-to-indicator trend relationship. Look at Figure 5.7, which is a daily chart on the

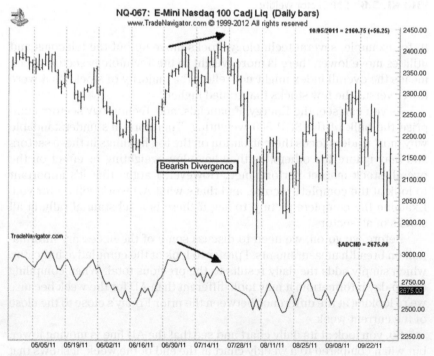

FIGURE 5.7 NQ-067: E-mini Nasdaq 100 Cadj Liq. (Daily Bars)

Nasdaq 100 futures. I use the futures markets charts, as they capture the European session markets movement, and therefore have fewer "gaps" in the charts, and I am using the cumulative AD line on the Nasdaq 100 Index. Notice the move in July 2011; as prices broke out and made a newer high, it was not accompanied by a move up in the AD line. In fact, the AD line made a lower high. If you drew a supporting trend line from the AD line low in June and connected it to the low made on July 18 and extended forward, a trend-line break would have occurred on July 28, thus confirming a trend reversal. As this chart shows, an incredibly violent sell-off in fact did occur.

Here are two suggestions on how you can make money on this type of setup: If you are versed in options strategies, simply buy put options on the Nasdaq 100 ETFs, the "Qs" (QQQ), or, you can buy (going long) an inverse-related ETF like the TYP. This is a three times inverse-leveraged ETF. This way, you are trading a security-based product with a directional trade bias.

Figure 5.8 shows a daily chart on the Russell 2000 Index (RUT); in the lower quadrant, the AD cumulative line is based on the RUT. Point A on the chart signals that the AD line broke below the trend line drawn

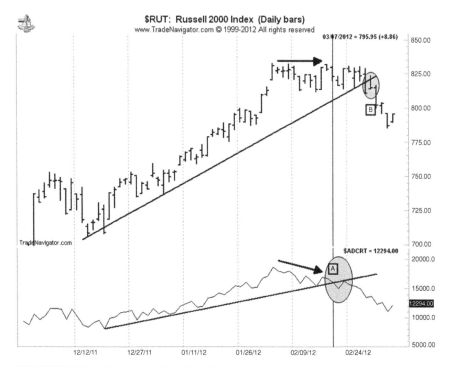

FIGURE 5.8 $RUT: Russell 2000 Index (Daily Bars)

by connecting the low from December 19, 2011, to the low made on January 6, 2012, and extending forward. While this signaled that there was trouble for the bulls—which developed seven trading days later, marked point B on the chart—the stronger and more reliable signal was evident in the declining trend in the AD line (as the arrow points out) while prices were chopping in a trading range. Eventually, a nice correction developed as the high on February 21 (Point A) was 831.01; by March 6, 2012, the low was 785.41, a nearly 6 percent correction in just 10 trading sessions.

I want to compare the Russell 2000 to the Nasdaq 100 during the same time. Figure 5.9 shows a daily chart with the AD cumulative line based on the Nasdaq 100. Notice we had a trend-line break here, as shown at point A. The difference here is that prices were rising, but so was the indicator. In fact, the AD line was making a higher high, and once it broke the trend line, that penetrating low was higher than the preceding low. There was no evidence of bearish divergence between price and the AD line as had existed in the Russell 2000 chart.

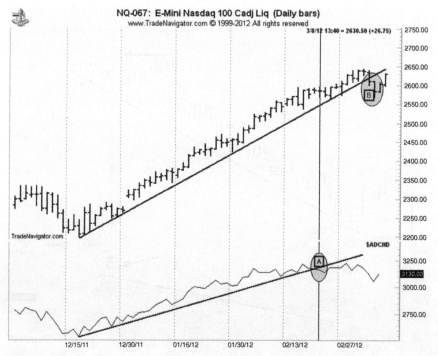

FIGURE 5.9   NQ-067: E-mini Nasdaq 100 Cadj Liq. (Daily Bars)

Now examine Figure 5.10 which is a daily chart on the Dow Jones as measured by the Dow Jones Industrial Average (DIA). The price action demonstrated steady uptrend, as did the AD cumulative line. This signals that stocks within the Dow were trading in tandem. Toward the end of February, the price of the Dow stalled, gyrating in a sideways channel. The AD line acted in a similar fashion. Then, on March 5, the AD line traded below the trend line at almost the exact time that the price traded below its uptrend line. What we did not see was a divergence in the AD line in relationship to the Dow prices. I must say that it was at this time in history that most analysts were looking and calling for a correction. The price charts show that we did experience a one-day correction, but nothing more. I believe a more serious correction would have developed if we had bearish divergence form not just in the Dow but in the Nasdaq and the S&P 500 as well. If you review Figure 5.1, we did have a trend-line break; however, there was no divergence pattern. That is a significant observation in the AD cumulative line as it relates to picking up sell signals.

FIGURE 5.10 DIA: SPDR Dow Jones Industrial Average (Daily Bars)
www.TradeNavigator.com © 1999–2012. All rights reserved.

Now let me play the role of the devil's advocate. Why in the world do I want to take a look at these four indexes when I can just look at the NYSE and the AD comparative line?

To answer that, let's look at the same time frame in the NYSE as we did in the other charts, as shown in Figure 5.11.

Notice here that the AD line was trending in sync with prices, but once the trend line was broken, as indicated at point A, we had a simultaneous trend-line break in price. Nowhere does a divergence develop like what occurred in the Russell. However, we seem to see a bigger correction in the NYSE than in the Nasdaq. What this tells me is that while one can use the NYSE for an overall market temperature using the AD comparative line, it is more useful to see which sector is the weakest and, in the case of the Nasdaq, the strongest. My advice is, if you are able to develop the AD lines for all indexes, take advantage of that information.

I would strongly suggest looking for bearish divergence in the AD line in relationship to prices. Furthermore, make sure you see a confluence of divergence across the various indexes to ensure that a stronger sell signal exists, especially when using daily chart data.

FIGURE 5.11 $NYA: NYSE Composite Index (Daily Bars)

www.TradeNavigator.com © 1999–2012. All rights reserved.

BULLISH CONVERGENCE SIGNALS

Now let's discuss the anomalies for bullish convergence that normally occur at market bottoms. Bullish convergence can typically indicate strong buy signals. Let's examine a few case studies. First, in Figure 5.12 we have a weekly chart on the DIA.

In August 2011, the stock market experienced a significant decline as prices show. We continued to see a consolidation toward lower prices that lasted into early October, but look at the comparative AD line—as prices trended lower, relatively fewer stocks went down in relationship to stocks that were rising. The indicator was making higher lows, while prices were making lower lows; this is, in essence, a classic formation of a bullish convergence buy signal.

Here is probably one of the very few examples throughout history where we had a bullish convergence set up a line with seasonal strength, since October generally marks the time frame when stock prices post their lows.

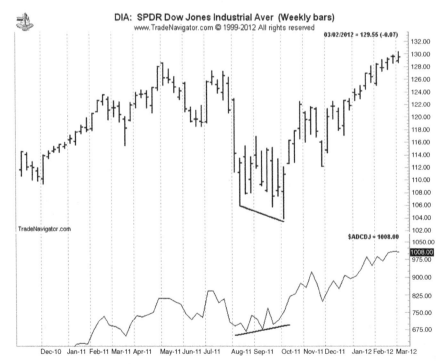

FIGURE 5.12 DIA: SPDR Dow Jones Industrial Average (Weekly Bars)

www.TradeNavigator.com © 1999–2012. All rights reserved.

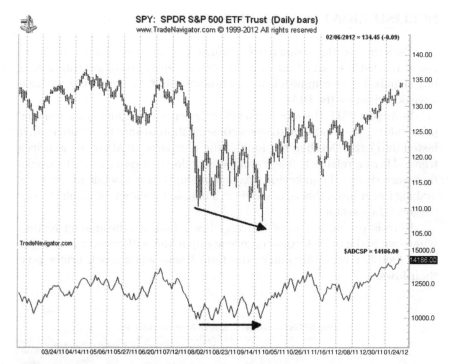

FIGURE 5.13   SPY: SPDR S&P 500 ETF Trust (Daily Bars)

Now let's examine Figure 5.13, which is a daily chart on the S&P 500, as measured by the ETF SPY. During that same period, from August through October 2011, you clearly see where prices made dramatic lower lows, but in the cumulative advance decline of the S&Ps. We did not make exact higher lows, but we did see a flat line against a support that could be drawn from the primary lows of the AD line. Even though the AD line did not make substantially higher lows, bullish convergence still existed, as the AD line did not make lower lows with prices.

Now let's switch to a daily chart and look at the NYSE Composite Index. Note in Figure 5.14 that a mini-correction began in November 2010; see how prices made lower lows at the same time. The cumulative AD line was creating a higher low, thus signaling a bullish convergence buy signal setup.

I hope this section illustrates the importance of bullish convergence and bearish divergence in the use of cumulative advance decline lines throughout the top stock indexes. There is a significant difference in the creation of tops versus bottoms of the markets. As the saying goes, "Tops

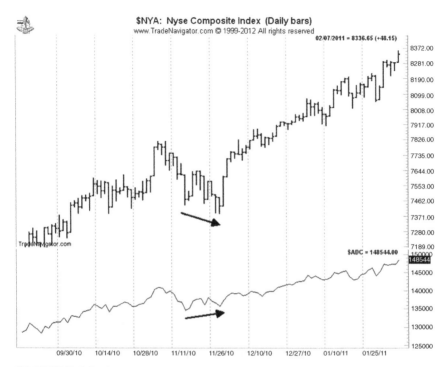

FIGURE 5.14 $NYA: NYSE Composite Index (Daily Bars)
www.TradeNavigator.com © 1999–2012. All rights reserved.

take longer to form than bottoms." Markets that post bottoms are typically more violent and short term in nature. Human emotions driven by fear tend to create selling out of panic; thus, we see most lows occur on increased volume at an extraordinarily fast-paced price change.

Most traders are looking to improve the quality of their research and market analysis. When looking at the overall health of a stock market rally, or examining the health and the destructive nature of a stock markets decline, I believe the most important tools to use to your advantage will be examining the trend or pattern of the cumulative AD line and identifying bullish convergences at the lows and watching for bearish divergence at tops.

SUPPORT AND RESISTANCE

So far, we have covered the importance of using the cumulative AD line in terms of using both trend lines and trend-line breakouts looking for bullish convergence at bottoms and bearish divergence at tops. When you apply simple trend-line charting techniques, remember to observe and to measure current prices as they relate to old highs or lows, points of interest, and to simultaneously examine the cumulative AD line values in relation to their past values in coordination with prices. If the price of a market is starting to make newer highs and the AD line is also breaking out of an old high, so that both the trend of the AD and the trend of prices are moving in tandem, then this indicates a strong rally and should not be faded. The strength of the trend is considered confirmed.

These three tips should be helpful for proper identification of price or indicator action in relationship or a trend line drawn:

1. Trend-line breakouts from old price points of interest.
2. Tests or challenges of trend-line breakout points.
3. Rejects of trend-line breakout points.

A rule of thumb for support and resistance is that what was once resistance typically turns into support, and vice versa. Compare past price action and then look at trend-line breakouts from old price points of interest, meaning whether market broke out above an old high or if the market broke down below an old low. This technique of using past price action or points of interest on the charts will help confirm strength or weakness, and that is why it's important to draw horizontal trend lines and extend out to the right and the left from those breakout levels.

It's amazing how a particular price level seems to attract or reject prices in the future. Logically, it stands to reason that if traders are buying a stock or an index at a specific level and keep losing, when the market rallies back up to that level, they will want to sell to liquidate just to break even. Remember that at every price high or low, someone sold the high and someone bought the low, and the reverse is true. So, when a market comes back to or breaks out from an old price point, those traders remember the agony of defeat, or the spoils of war, so to speak. And that's why the markets have a memory and gravitate toward certain price levels. The key is to see if there's enough positive energy to make prices run up to newer highs when they get to old resistance levels, and that's where drawing trend lines in both prices and in the cumulative AD lines comes in handy. In addition to trend-line breakouts from old price points of interest, we also see what we call "tests or challenges of the trend-line break." This setup not only shows up in price, but also occurs in indicators. Once the market breaks out of the old higher low, it will often come back to test that point of breakout, so look for pullbacks after breakouts to be what we call successfully tested.

And finally, we have trend-line rejects. This is where prices break out of an old support or resistance level, and just when the market expects the top on a rally and the absolute low to form at a bottom, the market continues its trend.

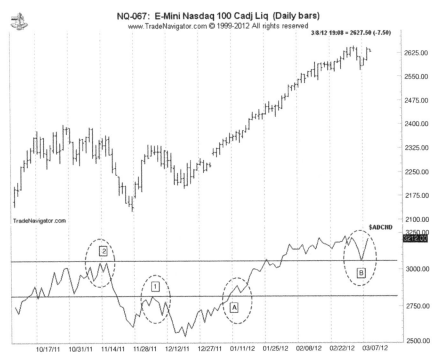

FIGURE 5.15 NQ-067: E-mini Nasdaq 100 Cadj Liq. (Daily Bars)
www.TradeNavigator.com © 1999–2012. All rights reserved.

Figure 5.15 shows a daily chart on the Nasdaq 100 with its respective cumulative AD line in the lower quadrant.

Let's first talk about trend-line breakouts from old price points of interest. As you can see, at point A we broke out above point 1, which created the horizontal line. You will see that this line is a point of reference of old highs and old lows. What's different is that once the AD line broke out above that horizontal resistance line in January 2012, there was a small pullback in the AD line, which successfully tested or challenged the trendline breakout point from the old high made at point 1. That old resistance level has turned into new support. You will notice that by mid-January, prices continued to rise until approximately January 25, where the AD line tested and old resistance marked point 2 on the chart. Again, the AD line backed off that resistance and then broke out above it. Coincidentally, prices continued to advance as well.

Now let's review rejects of trend-line breakout points. This is a very significant observation for traders, as many times when we tell ourselves that a market can't go any higher, the normal reaction is for greed and ego to take over and to start betting the farm that the high is in and load the boat on the short side. We call this a bear trap. In a bull or strong price rally, the market pulls back sucking short in, only to immediately reverse and continue higher. Bears or shorts get caught selling that low downdraft in the market, and then they have to scramble to cover their losses by buying back the short positions.

Please remember to trade the market on your terms—before you decide to sell believing a top is in, wait for confirmation of true breakdown in both prices and the indicators. Figure 5.16 shows a classic bear trap. At the beginning of March, we experienced a small correction in both the market and in the AD line as shown at point C. Notice that the old horizontal resistance level in the AD line turned into support. Once prices broke out above the old price high formed at point A, prices stalled or consolidated at point B; simultaneously, the AD line also broke out, thus setting a "line in the sand." A breakdown below that AD line level would now be a critical level to watch as confirmation for a top in the market. The key phrase here is a "break below that level." If you had waited to see not just a downdraft in

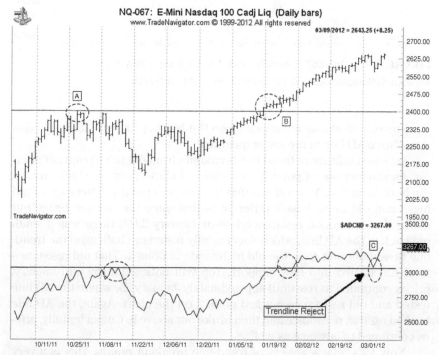

FIGURE 5.16   NQ-067: E-mini Nasdaq 100 Cadj Liq. (Daily Bars)

price, but also a break below that support and resistance line, you at least would not fall victim to a classic bear trap. By studying the relationship between the AD line and price and not specifically or singularly looking at tracking or charting prices, you will get a better-quality picture of the market's health. Using support and resistance techniques as described here is extremely important in using comparative AD lines.

INDICATORS AND MOVING AVERAGES

Just like I discussed in the previous chapter on comparative relative strength, we can apply a moving average on virtually any indicator, and the cumulative AD line is no exception. In fact, my friend, the famed technician Tom Aspray, has used this technique for decades. Again, just like any indicator, there is no holy grail, but a longer-term moving average can help determine the quality of the trend of the market as well as automating bullish and bearish trade signals based on crossover points between the moving average and the AD line.

The basic reasoning is not just to help generate the signals but, as we discovered, trend-line breaks within the cumulative AD line can give advanced warning of an impending directional price change. Then, since a moving average is literally a trend-creating tool in itself, it makes sense to formulate a moving average to this indicator. It can be argued that this is too technical or too time consuming, or is simply a bit of information overload. However, it stands to reason that if it helps my bottom line and increases my profitability, then by all means I will spend the extra minute or two it takes to set up the chart if it helps to give me an edge in the marketplace.

Take, for example, Figure 5.17. Here we have a weekly chart on the S&P 500 ETF SPY, with the cumulative AD line in the lower quadrant using a 20-period simple moving average (SMA). Starting with point A, we have a clean buy signal confirming an upswing in prices. This uptrend continued until point B, and once the indicator crossed below its moving average, it had successfully signaled a period of substantial price weakness from early May that lasted through late September until the AD line breakout at point C. From that point in time until point D, the AD line in relation with the moving average confirms a healthy price trend. Once we started to see the AD line break the moving averages, a whipsaw event unfolded as prices were in a corrective phase. Typically, this is where most traders are caught in a choppy market condition. From point D to point E, another corrective phase developed until prices resumed their advance with a moving average retest along the way in December 2011.

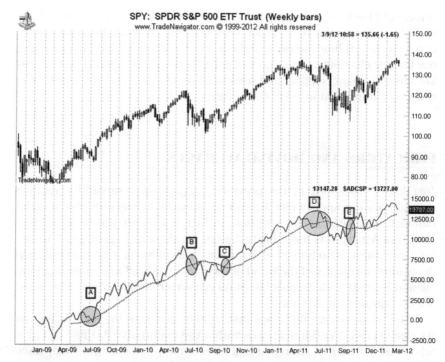

FIGURE 5.17 SPY: SPDR S&P 500 ETF Trust (Weekly Bars)
www.TradeNavigator.com © 1999–2012. All rights reserved.

Avoiding Whipsaws

A rule of thumb I like to follow is that after a long period of price appreciation as the price advance is very mature, typically, when that trend ends
that is when prices will consolidate before continuing or reversing the established trend. If you remember the old adage that tops take longer to
form than bottoms, then once a long-term uptrend develops, you will recognize that a consolidation phase will begin, and that might just save you
from getting caught in a whipsaw trading range.

This brings up one more important point: As a trader, I can't emphasize
enough the importance of using multiple time frames in your analysis. If we
are looking at a longer-term time frame, the weekly charts are a great asset,
but you need to integrate the shorter-term daily charts as well. I will admit,
the weekly chart did not give advance warning of a major price decline at
point B. This was the so-called flash crash.

However, the AD line to the moving average relationship departed or
separated significantly away from the moving average. This condition or

term between price and indicator to a moving average is called a *departure from the means.* When prices move too far from the average, the price action is considered overbought or oversold and is ripe for a correction. This is one more advantage of using moving averages, to help detect markets in the state of over- or undervalue. If we integrated a daily chart in addition to using a weekly chart at these points of interest, we could narrow our research to fine-tune our analysis to use shorter-term time frames to spot market reversals. As you can see in Figure 5.18, once the daily AD line crossed below the moving average, it gave an earlier warning, two days before that fateful market correction called the flash crash.

Don't forget that when using moving average studies, the shorter the time frame used, the more sensitive the moving average is to price changes. The moving average I used on the daily chart was a 14-period weighted moving average as labeled in the chart. It is acceptable to use multiple moving averages and look for a shorter-term moving average to cross above or below the longer-term moving average. This is another area of interest traders should look at when comparing various time frames on moving

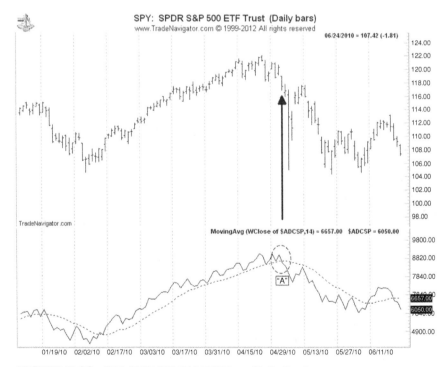

FIGURE 5.18 SPY: SPDR S&P 500 ETF Trust (Daily Bars)
www.TradeNavigator.com © 1999–2012. All rights reserved.

averages to the indicator. This could prove to be a more reasonable value for traders to explore in order to confirm trend reversals.

Advance-Decline Indicators

There is much to the subject of AD analysis. So far, we have covered comparative AD ratio lines using trend-line analysis, moving average analysis support, and resistance analysis. Now, to complete this chapter, it's important to discuss the work of several pioneers in this field and the development of the indicators that they created.

McClellan Index

In 2007, while giving a presentation on the Person's Pivot Indicator at the International Federation of Technical Analysis Society (IFTA) Conference in Sharm El Sheikh, Egypt, I had the pleasure of meeting Sherman McClellan, who developed the McClellan Oscillator and the McClellan Summation Index. I have been a big fan of both of these indicators, so it was a real pleasure to meet the creator in person, no pun intended. The McClellan Oscillator uses the data components of the advancing and declining stocks. The oscillator is the difference between the 19-day and the 39-day exponential moving average of the daily net advances, minus the declining figure. Most brokerage firms and trading platforms have the McClellan Oscillator already programmed, based on these default parameters, so you do not have to worry about becoming a programmer yourself.

The 19-day and 39-day moving average components approximately correlate to dominant and popular moving averages that correspond to market cycles, namely a one-month versus two-month time frame.

How to Use It

As the name implies, it is an oscillator, which gives indications of overbought and oversold market conditions. It also has a zero line crossover point, which helps to generate buy and sell signals. The oscillator is considered to be a short- to intermediate-term market timing indicator. This is debatable, but some believe readings below −100 help to identify market bottoms, and readings above +100 indicate overbought market conditions. As Figure 5.19 shows, using a daily chart on the S&P 500 (SPY), I overlaid three solid lines, one at +300, one at the zero line, and one at −300 and addition. I have overlaid two dashed lines, one at +150 and one at −150. Ditto market conditions experiencing heavier volume and more pronounced moves. I find the outer bands between −150 and −300 to be more reliable indicating market bottoms and +150 up to +300 indicating overbought market conditions.

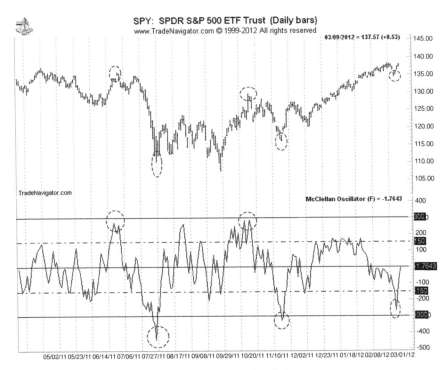

FIGURE 5.19 SPY: SPDR S&P 500 ETF Trust (Daily Bars)

Several of the techniques that we talked about in this chapter, such as trend-line breaks and rejection of supporter resistance, are applicable to this indicator as well. In addition, bullish convergences and divergences are useful as an oscillator showing overbought oversold conditions as, you can see by the circle marks in the corresponding price action, which shows that when the indicator falls near or below 300, we are at significant buy points. The inverse is true at near +300 readings, where the market shows when overbought conditions exist. As with any indicator, nothing is perfect and 100 percent guaranteed, but I believe you will find significant use in the McClellan Oscillator to help identify the strength or weakness of a trends direction. In addition, look for zero line rejections, as this technique is also useful in helping to uncover trend continuations when most are anticipating market corrections.

Let's look at this little closer by examining Figure 5.20. Again using the McClellan Oscillator, notice on the chart at point A that prices were making lower lows. However, within the McClellan Oscillator, prices were coming off of a –150 reading and the indicator made a higher low, signifying bullish

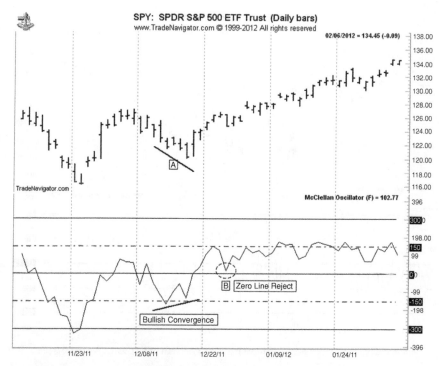

FIGURE 5.20 SPY: SPDR S&P 500 ETF Trust (Daily Bars)

www.TradeNavigator.com © 1999–2012. All rights reserved.

convergence as the market rallied. A small correction ensued. It appeared that the market may be forming a top, but notice the structure of the oscillator. It came back to the zero line and rejected it as it reversed course to a positive reading, thus giving a sign of strength in the marketplace.

This is not the end-all of techniques for using the McClellan Oscillator; however, most of the work that I've come across does not adequately discuss this indicator and the values it has for spotting trend reversals and trend continuations, especially for stock traders who are in positions that are highly correlated to the overall stock market's movement. Personally, I find this to be a vital indicator to use for short- and intermediate-term trend identification and price movement, especially using bullish convergence, bearish divergence, trend-line breaks, and as shown in Figure 5.20, where the zero line reject signals.

Now, what about the McClellan Summation Index? This is a cumulative sum of the daily McClellan Oscillator readings. It gives us a longer-range view of the market breath. Simply put, the value rises when the oscillator is positive. It declines when the oscillator turns negative.

When the McClellan Oscillator is positive, with readings above the zero line, the summation index will be rising. The actual readings of the summation index are just as important as the actual direction of that trend line. As you can see in Figure 5.21, the summation index shows periods of price weakness when the index falls below zero and shows periods of price strength when the index rises above zero. The index also lends itself to bullish convergence patterns and bearish divergence patterns. When the U.S. stock market was undergoing the significant sell-off from the financial crisis, when the actual low occurred in March 2009, as shown at point A on the chart, see how the McClellan Summation Index had a significant higher reading, thus forming a bullish convergence setup. As prices rallied throughout the next year, a bearish divergence pattern developed, as shown at point B. Yet this decline was short-lived as a bullish convergence pattern, but again developed as prices made a newer low, as point C shows. This proved to be another extension of a significant rise in stock prices until another textbook bearish divergence pattern formed at point D on the chart. News developed around the world in late 2011, as many believed another market crash would occur because the European sovereign debt crisis was unfolding due to the Greek bond defaults. However, the McClellan summation index generated a bullish convergence signal

FIGURE 5.21 SPY: SPDR S&P 500 ETF Trust (Daily Bars)

as shown at point E, thus setting up the U.S. market for another stellar market rally.

You'll find that the summation index will give hints of impending market stock corrections and market bottoms. Typically, a reading under –2,000 signals that the market is in an oversold condition, with the exception of 2008, when we had a daily reading of under –4,800. When the reading is over +3,000, we need to watch for danger signs of an impending top in the stock market. Several pioneers in the field of technical analysis brought to light the use of moving averages overlaid on an indicator to help generate buy and sell signals. With that stated, Figure 5.22 is a 14-period SMA overlaid on top of the McClellan summation index.

As the chart shows, several buy and sell signals are generated. I believe it would be more useful to look for moving average crossover buy signals from the extreme oversold readings near –2,000 and sell signals from the +3,000 level in order to confirm your suspicions of a market reversal from a significant high or low price point.

Arms Index

Good traders are observers of the current health of a market trend, but eventually we fall into the trap of becoming prognosticators in order to

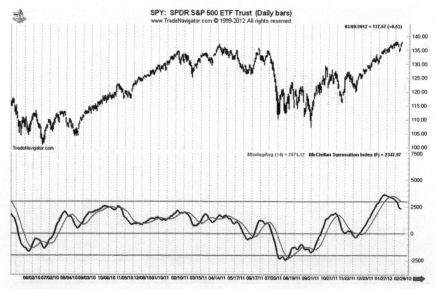

FIGURE 5.22   SPY: SPDR S&P 500 ETF Trust (Daily Bars)
www.TradeNavigator.com © 1999–2012. All rights reserved.

see when the change in the trend is likely to occur. This is not a bad thing. I believe that using technical analysis in the correct fashion and using the techniques and indicators that we have described so far will help you to uncover when there is a higher probability, or simply stated, a better chance of buying or selling in the marketplace. One more tool in market breadth analysis was developed by Richard Arms. Back in early 2005 at a conference in California, not only did I have the pleasure of meeting Mr. Arms, but we sat and had lunch, as we were both speaking at the same time. Because of that, I was unfortunately unable to sit and listen to his presentation. My whole life has been devoted to trading, so to actually meet this icon in the field of technical analysis was a privilege. The Arms Index was created by comparing the ratio advances to declines, and then the ratio of advancing volume to declining volume. Originally, it was called the short-term trading index (TRIN). It is still referred to as the TRIN to this day.

How to Use It

This is an inverse or opposite indicator in relationship to the direction of market price. The ratio line above one point reflects more volume in declining issues, and is negative. A falling line below one point reflects more volume coming into the market in a bullish stock market and is a positive indicator. In Figure 5.23 we have the raw Arms Index, or TRIN indicator,

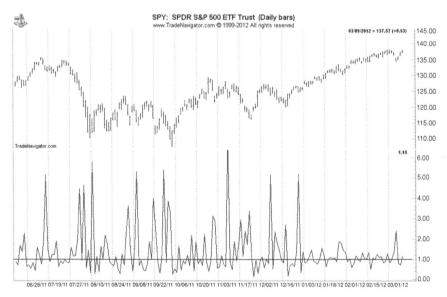

FIGURE 5.23 SPY: SPDR S&P 500 ETF Trust (Daily Bars)
www.TradeNavigator.com © 1999–2012. All rights reserved.

and as you can see, it looks like an EKG reading. However, the concept of combining up versus down issues and applying them versus down volume is very logical. Therefore, one would want to use a moving average component. Richard Arms uses a 21-day smoothing for intermediate-term price objectives and 55 days for longer-term use. Remember, this is an inverted indicator, so when the 21-day breaks below the 55-day moving average, a buy signal is generated. The opposite is true when a 21-day average goes up above the 55-day average; a sell signal is generated. My friend Tom Aspray created a 10-day average versus a 30-day average for this indicator.

If you believe in market contrarian or extremes, then the Arms Index theory is beneficial since it is perceived that if a reading above 3.00 indicates heavy volume on the sell side, then the market may be at an important bottom, what we call *capitulation point*. This is an indicator that you can apply a moving average component, which is more useful or helpful in smoothing out the data to generate less false signals. The moving average components are illustrated in Figure 5.24. Mr. Arms recommends a 5- day moving average of the Arms Index.

In Figure 5.25 we have a 10-period versus a 21-day moving average of the actual Arms Index. To make a more fluent market analysis, we have inverted the scale and the Arms Index. The Arms Index calculation itself gives us a number that can be infinitely large, but it cannot go below zero. That means the distance above 1.00 gets larger much more easily than the distance below

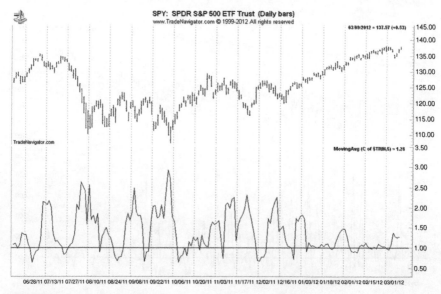

FIGURE 5.24   SPY: SPDR S&P 500 ETF Trust (Daily Bars)

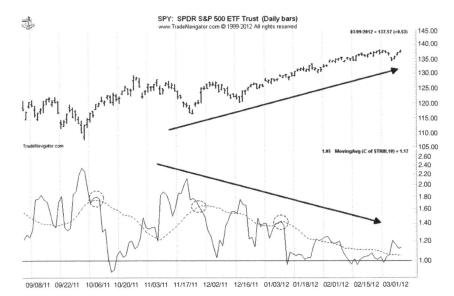

FIGURE 5.25 SPY: SPDR S&P 500 ETF Trust (Daily Bars)
www.TradeNavigator.com © 1999–2012. All rights reserved.

1.00 becomes smaller. We can adjust this by changing the vertical scale to a log scale. We still keep the 1.00 point as neutral for the index; we use this as the 21-day moving average of the Arms Index moves closer to the neutral line. It gives a strong indication of a potential bottom in prices. In addition, notice that when the 10-period moving average crosses beneath the 21-period moving average, prices increase. The closer we get to the 100-point, the more we tend to see bottoms being formed in the market.

CONCLUSION

Market breadth indicators can help you to determine whether a market is capable of extending gains or if the market has exhausted itself. We can apply many forms of technical analysis from simple trend line to complex moving averages. The key is how you identify and have the confidence in seeing past the store price action as it relates to these indicators to help you make your trade decisions. There are other methods of looking at breadth analysis. If you look at all the stocks in the S&P 500 to confirm if the trend is strong, see how many of the stocks within that index are above specific time-period moving averages. You can also look at an overall percentage of the components of stocks above their 200-day moving average. And you can look at the percentage of component stocks near 52-week highs within

4 percent and the percentage of component stocks at or near 52-week lows within 4 percent. I use 4 percent as an arbitrary percentage number. Say, for example, the market made a new 52-week within the last two weeks. If there's been a small correction, you'll still be able to pick up the fact that the stock is near its 52-week high or low, depending on your criteria or search. This method is a better way to gauge how healthy the market is. In addition, you will also be able to detect if the market is at an extreme overbought or oversold condition based on the number of stocks at or near highs and lows, as indicated with a 52-week look-back window.

Once again, we can look at these four points to help determine a stock market's health:

1. Index components—stocks above or below 10-, 20-, and 50-day moving average.

2. Percentage of components above 200-day moving average.

3. Percentage of components at 52-week highs.

4. Percentage of components at 52-week lows.

CHAPTER 6

Volume
Analysis

Whether you are a beginner or advanced trader, you need to address what goes into the decision-making process for whether to buy, sell, or hold. The decision-making process also includes whether to add to a trade, lighten the position size, adjust stops or hedging strategies (such as selling calls against long stock positions), or implement a collar strategy. Right, wrong, or indifferent, knowing when to get in and when to get out is the critical decision-making point for any trader.

Traders are constantly making important decisions, and making good ones and avoiding terrible ones is not an act of fate. It is a skill that can be learned, polished, and perfected. It is thought the repetition of executing constructive trading plans that one becomes a more successful seasoned trader. There's a fine line between trading smart with high frequency and just constantly trading. On the other side of the coin, some traders state that to be successful, you shouldn't trade often. I believe that to make successful decisions, there are techniques to enhance your effectiveness, and success does come from repetition by making better-educated decisions. Knowing that, perhaps you'll trade with more frequency, but with more purpose. Here is a case in point; do you get better at golf by swinging smarter but not often? If you learned to swim at an early age, this is not a skill at which you would have wanted to apply the methodology "swim smart but not often." You probably took lessons and practiced way before letting go of the instructor's hand, kick board, or inflatable life vest.

Trading and investing are similar—you need to practice and work through the steps of conceptualizing a trade, executing, and following through. In later chapters, we will cover putting together a checklist, a set of criteria or algorithms for those who are looking to program computer scans for trading opportunities. But first, I want to cover what I think is crucial in substantiating quality trades.

As I've said before and will say again and again throughout the book, there is no holy grail of one methodology for trading, and, believe me, not every trade is going to be a winner. But well-thought-out plans based on sound research from factual data and followed through with good execution are what you should strive for to become a profitable trader. It is through repetition and consistency that one achieves successful results.

In this book, we will present dynamic material that is engaging and practical, so that no matter what level of trader you are, you will be able to apply it to your business. In fact, in this chapter, we are going to compare and contrast various situations to help you refine your ability to distinguish between smart and poor decision-making analysis so that you will be able to identify higher-probability trading opportunities.

Think about what goes into influencing your decision-making process on a psychological, financial, and emotional level. If you examine that, perhaps you shall be able to better sidestep the potential mistakes that most traders make. Questions start to pop up in one's mind, such as: Will this position make up for the last trade? How much of a loss can I afford to take on this trade? How much will I make on this? Do I have the time to watch this trade? First, the last trade should have nothing to do with a new position. Most likely, a new trade will have a completely new matrix and set of variables. Second, while it is true that most analysts use either fundamental or technical tools to formulate a price objective, it is prudent to advise you that market conditions change. Profit objectives can easily be missed and can easily be over- or underestimated.

With that said, how can we gauge the potential for a move? One of the best measures is what I call the fifth element of data, volume analysis. Remember, the first four bits of data are the open, the high, the low, and the close, otherwise referred to as prices.

Volume is considered the lifeblood of any marketplace. Volume shows us whether there is participation and helps define liquidity. Price tells us what the value of a product is, but volume tells us how it happened. I suppose this is when I could start to use metaphors to help you relate why volume plays an important role in trading, but I would rather get to the point and show you it can work to give you an edge in the market. I am not going into the details of all the specific volume indicators that are available. There are some really good ones and others with redundancies, and some are three times removed from the raw data, such as an oscillator of the difference between moving averages of volume and volume itself. One such indicator is the Chaikin Money Flow Oscillator, created by Mark Chaikin. There are many books and articles written on market breadth and volume indicators. Greg Morris has *The Complete Guide to Market Breadth Indicators* (McGraw-Hill, 2005) and John Murphy's work in his book *Technical Analysis of the Financial Markets* (New York Institute of Finance, 1999) covers more indicators as well. However, I want to illustrate and focus on a simplistic time-tested tool I currently use. But my goal in this chapter also is to teach you techniques so that you can use a specific indicator and volume more effectively.

Simply stated, the definition of volume is the number of equity or stock shares or futures contracts traded in a market during a given period of time. End-of-day volume for a stock is simply the number of shares that trade hands from buyers to sellers. If one buys 1,000 shares, then the volume for that period increases immediately by 1,000 shares based on that transaction.

The rule of thumb on volume theory is when prices are rising accompanied by a rise in volume, then there is the belief that the market is under a healthy and sustainable move. If the market is rising and the underlying volume levels are decreasing, the theory states that this is a weak or unhealthy rally and any further price gains will probably not be sustained.

Both statements are true to a degree, but in the past eight years or so, we have experienced substantial bullish moves in markets while in a low volume environment. This trend of declining volume while prices are rising is completely contradictory to what all technicians have relied on and used as a guide for decades. So what could the reasoning be as to why we see this contradiction?

I believe it is based on several factors. One factor is that more hedge funds are globally based use derivative products such as options and exchange-traded funds (ETFs). An option trader can take on a synthetic long position, which entails selling a put option and buying a call option, thus masking a long stock trade. Another concept is that high-frequency traders (HFTs) significantly add to daily volumes totals but reduce transactions on extremely volatile days, which in theory will reduce volume transactions.

Let's examine a case in point. Look at Figure 6.1; here we have a significant bullish trend in the gold market as illustrated using the ETF GLD. At the time the price was moving higher, there were many disbelievers because of the theory that price increases need to be sustained on a rise in volume. This rally had a declining trend in volume, and as the chart shows, the price did, in fact, continue to rise despite a declining trend of volume.

Now let's look at Figure 6.2, which is the same chart of (GLD) during the same time period using a volume indicator rather than volume by itself. You can clearly see prices were rising while at the same time the volume indicator was rising and making newer highs. What's the difference?

The difference is that one is an actual recordable volume table and the other is an indicator called on-balance volume (OBV), which was created

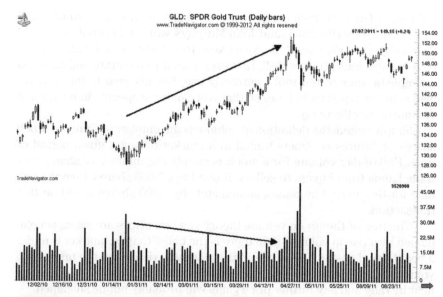

FIGURE 6.1   GLD: SPRDR Gold Trust (Daily Bars)
www.TradeNavigator.com © 1999–2012. All rights reserved.

FIGURE 6.2   GLD: SPDR Gold Trust (Daily Bars)
www.TradeNavigator.com © 1999–2012. All rights reserved.

by Joe Granville in the 1970s. Here is how it works: The on-OBV indicator adds to a running total the volume of each bar with a higher close than the bar before and subtracts from the total the volume of each bar with a lower close. The running total is plotted as a line. The use of both price and volume provides a different perspective from price or volume alone. Because OBV begins accumulating values from the left of the chart, the numeric value of OBV will depend on the data available in the chart. Therefore, the relative value, or trend direction, of OBV is more important than its numeric value.

This is just one of the many volume indicators available to investors on most any trading platform or brokerage firms that offer a charting software package. I am going to delve a bit more into this tool in just a bit, but I thought it would show that there are better tools out there to use to help us uncover hidden value in the market, whether the trend is strong or weak.

Now let's look at one more situation in the SPDR (SPY) Index using volume bars. As you can see in Figure 6.3, from the low in March 2009, the price trended significantly higher for a substantial period of time. Look at the trend of the overall volume. See how it trended lower? As a result, there were many prognosticators who were warning investors that the rally was unsustainable, as the move was not accompanied with a rise in volume.

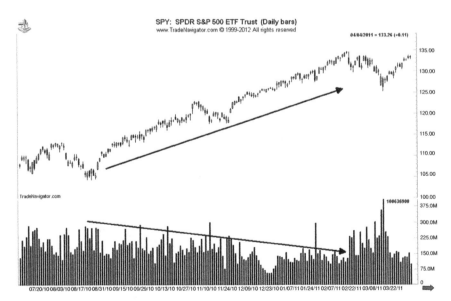

FIGURE 6.3 SPY: SPDR S&P 500 ETF Trust (Daily Bars)
www.TradeNavigator.com © 1999–2012. All rights reserved.

Here is the problem that this can cause: Without looking further into the facts, it could cause a trader or investor to completely avoid getting into the market, thus missing what is now called a once- or twice-in-a-lifetime buying opportunity. Or worse, what did happen to many was to sell short, believing the market was ready to crash again. As you compare Figure 6.3 with just the volume bars against Figure 6.4, which is the same time frame and same market using SPY, look how the OBV indicator trended higher in price, confirming a bullish trend. Perhaps the overall volume in the market was lighter, but was this missing volume as a result of offsetting positions taking place in ETFs or options strategies? Clearly, the better tool in this sample of data was the OBV Indicator.

While it was true the trend of the volume was not increasing with price, clearly this is a case where you want to explore what the volume measurements are on days or weeks when prices rise, but also the volume relationship on down days and weeks. In addition, as we discussed in the preceding chapter, how about adding a breadth study to see when the overall index rises is the running total rising and are more stocks moving higher versus lower? In Figure 6.5, we have prices of the market in the upper quadrant with the cumulative advance decline indicator specifically for the Standard & Poor's (S&P) 500 under that, then the OBV Indicator and the volume bars at the bottom of the chart. This is the same sample time period as shown

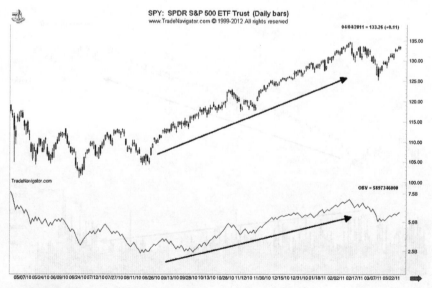

FIGURE 6.4   SPY: SPDR S&P 500 ETF Trust (Daily Bars)

www.TradeNavigator.com © 1999–2012. All rights reserved.

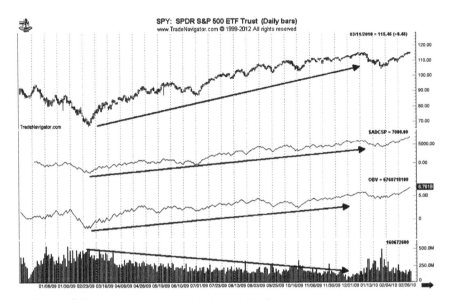

FIGURE 6.5 SPY: SPDR S&P 500 ETF Trust (Daily Bars)
www.TradeNavigator.com © 1999–2012. All rights reserved.

in Figure 6.4, and as you can see, the breadth or condition of the market as a whole was indeed healthy and corresponding or in gear with both the uptrend in the OBV indicator and prices. The volume bars, though, were trending lower.

As you look at this comparison, it almost makes you want to believe that as volume was trending lower, the overall market price was actually in a healthier condition. The price trend did have longevity. In fact, we can see from the volume bars, as prices peaked temporarily in late January 2010, volume finally started to trend higher, but notice that prices started to decline. You can even see that the actual peak in the volume bar was created on February 5, 2010, the same day the exact low was made before the market continued to resume the uptrend. If you look at the bottom left of the chart, you will see where the heavy volume comes in as the market is creating the low from January into March 2009.

According to this small sample or this one situation, it appears that increasing prices tend to be accompanied by declining volume trends and that when the market makes bottoms, we see heightened volume levels. This is an interesting observation, which we will expand upon in this chapter, since we do see heavier volume attributed to what we call selling climaxes.

Finally, looking at Figure 6.5, as prices began their short-term correction in February 2010, we observed that volume was finally starting to pick up.

At the same time, if you used the trend-line technique that we applied on the comparative advance-decline (AD) lines from Chapter 5 on both the OBV indicator and in the cumulative AD line, you will no doubt see a nice trend-line break alerting you to this short-term top that occurred in the market.

Let's expand on this observation, as it is very important for you to know how to identify a change in market conditions. When price is rising and volume bars are trending lower, a red flag should go. Once you are in a trade, it is important to monitor the market to determine how it will affect your positions. The indicators we are using are there to help us take action either by taking some portion of our positions off and adjusting our stops up to protect what we have earned or simply exiting a trade entirely or putting on a protective option strategy.

I have zoomed in on that peak made in February and drawn in the appropriate trend lines to illustrate that top pattern. The price trend line broke almost halfway into the correction. The cumulative AD line broke its trend line a bit earlier, as indicated at point A on the chart. Now focus your attention at point B, which is the OBV indicator; not only did it break its rising trend line, but see the dotted circle—it also created a head-and-shoulders pattern. This is a very important aspect of using indicators. We will and do see traditional patterns within the indicators themselves that may not show up in the price charts. The one rule for a head-and-shoulders pattern to become completed is that you look for the neckline to be broken, which, as you can see, occurs simultaneously at the point in time that the uptrend line is broken on the indicator. Point C on the chart illustrates the rising trend in volume, showing that selling is picking up pace right up until the selling climax occurs on February 5. You will also notice that the day the low was formed created a "doji" pattern on the candlestick chart, which also follows up with the high-close doji pattern that we will cover later.

The use of the OBV indicator and both the trend-line break technique and combining the rule of the head-and-shoulders neckline break gave warning of a correction in the market on the close of January 20, 2010. That was at 113.89. Just 12 trading days later, SPY hit a low of 104.58.

As we covered in the previous chapter on market breadth—or the internals—and the benefits of examining the four top indexes, here is a classic example where that technique will help guide you to confirming if the market may be ready to experience a correction. Examine Figure 6.7. Here we have the SPDR DIA representing the Dow Jones Industrial Average (DJIA). As you can see on the chart, a very similar pattern exists using the cumulative AD line on the Dow, as labeled on the chart ($ADCDJ). A trend-line break does occur on January 20, and I have taken the liberty to overlay a vertical line that also shows the corresponding trend-line break on the OBV indicator and the simultaneous head-and-shoulders neckline

FIGURE 6.6 SPY: SPDR S&P 500 ETF Trust (Daily Bars)
www.TradeNavigator.com © 1999–2012. All rights reserved.

break pattern that developed on the Dow's indicator at point B. The market closed at 106.02 on January 20, and the low was created on February 5 at 98.36, which translated to a 766-point Dow move.

HINDSIGHT IS 20/20

The saying goes that hindsight is 20/20, and if we look hard enough, we can make almost any chart support our case, usually after the fact. But we do see patterns repeat themselves. The technical analysis and indicators we have to work with—while some are most definitely better than others—will not be able to give us the insight to accurately predict what the outcome the markets will be as a direct result of using the indicators or by examining price patterns. They do give us fair warning on most major market moves. It is up to us how we act and closely monitor the market conditions with the tools and data we have at our disposal.

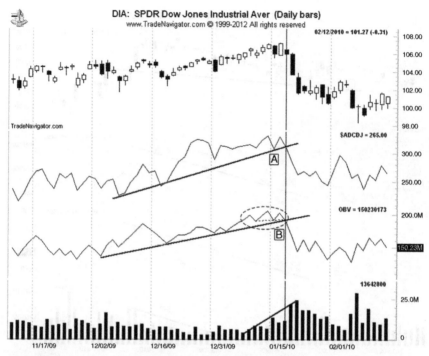

FIGURE 6.7   DIA: SPDR Dow Jones Industrial Average (Daily Bars)
www.TradeNavigator.com © 1999–2012. All rights reserved.

As you may well be aware, after the low was made on February 5, the stock market reversed from that low and the Dow (DIA) traded to a new yearly high of 112.08 by April 26, 2010, a 14.48 percent gain in just under 12 weeks. That was eight days before what became known as the flash crash on May 6, 2010. There were many signs of an impending correction; the most basic was the seasonal tendency for stock markets to decline in May. Remember, in Chapter 2, we quoted Yale Hirsch's observation made in the *Stock Trader's Almanac*: "Sell in May and go away." Let's examine the volume aspect, since that is the center of focus in this chapter. The question is: Would this technique work—did the indicator stand the test of time? The answer is emphatically yes, and as a matter of fact, there was an interesting pattern that formed within the OBV indicator: a head-and-shoulders top formation with a neckline break.

In Figure 6.8, we had a very similar breakdown in the cumulative AD line, as shown at point A. The intersecting vertical line shows the point of trend line break that occurred on May 4, two days before the flash crash. Notice that, as the Dow was making newer highs, the AD line was

FIGURE 6.8 DIA: SPDR Dow Jones Industrial Average (Daily Bars)
www.TradeNavigator.com © 1999–2012. All rights reserved.

struggling to make newer highs as well. In addition, the day the exact high was made, on April 26, a doji candle pattern formed a very ominous sign of indecision, one that was signaling that this bullish trend was in question. But it was the OBV indicator that had created a head-and-shoulders formation that I believe was a major warning flag. Not only did the intermediate-term uptrend line break, but so did the neckline trend, as shown at point B. The volume bars started to increase once again, just like they did in February, just 12 weeks earlier. One last point is the highest volume bar was made on the day of the flash crash and the day after. Even though prices came back to test that low and did, for a time, carve out a newer price low, the market did not trade on that same level of transaction volume. As prices dipped to lows, we did see that selling occurred on extremely high volume, which is usually a good indication of a selling climax.

This setup between the trend-line breaks and, most importantly, the head-and-shoulders top formation in the OBV indicator is a most useful setup, and I trust you will be on alert for these patterns in the future to warn you of impending tops, whether they are of great magnitude or minor corrections.

CURRENT EVENT ANALYSIS

Now that we have covered how to use the OBV indicator with trend-line breaks and incorporating patterns such as head-and-shoulders formations, I also want to emphasize the importance of the relationship between that indicator and volume bars. We have covered a small sampling of this indicator to actual volume relationship, and so far, it appears that when prices rise, it's typically on declining volume, and when the market falls, the bottom in prices is typically associated with a high peak volume day.

Let's fast-forward and focus on the most recent market action. In the first quarter of 2012, the stock market had rallied toward nosebleed levels, with extremely minor corrections lasting a day or two before accelerating upward. Everyone was calling for a correction, yet the market continued to advance. Apple's stock traded to an intraday high of 600.01; the market seemed unstoppable. In fact, the Commodity Futures Trading Commission's Commitment of Traders (COT) data showed that small speculators were short the whole way up.

I myself was a petrified bull. I was mildly long and using the rally to lighten my long positions. Hindsight, as we know, is 20/20; I should have doubled up on my longs, but instead, I was cautious. The good news, and the lesson learned here, is I was not selling short the market. In fact, staying true to the analysis that I am sharing in this book, at PA Stock Alerts, we were long a select group of stocks in the financial and energy space. The reason is this: These sectors were in a seasonally strong time, and the market in general was maintaining the bull trend. As the old adage goes, the trend is your friend until it ends. Examine Figure 6.9, which is a daily chart on SPY with the OBV indicator in the middle quadrant and the volume bars at the bottom of the chart. This chart has a very similar characteristic to the significant rallies we covered from the low of 2009, the move in 2010, and the rally in 2011 in the sense that the OBV indicator was trending higher in concert with prices, while at the same time, the trend in the daily volume was declining.

Seeing if the OBV indicator has formed a head-and-shoulders top with a trend-line break from the time this book is being written to when it goes to press and then to when you start reading will serve as a great case study. But as the chart shows, until we have a trend-line break or a pickup in volume, or the seasonal "sell in May and go away" theme plays out, the best choice is to continue to ride the trend until these conditions change.

FIGURE 6.9 SPY: SPDR S&P 500 ETF Trust (Daily Bars)
www.TradeNavigator.com © 1999–2012. All rights reserved.

INDIVIDUAL STOCKS

When you examine a chart with volume bars, it may be difficult to spot subtle changes or shifts in the volume levels. It is changes in patterns that give us a read or clue as to a market's strength or weakness. Is OBV the best indicator out there? Some may take the point of view that this indicator is not the greatest for all markets; I argue that it is one of the more simplistic and easiest to use. The key to remember when using this indicator is if prices are rising, then the OBV Indicator should rise in tandem with prices. If prices are rising but we see OBV flatline, then the indicator is not confirming the rally and therefore, one should be suspicious of that rally. Use of trend lines or overlaying moving averages is appropriate to use in conjunction with this indicator. One of the pitfalls of this indicator is that it assigns a positive and negative value to up and down days. Suppose a market forms a doji or gaps higher and closes closer to the low of that session. Does this indicator account for that sufficiently? I believe you will find it does a good job compared to studying volume bars alone.

Examine Figure 6.10, a daily chart on Apple (AAPL) as it was rising to the stratosphere, hitting the $600 milestone. At the end of 2011, prices were in a steady uptrend, as confirmed by the OBV Indicator, and in typical fashion, volume bars were trending lower. Then, the first major gap up occurred on January 25, 2012; the volume spiked, as shown at point A on the chart. Notice that the OBV Indicator broke above a previous resistance level and was now acting as support. What the indicator was showing was that the move was sustained and buying pressure was still evident. For many using just the volume bar analysis, it may have given a false sense of a blow-off top. Then, as the market continued the rally into February, the OBV Indicator was rising in gear with prices. This, in effect, was confirming that this move was healthy—until February 15, when the market gapped higher and closed sharply lower, triggering what appeared at the time to be a key reversal formation. But once again, the volume bar, as illustrated at point B, may have given yet another false blow-off top signal. At this juncture, look at the OBV Indicator. First of all, it did not break below the trend-line support, and it did not reflect a bearish head-and-shoulders pattern. What it did was pause and form a small wedge-like pattern until the OBV line broke out above the dashed resistance line. This triggered another bullish confirmation. As of the time of writing this book, Apple stock is trading over 600; we have yet another high-volume bar, as shown at point C; the OBV Indicator is in a solid uptrend; and there is no trigger to sell stock, buy put options, or get bearish on this stock simply because it is high priced. Selling a stock simply because you think "it can't go any higher" is not a sell signal. That is a market opinion, and not based on factual data. You should be making trading decisions based only on a solid trading plan. When AAPL or any stock has gone what we call parabolic (straight-up), typically we will get a clue that the market is topping out. You need to wait for that clue. I believe the OBV Indicator will alert you when that happens if you wait and watch for it. When you start guessing when the bottom or top is in a market, most likely the first 10 times you are going to be wrong, and that will end up costing you money. Believe me, I know some traders out there were saying, "It can't go any higher" or "I am I sure it will come down eventually," but realize that the vast majority were saying that at 350, 425, 450, 475, 525, 575, and then at 600. If these folks were buying or writing a bearish option strategy, odds favor the fact that on this situation, they lost money either from time decay (theta) or short call strategies that went intrinsic (in the money) on them. Once again, by looking at this price chart in Figure 6.10, we see that the trend was still intact, the OBV Indicator was moving with prices, and the volume bars were not a big help, except for illustrating that there was an increase in volume transactions from about $500 per share up to $600.

In my opinion, using OBV to confirm trends in individual stocks is not only effective, but I believe it is also s a gem of an indicator for the computer-challenged or start-up trader. It will not only help you to determine whether a bull trend is developing, it will also confirm the trend's strength.

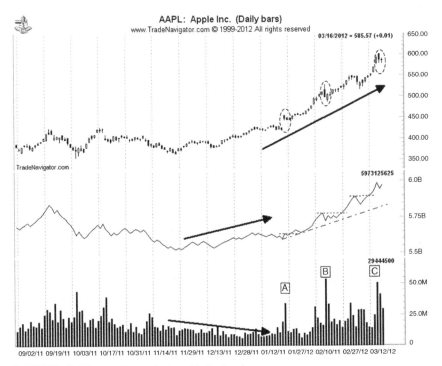

FIGURE 6.10 AAPL: Apple Inc. (Daily Bars)

Remember what I wrote about Starbucks? Believe me, in writing this book, my consumption of their coffee helped boost sales so much that I probably added at least 3 percent to the stock's value from January through April 2012.

All joking aside, look at Figure 6.11, a weekly chart on Starbucks (SBUX). Throughout this move, volume overall has trended lower as price has risen in sync with the OBV Indicator, with a few exceptions. SBUX's price has been engaged in a solid uptrend from the March 2009 low. Let me point out the few corrections that have materialized along the way, including the August 2011 sell-off shown at point A. See how the volume spiked, hinting that we could see a significant decline? The OBV indicator did retrace in step with prices, as point C shows, but notice that it held a support level drawn from the last low point from point B.

At the point in time shown at point A on the chart, the volume bars created a spike, as shown at point D, suggesting a blow-off top. There was a heavy surge in volume as prices started to decline. Using the OBV Indicator gave a slightly different analysis, as the line at point C did not break the support line. Prices then consolidated, regrouped, and continued marching along with the dominant bullish trend. Once again, when comparing price and volume, use the OBV indicator. It can give you a more detailed look at the overall volume trend and help confirm market participation.

BEARISH DIVERGENCE

We want to check for convergence and divergence patterns as well, and the OBV Indicator helps to provide these patterns. Again, bearish divergence is when prices rise and the indicator declines; thus, they diverge from each other's respective trends.

A typical short-term bearish divergence in the OVB Indicator will resemble a pattern similar to the one in Figure 6.12. Prices make a high, then a correction or pause, if you will; the OBV indicator posts a high and pulls back in line with the price pause. Then prices will make a follow-through higher high, but the indicator does not. Confirmation that the rally has failed comes as

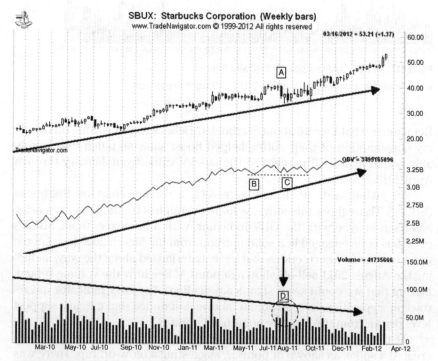

FIGURE 6.11   SBUX: Starbucks Corporation (Weekly Bars)

www.TradeNavigator.com © 1999–2012. All rights reserved.

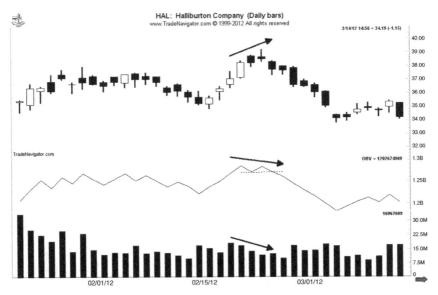

FIGURE 6.12 HAL: Halliburton Company (Daily Bars)
www.TradeNavigator.com © 1999–2012. All rights reserved.

the OBV Indicator makes a newer low in concert with a decline in price. This signals that the sellers are taking over. As you can see from this example, in Halliburton (HAL),the volume bars were a bit misleading since the surge in prices was on a rise in the volume bars, and as prices started to correct lower, the volume bars also declined. The OBV Indicator is more useful in tracking the price trends flow as far as illustrating buying and selling pressures.

As far as the characteristics of an intermediate- to longer-term bearish divergence pattern to form, it is important to examine the OBV Indicator's reading at previous price peaks. Typically, I would not like to see a newer high to form more than 30 days. The previous highs usually are tested within a shorter period of time, say within two weeks. From the time the first peak high is made, prices pull back and will pause or consolidate. Then, as bulls take charge again and momentum builds, prices advance. The key here is to realize that what creates the bearish divergence is that this new secondary high does not have the participation behind the move. There are fewer buyers, and perhaps the secondary high is created by slight short covering. This may help explain the fundamentals behind this weak secondary price peak. In any event, the OBV Indicator helps identify these weaker uptrends and gives a lower high reading. Examine Figure 6.13; as the chart on the GLD shows, the volume bars do not change significantly to alert you of a weak or potential bull trap like the OBV Indicator does.

FIGURE 6.13   GLD: SPDR Gold Trust (Daily Bars)
www.TradeNavigator.com © 1999–2012. All rights reserved.

BULLISH CONVERGENCE

When prices decline and make newer lows while the indicator simultaneously makes higher lows in correspondence with the secondary low, the relationship between price and the indicator converges or "comes together."
This pattern is evident, as shown in Bank of America (BAC) at the beginning of January 2012. As you can see at point A on the chart in Figure 6.14,
the OBV Indicator was moving higher as prices were trending lower.
As the market started to lose the selling pressure every time it made a
newer low, prices had little follow-through to the downside. Buyers were
stepping in, either those establishing new positions, or those who previ-
ously sold and were buying back, thus covering the shorts. What develops
is this pattern known as *convergence*. This is a very formidable and high-
probability buying formation. After a market has a long-term price decline
and the pace of price change diminishes or does not make a strong price
decline, meaning we do not have significant lower lows, the key to look
for is the higher low readings in the OBV indicator. Again, this is a bearish
divergence between price and indicator. Prices make a newer low, but the
indicator does not.

FIGURE 6.14 BAC: Bank of America Corporation (Weekly Bars)
www.TradeNavigator.com © 1999–2012. All rights reserved.

SELLING CLIMAX

Volume bar analysis is still extremely useful; I do not want to give you the impression that it should be replaced entirely by the OBV Indicator. When we have violent price declines, or what technicians refer to as a "V-Bottom formation," typically the selling climax is confirmed by a surge in volume as longs throw in the towel, otherwise referred to as *capitulation.* Here, as well, if a low was made on significant volume, it will add a level of confirmation that a low is in place. Examine Figure 6.15; notice we have SPY showing that the low in February 2010 was made after a significant decline on extremely heavy volume. The actual candle pattern, as illustrated at point A, was in fact a doji formation. Typically, these indicate indecision and can give hints to a market reversal. The low created on a spike in volume certainly fits the description of a selling climax. To trade this, we look for confirmation that the low is in place. This chart low actually created

FIGURE 6.15   SPY: SPDR S&P 500 ETF Trust (Daily Bars)

the high-close doji pattern I have published in many of my books. This is a high probability buying setup. We will go over this formation in detail in a later chapter.

EXHAUSTION TOPS

Just like for a selling climax, volume bars are very useful in determining if a market is in a blow-off or exhaustion top phase. Examine Figure 6.16, a daily chart on U.S. Steel (X). As the trend advanced higher at the end of January 2012, there was one more thrust that made a newer high. Just preceding that high, the market advanced with a huge spike in volume. Then, three days of continuous higher highs occurred, as point A shows, marking the high of the move, with small or narrow range candles forming. Now here is the key: The new high for the move was made with a subsequent decline in volume. Little follow-through in price after a huge surge in volume is a warning flag that the market may be in for a correction. Here again, we look for confirmation of the actual reversal to occur. Candlestick analysis shows that a bearish engulfing pattern had formed three days after the exact high was made, and then the price reversal was under way. Spikes in volume should alert you that something is occurring in the market. We will

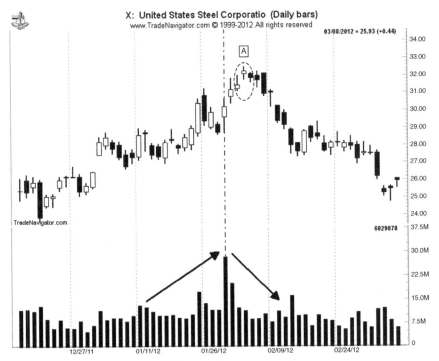

FIGURE 6.16 X: United States Steel Corporation (Daily Bars)
www.TradeNavigator.com © 1999–2012. All rights reserved.

either see these at market bottoms or as a market nears a top, and we also see volume spikes during a strong trending market from time to time. The key is to look at the overall market and examine where prices came from. Watch for price failure, or, as in the case in Figure 6.16, watch if the market makes newer highs with declining volume after the spike. That may help alert you to an exhaustion top. This observation my just keep you from buying at the top of a move.

TRADING PATTERNS

Wedges

Just as you may have studied or have used with price charts, traditional patterns can and should be applied to indicators such as OBV. We looked at several other patterns, like head-and-shoulder tops, in Figures 6.7 and 6.8,

FIGURE 6.17   FCX: Freeport-McMoran Copper & Gold (Daily Bars)
www.TradeNavigator.com © 1999–2012. All rights reserved.

then the bullish convergence and bearish divergence pattern. Now let's examine Figure 6.17, which shows a wedge formation both in price and in the OBV Indicator. As you can see, at point A on the chart, the volume line broke out above the overhead resistance level, confirming the price move up and away from the higher gap opening, as shown at point B. This type of setup requires you to be diligent and patient, as well as having a keen eye for gap moves. Many software programs like Genesis and TradeStation can be programmed to scan and alert you for gap moves. What makes this a more interesting setup is the breakout of the volume associated with prices. This gives strong confirmation to go with this breakout. It is also an interesting note that Freeport McMoran (FCX) Copper & Gold, Inc., as the name implies, produces copper. One can assume that if copper prices rise, or if demand for copper increases, then they may see increased revenue and share prices could move up. That's the theory, at least. Knowing these guys are in the copper business, you should be aware of the seasonal tendency for copper to bottom in late December. So if you line up your trades by seasonality and sectors by month, then this stock should be on your radar screen. The OBV wedge breakout formation provides added confirmation to go long between the 38.00 and 40.00 levels, with stops below the swing low under 36.00. Granted, prices peaked at 48.96 on January 26, 2012, with a long-legged doji. It was certainly a nice trade since prices rose over 20 percent in less than 12 trading session, giving plenty of room to take money off the table. In fact, this was a trade made from our research at PA Stocks for these exact reasons. I am sharing this, as these are the sequence of events and techniques that I use to unveil clues or help confirm trade setups just like this one. OBV breakouts from a compression, over time forming the wedge pattern, is a powerful confirmation tool.

Inverted Head-and-Shoulders

Inverted head-and-shoulders are very strong bottom patterns. They are the reverse of a head-and-shoulders top formation, such as those shown in Figures 6.7 and 6.8. The next chart, in Figure 6.18, is a weekly chart on Caterpillar (CAT). Did you notice that the symmetry of the inverted head-and-shoulders formation is more defined in the indicator than in the actual price chart itself? This is a common occurrence, which is another great reason to use price and volume together. You may get a better picture from the indicator itself rather than prices. The exception is the measuring technique when applying pattern analysis to indicators. For example, once the so-called "neckline" is violated, the rule of thumb is to measure the distance from the head to the neckline and project upwards to determine a resistance or profit objective. Since the OBV Indicator is not a price value, this is not applicable. What is useful is seeing the volume levels correspond

FIGURE 6.18 CAT: Caterpillar, Inc. (Weekly Bars)

with prices. Once the OBV line breaks out above the neckline resistance, if there is a pullback, the OBV line should not go back under the newfound support created by the neckline. The pattern within the indicator will help confirm a breakout of prices.

Time-of-Day Patterns

Examine Figure 6.19; using a 60-minute chart during the open outcry session on SPY, notice that the heavy volume spikes seem to occur during the first two and last two hours of the trading sessions. This creates a U-shaped pattern of volume every day. That is why I took the liberty to place a U above those volume bars in each respective day. The reason I wanted to bring this up is that as you develop as a trader, you will be watching for patterns to repeat and you will be also be looking for when patterns should occur and then do not. That is a clue that something is up. Big up and down daily price reversals tend to hold a steadier volume all day than a U-shaped pattern. So, if you are in a long trade and the pace of price change is very aggressive and you are considering taking money off the table, watch the intraday volume levels to see what they reveal. If volume is not backing off significantly, especially during the lunch or midday session as it normally will do, then this may be a clue that the buying pressure is still quite significant and you may wish to hold on to

FIGURE 6.19   SPY: SPDR S&P 500 ETF Trust (60-Minute Bars)
www.TradeNavigator.com © 1999–2012. All rights reserved.

your long positions a bit longer. In fact, HFTs are apt to look for these situations, and that may be a reason we see certain trading sessions not always adhere to the normal U-shaped volume patterns during strong trending days.

VOLUME AND HIGH-FREQUENCY TRADERS

HFTs are literally individuals, companies, or proprietary outfits that take trade ideas and specific sets of algorithms and program them into super-light-speed computers and servers for trade execution. Larger HFTs' proprietary firms (prop firms) can contribute anywhere from 2 to 10 percent of the average daily volume for many stocks. If the average daily volume of a stock is five million shares, an HFT would account for between 100,000 and 500,000 shares per day! At times, this is what is to blame for excess volatility, and it has become an issue on Capitol Hill. Others, including myself, recognize this field as having improved the liquidity in most stocks and ETFs and brought about more efficient markets.

How they accomplish this, or shall I say at the heart of high-frequency trading, is not just state-of-the-art hardware, but also software and how the interaction between the two can be worked to maximize performance. Speed, security of proprietary algorithms, and technology are critical and now are easily available. Many so-called high-frequency traders use Sun Microsystems, Hewlett-Packard, and Dell servers. Programming can be complicated, and believe it or not, Excel can be used on some software vendors. The main essence is bandwidth and processor speed. This raises a concern about fair access to market data in order to interpret and then act on that information since it seems these institutional type traders are gaining an unfair advantage over the normal retail speculator. That not only includes the downloaded data, but also news release of information that's transmitted via exchanges, government agencies, and/or private weather companies.

As they say, "the devil is in the details," and for HFTs, the details are in the technology that delivers the speed of information and execution, which is what gives the HFT the upper hand to a degree. The reason I bring this subject up is quite appropriate, especially for this section on volume. As I mentioned, ever since the flash crash in May 2010, HFTs have been on the regulatory agencies' radar screens. It has been estimated that HFTs account for more than 60 percent of U.S. equity share volume.

There are several terms and concepts that I want to include in this book for the novice trader so that the terms do not scare you. For advanced traders who know all about HFTs, please skip to the next chapter.

VOLUME WEIGHTED AVERAGE PRICE

Volume weighted average price (VWAP) equals the dollar value of all trading periods divided by the total trading volume for the current day. Calculation starts when trading opens and ends when trading closes.

Dark pools are for buying and selling large blocks of stock security orders without showing the amount of bids or asks or the identity behind the orders. Orders rest in an alternative trading system (ATS) that matches buy and sell orders for execution without first routing an order through an exchange or other electronic communication networks (ECN). These dark pools were created to enable the user to execute a large block order without impacting the quotes on level II or public quotation services. Broker-dealers and large institutional firms have their own in-house dark pools, which allow for conditions of anonymity.

Algorithm Factors

1. Order Entry: As volatility increases, the algorithm becomes increasingly more aggressive in order execution or entering larger block orders.

2. Price: When the best-selected price becomes more favorable, the algorithm will execute or release more orders to be filled.

3. Bid/Asks: The wider the spread or difference between bid and ask is, the more passive order entry the algorithm initiates.

4. Price Direction: The more stock prices that are printing, the more aggressive or more passive the algorithm becomes as needed to execute the desired amount of shares.

5. Momentum: If there is a strong trend in the stock price as set by more frequent higher highs higher lows, the pace of price change accelerates; the algorithm is programmed to be more aggressive in order entry. This is the multidimensional sensitivity profile.

An order entry algorithm can be programmed by measuring these factors to help determine the optimum strategy to execute large block orders. Most HFT platforms allow a trader to take over direct control of participation rate. It's not just the change of price, but the change of liquidity. Remember, most traders are not looking for the lowest price to buy; rather, they are looking to get the best average price. When order flow dries up, a trader must reduce his or her order sizes; otherwise, it could significantly impact the overall market. Where a dark pool feature can come in handy is in allowing the trader to control the minimum fill size so that multiple small fills will not leak out into the marketplace. The showing of the hand of this particular institutional trader helps hide both the potential orders and perhaps, the the trading methodology, such as increasing buy orders on arise on every penny increment of a specific size of order.

What they are using is a machine to better execute and implement their strategies. In other words, the machine does what they were going to do anyway. Companies like Trading Technologies (TT) and Stream Base allow users to build, test, deploy, and modify trading systems. Most importantly, many have algorithmic trading features built in, as well as transaction cost analysis (TCA), which is an integral part of the high-frequency trader's business model.

Hopefully, you now have a better understanding of what a high-frequency trader is. It is just another entity or trader with just a little bit larger order to fill than the average retail investor. Two of the key metrics for HFTs are not only market condition or trend direction, but volume and the bids and asks, which play an important role in the way they execute their orders.

CHAPTER 7

Patterns, Indicators, and Oscillators

In Chapter 6, I touched on a few patterns within the indicators, like the wedge and the inverted head and shoulders formation. We also touched on convergence and divergence between the volume indicator and prices. I am not sure I put the cart before the horse as far as describing what those formations are or the nuances and or trading rules are for these setups, but I will take that opportunity in this chapter.

If you have traded before and studied much on the subject of technical analysis, as I suspect some readers have, then this chapter may help reaffirm your understanding of what certain patterns and formations indicate. In almost every chapter, I have stated that nothing is 100 percent. However, when patterns form, they have a certain characteristic of an outcome in both instances of when they work and, almost as importantly, when they do not work out. In other words, I know what I can expect a loss amount to be if a momentum play fails. Then, when I combine an indicator to help confirm buying or selling pressure, such as the on-balance volume (OBV) indicator, I have that much more confidence to pull the trigger and execute an order to enter a trade. This is what I want to review and explain in this chapter.

Before we begin, let me state that it is always best for beginners and intermediate traders to construct a journal or a checklist of items to review before placing a trade. As you become a consistently profitable trader, writing down what worked, what didn't work, what lesson was learned on each trade, this will certainly help you reinforce positive trading habits.

It is hard at times to remember what resources were used and what steps did you follow two months or two weeks after a successful trade.

At best, we might remember we made money on a specific trade. Heck, I have trouble remembering what we had for dinner two nights ago, let alone what the setup was to enter a trade that occurred two months ago! So it is important to have a journal.

After each trade, you should write down how you came to your decision, what the outcome was, and what you would do differently, if anything at all.

In my opinion, here are the patterns to learn, not based on their rate of success so much as on the order of frequency and reliability that I have observed over the years. First, let's start with the chart type. I use candle charts, as I will explain below. There are many types of specialty charting styles to use such as the simple bar chart, point and figure, market profiling, tick charts, close line (we use these for relative strength or spread charts), and more charting styles that also integrate candlestick philosophy such as Renko charts and others that incorporate volume in the bars such as Equivolume charts.

CANDLESTICKS

This section is going to focus on candlestick charting and is only going to cover my top patterns with trading rules on entry and exits. If you need further information on candle chart patterns, there are several books written on the subject from Steve Nison, Greg Morris, Tom Bulkowski, Steve Bigalow, and even my second book, *Candles and Pivot Point Trading Triggers*, published by John Wiley & Sons (2006). All of these books cover the subject in great detail, and the latter includes a nice section on a statistical back-test study on the frequency of which candles form at tops and bottoms on various markets for day traders.

The reason I prefer candlestick charting is that it has a distinct advantage over bar charting due to the fact that the candle provides immediate visual recognition of the open, high, low, and close. Many traders who employ candlestick charting techniques set their charts so that the candlesticks are a certain color for a higher close or a lower close. (i.e., white for a higher close, black for a lower close). For the purpose of this book, a candle with a higher close than the open will be referred to as a white candle, as shown in Figure 7.1.

A candle with a lower close than the open will be referred to as a black candle as shown in Figure 7.2. A single candle does not tell you if the close is higher or lower than the previous time period. The single candle only shows whether the close is higher or lower than the open for each candle.

Each candle has different characteristics that provide insight into price movement by distance between the open, high, low, and close. The candlesticks formed for each time session also indicate if the price movement

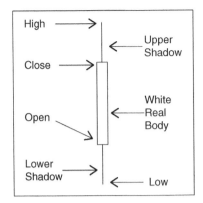

FIGURE 7.1 White Candle

shows a level of increasing or decreasing pressure by the size of the candle, or its "real body."

The emphasis on the body is based on the belief that the most important price action for the period takes place between the open and close while the price action outside the body the upper and lower shadows is less important. However, it is important to note that the shadows can visibly show price rejection, particularly at key reversal areas.

The components of a candlestick are derived from the open, high, low, and close. The main components that we need to identify are:

- Relationship between open and close of the candle body.
- Real body's color.
- Shadows and correlations to candle body.
- Size of shadows.
- Range or length of candle.

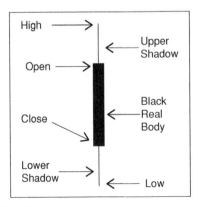

FIGURE 7.2 Black Candle

As I wrote about in my second book, *Candlestick and Pivot Point Trading Triggers*, from John Wiley and Sons (2007), candle charts will give us immediate identification of the current market's environment and the market participants' acceptance or rejection of a support or resistance level in a clearly visual manner. Candle charts also give us a clue as to the momentum of the market price. Momentum measures the velocity of a price move in an uptrend or a downtrend. Candle charts also aid in determining whether the market's velocity has slowed and if the rate of price change is decelerating. For momentum to increase in value, recent price gains must be greater than older price gains.

So a candle chart will show a long white candle with a higher close than the past or prior highs. If recent price gains are the same as older price gains, momentum will be flat, even if the market is still going up. Candle charts will most likely show spikes or long shadows, signifying that the closing price is backing off the highs and therefore bullish momentum is declining.

If recent price gains are less than those of before—even if prices are still rising—meaning higher highs but the same or lower closes, then the rate of change will have slowed further and the momentum will drop.

Since momentum measures the velocity of a price move, valuable information is provided by identifying the open close relationship to the high or low of each respective candle. This can help us identify is the market is overbought or oversold. When price reaches a top or bottom, momentum will level off or begin to decline, often well before the actual peak or trough.

THE DOJI

The doji is where the opening and closing prices are equal or very close, defined by a few points or "ticks," as Figure 7.3 illustrates. My technical definition of a doji for system programming code is if the open–close relationship is less than 8 percent of the overall range for that session. This candle typically indicates indecision, not necessarily an absolute change of direction. For example, for a daily time frame, if the market opens higher, then trades higher as the session progresses, and then trades down and forms a low, thus establishing a range for the day as confidence is lost from buyers and sellers, then we see the market close about where it started. This is the doji pattern.

Dojis are the most powerful single candle pattern as an indicator of a market top and bottoms, but more confirmation is needed than just this single formation. In my years of trading, as I observed these formations, I realized there was a common denominator that occurred when a price reversal occurred. It generally happened after a long trend or a significant pace of price change occurred.

FIGURE 7.3 The Doji

Typically, a doji would form toward the end of the trend; more times than not, it would coincide near a pivot support or resistance level (we will go over pivots in Chapter 10)—so much so that my second book, as mentioned before, became quite popular. This chapter will review these candle patterns and the specific rules that apply to placing entry and stop orders.

REVERSAL PATTERNS

Up to now, we have covered how to determine a market's trend and health or condition using seasonal analysis, consensus studies, indicators, and comparative strength analysis. This is considered analyzing the markets for setting up a trade.

So when do you know when to act on entering a position, the physical act of pulling the trigger? Once you have done your homework and selected the vehicle you wish to trade, whether it is a stock, an index exchange-traded fund (ETF), or an options strategy, the decision is usually made from a condition or series of criteria.

Several of my favorite triggers are based off of candlestick formations and are based on a set or rules. This is the part that defines a successful trader, having the ability to be disciplined enough to follow the trading rules. This is how one becomes a master stock trader: Plan the trades and then trade and act on the plan when a trigger or signal is alerted. Many of the best trades come from reversal patterns, meaning that after prices have been in a prolonged downtrend and are just entering a seasonal period when prices bottom out, we need to look for a reliable pattern that suggests a reversal may occur and prices will move higher.

Inversely, after prices have been moving higher and we enter a seasonal weak period, how do we know when to exit a long position or take a short position? This is what you will learn in this section.

High-Close Doji (HCD)

Basically, after a defined downtrend has occurred and as the selling pressure begins to dry up, we tend to see the doji appear, indicating indecision and weakness of sellers to maintain downward trend. As Figure 7.4 shows, we look for a candle to close above the doji's high with these rules:

1. After the doji forms, once a candle closes higher than the doji's high, enter a long position on the open of the next candle, no greater than 0.008 percent of the closing price. This helps to minimize slippage and avoid missing a trade.

2. This higher close above the doji's candle high needs to occur within three time frames; otherwise, the signal loses its reliability. The image in Figure 7.3 shows the close greater than the doji high on the next time frame, which is considered one time frame.

3. Stops are placed below the low of the doji or the lowest low of the past four bars.

4. For trading automation, you can use the half (.05) percent price rule, meaning place the sell stop a half of a percent of market price value below the doji's or lowest lows price level.

Typically, I will enter a trade with my full position or maximum lot size when trading an ETF or a futures contract. There are several exit strategies to employ, such as the 100 percent risk rule, where I will exit half of my positions on the amount equal to the risk factor, and then adjust my stops on the balance of positions. One other technique I teach is to trail the stop until we have the first lower close below a prior time frame's low. This generally signals an end to a bullish uptrend. One more observation about the HCD setup is that typically, it will trigger an entry in a trade between two and five time periods before my Person's Pivot Study (PPS) momentum indicator signals a buy.

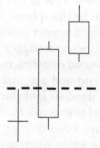

FIGURE 7.4   Candle Above the Doji High

Examine Figure 7.5; using TradeStation software, an HCD was detected in AK Steel (AKS) on March 9, 2012. This was one trade where the entry was on a Monday; as the open was a little lower than the close at 7.26, the stop placement was under the lowest low of the past four time periods at 6.80. Using the stop loss 0.005 percent rule, the initial risk would be at 6.76, just over 7 percent or $0.50 per share from the entry price. The first profit objective would be 7.76 per share. Within five days, the stock exploded to a high of 8.65. The trailing stop method had you exit on March 21 on the close at 8.12 per share. This was the first lower-closing low or the second black candle after the peak in price was made.

The age-old question is: What is the definition of a downturn? When technicians state that the market is correcting after a long uptrend, this can also mean either prices are moving lower or in fact they are trading sideways.

A downtrend can be defined as a market that trades under a longer-term moving average over a specific number of time periods, Another definition would be if prices or the current bar's or candle's close is within 1.75 standard deviation from the 10-day period moving average; this is similar theory to the concept of Bollinger Bands. If these criteria are met, then a market is defined as in a downtrend and then look to scan for buy setups.

One technique I look for in a stock as a buying opportunity is after having been in a downtrend once the stock price trades under the

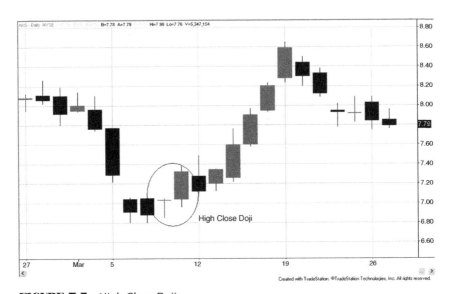

FIGURE 7.5 High Close Doji

50-day weighted moving average (WMA), and forms a completed HCD pattern, then I feel more confident in this trade, especially when the stock is either in an index, industry, or sector seasonal strong period. For one thing, the stock trading under the moving average is likely in an oversold market condition and ready to move higher. Another useful trick is, if you are looking at a weekly chart, change the moving average setting to a 10-period, which translates to a 10-week or 50-trading-day moving average. As you progress in your trading and incorporate computer scanning features, this bit of information will become very helpful in mining out trade signals.

Examine Figure 7.6; this is an HCD trade setup using a weekly time frame on Toll Brothers that the scan feature did in fact accurately identify. The HCD pattern is not exclusively for use on a day chart; this pattern works for end-of-week, end-of-day, and intraday as well. We have many examples of the bullish HCD setup throughout the book, as well as the bearish LCD, in which the rules are reversed, as described next.

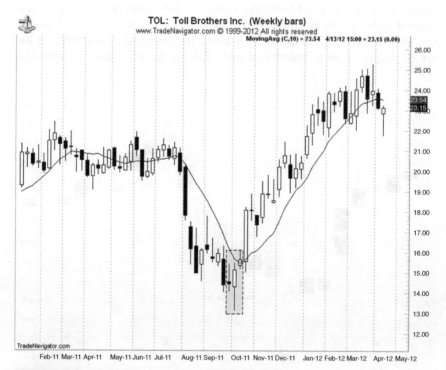

FIGURE 7.6   TOL: Toll Brothers Inc. (Weekly Bars)

Low-Close Doji (LCD)

The LCD setup is simply the opposite of the bullish HCD pattern; once a market has extended the price trend to the upside, typically the buying pressure becomes exhausted and the market signals an overbought condition. This first sign can come in the shape of a doji. Again, once this candle pattern appears, it indicates indecision and weakness of buyers to maintain the upward trend. The rules and sequence of events are as follows:

1. After a prolonged uptrend, once a doji forms and a candle closes below the low of the doji, enter an order to sell on the close or next open, at no less than 8 percent of the closing price. This helps minimizes slippage and potentially avoids missing a trade.

2. Pay attention, as this lower close needs to be within three time periods of the doji formation; otherwise, the signal losses its relevance. The setup in Figure 7.7 shows the second candle after the doji initiated the trigger to sell.

3. The stop is placed above the high of the doji or the highest high of the past four candles from when the trigger to enter was created. For trading automation, you can use the 0.5 percent price rule, meaning place the buy stop a half of a percent of market price value above the doji's or highest high price level.

4. Enter the trade with full lots based on the anticipation that the resistance area will not be tested a second time

Examine the weekly chart on Dean Foods (DF) shown in Figure 7.8. As you can see, the trend was up, the market price was above its moving average, a doji formed, and then the third candle closed below the low of the doji for the week ending June 10, 2011. When the market opened that next Monday, notice that it did open higher, which is a good thing if you are looking to sell, as it gave a better price. Remember, we do not chase a market. The rules are specific that we will give it a little wiggle room, but

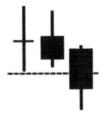

FIGURE 7.7 Second Candle

FIGURE 7.8 DF: Dean Foods Company (Weekly Bars)
www.TradeNavigator.com © 1999–2012. All rights reserved.

no more than 8 percent of the closing price. A short position would be entered at 12.57; the stop-loss would be half a percent (0.005) above the highest high of the past four time frames from the entry as indicated at point A on the chart. The high was 13.90, so the stop would be entered at 13.97. The results speak for themselves and the exit strategy of reducing half the position on a 100 percent match of the risk factor or trailing a stop can be implemented.

Gaps Patterns

Prices that open significantly higher or lower than a previous established range (high or low) create what is called a *gap*. Most stocks—and now, ETFs—that may be affected by a news-driven event when the markets are closed create these occurrences. Gaps can form in the futures markets, but since we trade virtually 24 hours, the common time frame for a gap to occur in these markets would be from some news-driven event between Friday's close and Sunday night's open.

Gaps on stocks can be created from an earnings report or a political change in the sector that the particular stock trades in. For example, if a ruling occurs to increase subsidies for ethanol producers, this could have a very positive impact on a company like Archer-Daniels Midland. The initial demand for purchasing this stock in the preopen session could cause the market to gap higher.

There are several trade concepts to use with gaps. In candle analysis, we call a gap a *window*. A rising window is the open area created when prices surge to the upside. Here, a strategy is to buy once the gap is filled or the occurrence is as the "window is closed." The opposite is true in a declining market.

I am not much of a believer of fading a rally in anticipation of a gap to be filled immediately. In other words, without confirmation from other indicators, I do not sell after a higher gap opening just because a theory suggests prices will come back down to fill the gap. . I would rather go with the dominant trend and then buy the pullback as prices regress towards the gap opening left on the price charts. One of the main gap patterns that I do like to trade is the three-gap method, where the first gap is called a breakaway gap, which occurs when prices gap up or down from a trend or consolidation level. The second gap is called a measuring or midpoint gap, and the last of the three is called the exhaustion gap. The distance from the top of the move to the midpoint, or the measuring gap, should be approximately equal to where the move will end. Once a third gap does form, especially if it ends near this measuring objective, the downside price pressure should "exhaust" itself. This is where bulls throw in the towel, so to speak. Again, this is not an exact science, but when we add indicators to help confirm a price reversal, a three-gap method is quite a nice setup to identify, especially in longer or older established trends as this exhaustion helps identify a potential capitulation from those holding long positions in a downtrend.

Examine the chart in Figure 7.9, where we have Netflix (NFLX), which formed a textbook example of a three-gap formation.

Here is a stock that hedge funds loved to short on the way up. Once it broke its support, a breakaway gap was formed, then as the trend started to mature, a secondary or measuring gap was formed. This was, at the least, besides a measuring tool, a technique to use hinting that the market was not ready to bottom out. Finally, on October 25, 2011, the stock cratered, forming a 35.71 dollar "gap" from the prior day's low of 115.10 to the high that day of 79.39. As you can see, the stock tried to rally to fill in or close the window, but failed as it resumed the downtrend for another 26 days before bottoming out at 62.37 on November 30 of that same year. The stock price did rally back to a high of 133.43 by February 7, 2012. So what would have helped trigger a long in this stock near the lows? The daily chart gave

FIGURE 7.9 NFLX: Netflix, Inc. (Daily Bars)

you a heads-up that a potential low was near as the three-gap technique alerted you to a potential rally. But there was no trigger to go long. However, if you combine longer-term graphs in your analysis like a weekly chart, then we can see if there are nay patterns that can uncover potential buy signals. Examine Figure 7.10, which some considered a "target-rich environment"—at least the believers of the HCD pattern. There were actually two HCD patterns created. Whether you were trading this stock or trading options on stocks, the illustrations here show how to successfully incorporate several patterns like the gap method and doji patterns on multiple time frames.

Another prime example of a three-gap method was actually covered in our live trading room as a year-end potential tax-related selling victim. The company was Sears Holding. Typically, stocks that are losing at the end of the year get dumped for tax benefits. Many tried-and-true believers of this strategy look for stocks in the S&P 500 that are losing at year's end and look to buy.

Sears came up on the radar screen as one of these stocks. In addition, the three-gap method was present, but if you examine the daily chart in Figure 7.11, while the third gap does indicate exhaustion, notice the

FIGURE 7.10 NFLX: Netflix, Inc. (Weekly Bars)
www.TradeNavigator.com © 1999–2012. All rights reserved.

similarity to Figure 7.10; it takes time for the market to actually bottom out, just as was the case in Netflix.

Nine days after the third gap was created, you will see a doji formed almost the low of the entire move. It actually created an HCD formation, as shown in a close-up in Figure 7.12. The moral of this is that the three-gap method is not fiction or a myth or a pattern that rarely shows up in longer- to intermediate-term strong trending market conditions. I find the three-gap pattern to be reliable as long as you are aware that they do not, in my experience, show immediate results. We need to look for a trigger or some bit of confirmation to signal the price trend is ready to reverse. High- and low-close dojis are two such tools or trigger mechanisms that are helpful, especially when integrating your search from daily and weekly time frames.

Island Gaps

The most bullish and or bearish of all gaps is called the island top or island bottom gap. In candlestick analysis, we call that the "abandon baby"

SHLD: Sears Holdings Corporation (Daily bars)

FIGURE 7.11   SHLD: Sears Holding Corporation (Daily Bars)

formation. In the example in Figure 7.13, we have a daily chart on Green Mountain Coffee Roasters (GMCR), which formed this rare price action gap on March 9, 2012.

The market "gapped" sharply higher on February 2, yet in a 24-day period, the market price traded above that gap level without pulling back to fill the "hole." It was the 25th day when prices opened sharply lower than the past gap, which in reality, created an island top formation, as shown in the shaded area.

The market traded for eight sessions without being able to fill in that gap. It was this inability to fill the gap that made this a classic island top formation. Generally, we see island tops cause a more immediate bearish price reaction and are not so long in the making as this example. As a trader, keep this formation in your arsenal of trading tools, as it is an extremely high probability trade signal. We will cover head-and-shoulders top formations in a bit; just remember this chart, since this stock was creating the island top formation at the same time it also created a head-and-shoulders top pattern. You will also note there is an LCD formation that was created

FIGURE 7.12 SHLD: Sears Holding Corporation (Daily Bars)
www.TradeNavigator.com © 1999–2012. All rights reserved.

at the highest peak price as well. This brings me to another point: As a trader, watch for multiple patterns within patterns to form and do not ignore the bigger picture.

A more classic island bottom formation can be found in Figure 7.14, which is a daily chart on Well Fargo; most of you may be aware of this bank, as it is listed in the ETF XLF. The interesting point is that we have not one, but two island bottom patterns created. The larger one is from the gap lower open from November 21 and then the higher open six days later on November 30. I highlighted the two-day island bottom from November 23 and then the higher open on November 28, once again showing how to identify a pattern within a pattern.

In the spirit of comparing a stock to the underlying sector such as Wells Fargo in the Financial Select Spider XLF, examine Figure 7.15, as this shows the similar gap formations with one exception—the larger island gap formation was filled in the XLF. But the two-day island bottom remains intact as of the writing of this book. It may be a long time before this gap is filled, and yet at the very least it goes to show the power of island tops and

FIGURE 7.13 GMCR: Green Mountain Coffee Roasters (Daily Bars)
www.TradeNavigator.com © 1999–2012. All rights reserved.

bottoms. More importantly, it is a nice technique to compare the underlying stock and the sector to see if the buying pressure as is the case with an island bottom is simply on an individual stock or isolated situation or if it is in a sector wide situation as is indicated with the island bottom gap formation in the XLF. Either way, if you identify island tops or bottoms in a sector, look at some of the top holdings in that sector to see if individual stocks have that same patterns.

CONTINUATION PATTERNS

We have covered some of the more reliable reversal patterns in the previous pages. What about identifying patterns to give us a heads-up or clue as to whether or not a market may see a trend continuation? After all, markets go through periods of strong trends and then pause or consolidate before either reversing the trend or continuing in the original direction. Here are

FIGURE 7.14 WFC: Wells Fargo & Company (Daily Bars)
www.TradeNavigator.com © 1999–2012. All rights reserved.

some of the more reliable continuation patterns and how to use them to your advantage.

Wedges, Triangles, and Pennants

Typically, these three patterns are described as separate patterns. Triangles are shorter term in nature and have three distinct shapes and names: symmetrical, ascending (bullish), and descending (bearish). Pennant formations are more elongated, and wedges can also be classified as rising wedges, which form after longer-term uptrends and are bearish, as they indicate a top is forming. Falling wedges typically form after longer-term declining trends and are associated with bullish reversals.

As we showed in Chapter 6, the wedge formation in the OBV indicator in Figure 6.17 reveals a compression of buying pressure, and once prices break out we can assume the breakout will continue in the original trend direction.

FIGURE 7.15   XLF: Financial Select Sector SPDR F (Daily Bars)
www.TradeNavigator.com © 1999–2012. All rights reserved.

I like to look for wedge formations in stocks that have been in an up-trend. Typically, as the diagram in Figure 7.16 shows, the measuring technique we use is to take the distance from A to B and then measure that up from the apex where a breakout occurs to determine the approximate upside or breakout price target. Prices should never completely fill in all the way to the point of the apex.

One observation is that there are times when prices will break out and continue higher, and then there are other times when prices break out but will come back to retest the point of breakout.

One example is shown in Figure 7.17, the daily chart on Abbott Laboratories. The distance from A to B, extended up from the breakout points as shown at point C, measures up to point D. As of the writing of this book, that objective was matched almost exactly. Typically, we can and do see price breaks test the so-called breakout point. Once you identify a wedge breakout pattern, check to see if volume is in gear with the price move.

Wedge Formation

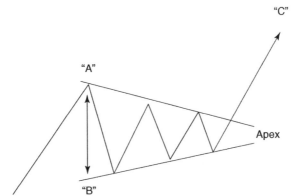

FIGURE 7.16 Wedge Formation

FIGURE 7.17 ABT: Abbott Laboratories (Daily Bars)
www.TradeNavigator.com © 1999–2012. All rights reserved.

For a bullish wedge formation, here are the rules of engagement (bearish rules are just the opposite):

- Wedges may occur in an uptrend or a downtrend.
- They must touch the top and bottom trend line a minimum of two times (four touches total).
- Price should break out of the wedge in the direction of the current trend.
- Typically, the breakout should occur within 75 percent of the width of the wedge.
- Buy partial positions on a closing breakout above the resistance trend line, as many times the market will pull back to challenge the point of breakout.
- Place the stop losses 8 percent below the last swing low that created to support trend line.

Bracket Order Strategies

Enter a buy-stop above the last known high within the resistance line and a subsequent sell stop below the low of the support line. Orders may be placed on both sides of the triangle; if the buy order is filled, the sell order becomes the stop-loss order.

If you combine the seasonal analysis theory we touched on in Chapter 2 and apply a seasonal trend tool as well as the on-balance volume indicator, these are great confirmation tools. Examine Figure 7.18, which is a daily chart on Starbucks (SBUX). At point A on the chart, prices did break out of the wedge formation. In fact, this was anticipated according to the seasonal trend because prices tend to rally in this stock from late February into mid-April. See how prices retested the point of breakout but the resumption of the uptrend was confirmed by the breakout above the resistance line in the OBV indicator as shown at point C? The indicator was in gear with prices, reflecting there was significant buying pressure. The one exception to the rules stated above is that the rally surpassed the measuring technique. The point is, I wanted you to see how these techniques can be applied in modern times.

Head-and-Shoulders

One of the more common and frequent top patterns is the head-and-shoulders formations. Remember, in the GMCR chart in Figure 7.12, we had an island top formation, and yet within the island gap was a head-and-shoulders pattern. As the graph in Figure 7.19 shows, this setup has three peaks, with the middle one taller than the others, thus giving it the nomenclature of a

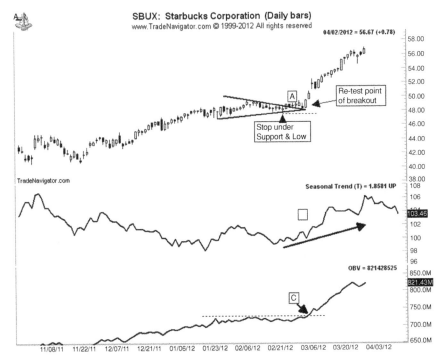

FIGURE 7.18   SBUX: Starbucks Corporation (Daily Bars)
www.TradeNavigator.com © 1999–2012. All rights reserved.

head-and-shoulders pattern. The neckline is drawn from the corresponding lows or reactionary pullbacks from these minor peaks or shoulders. The neckline is an important feature, as it is a component of the measuring technique and the identifying point of breakdown in prices. As for the measuring technique, to reach a downside price objective, measuring the distance from the top of the "head" down to the neckline and then extending out will give you a minimum price objective of where to expect prices to go.

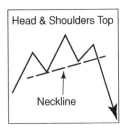

FIGURE 7.19   Head-and-Shoulders Top

FIGURE 7.20   APA: Apache Corporation (Weekly Bars)

Let's examine a more recent head-and-shoulders formation, as shown in Figure 7.20, with the weekly chart on Apache Corporation (APA). This stock certainly displayed a symmetrical formation in that the distance from left shoulder to head and head to right shoulder matched up. Unfortunately, the breakdown was so severe that it was hard to get a good risk profile on the trade to sell short. However, for options strategists, this pattern can be very helpful, as one can implement bearish positions such as credit call spreads or debit put spreads.

Enter the trade with half lots, anticipating the return of price to the neckline. Once price reverses at the neckline again, enter the remaining lot positions.

Exit the trade on the open of the session after a candle has a higher closing high, especially when the price projection has been met.

Inverted Head-and-Shoulders

The inverted head-and-shoulders bottom pattern is the opposite of the bearish head-and-shoulders top. Typically, after an extended move to the downside, we see the bearish momentum begin to show signs of exhaustion. Capitulation can be measured by an increase in volume. On the first low, or left shoulder, prices make a low rally up, and then the next trough is a lower low. This we call the head, but this trough does not make a significant lower low. The last low, or trough, of the formation does not break the low of the head. Finally, price moves through the resistance area created by the last two peaks, or the neckline. That is when a buy signal is generated. We typically do see prices come back to test the neckline. One other casual observation is that I like to see a symmetrical or equal distance from the distance of the left shoulder to the head match the distance from the head to the right shoulder, just like in a top pattern. However, if we can see a slope in the neckline, both lower and higher, the latter is more of a bullish indication. The graph in Figure 7.21 is a typical representation of the inverted head-and-shoulders pattern.

Figure 7.22 shows a weekly chart on Mylan Inc. (MYL), with what is identified as an inverted head-and-shoulders bottom formation. The distance or symmetry between the head and shoulder is in the right perspective; however, the slope of the neckline is descending. Also note that once a market does break out above the neckline resistance level, a head-and-shoulders price pattern tends to retest the point of breakout. Therefore, I tend to enter when the initial price breakout occurs with a partial size position. Another reason is that as reliable as pattern recognition is, remember, nothing is 100 percent guaranteed. Usually, once the breakout occurs, the risk profile tends to be more significant, but this pattern does have a high probability of success.

When you believe a bullish pattern exists, that is when it is time to apply a confirming indicator. One of the better tools to use with head-and-shoulders formations is volume analysis. As the chart shows, at point A, we have a moving average applied to the OBV indicator. This is a concept we will cover in Chapter 8. The crossover in the OBV Indicator above the moving average value triggers a buy signal confirmation.

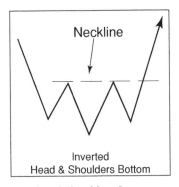

FIGURE 7.21 Inverted Head-and-Shoulders Bottom

FIGURE 7.22 MYL: Mylan Inc. (Weekly Bars)
www.TradeNavigator.com © 1999–2012. All rights reserved.

For now, focus on the point of the indicator at the same time as when the left shoulder was formed, then look at the low point in the OBV indicator when the head was formed in the price charts, and the same goes for the low on the OBV at the point in time when the right shoulder was formed. What you should see is that as the prices made a newer low, forming the head, the OBV Indicator made a higher low. As the right shoulder was formed, the OBV made an even higher low. This is the type of volume confirmation we look for, which shows that the selling pressure has dried up and market participants are accumulating positions.

In my observation and experience, declining necklines are still reliable patterns, and they are more frequent formations. A downward sloping neckline due to the market's being in a declining trend is likely to experience less of an immediate and substantial breakout. Perhaps it is because it takes time for buyers to join in on the new trend. In any event, the measuring technique still applies: Taking the distance from the head to the neckline and measuring up will give you a good expectation of a price objective.

Let's go back in time to the March 2009 low. Some say it was the buy of a lifetime; others have called that low the buy of a generation. For the record, I was bullish based on technical reasons, and I was buying stocks. In hindsight, I would rather have bought longer-term, deep out-of-the-money call options on the broad index such as the SPY, but as the saying goes, hindsight is 20/20. I stated in the Introduction section that I see more buying opportunities in the years ahead; that is why I am sharing these techniques. We will have more scary market crashes that will present great opportunities.

So, with that said, let's examine the pattern that you can identify as a bullish formation. Back in March 2009, besides the fact that the S&Ps made a new lower low, there existed a divergence between indexes. The technology sector did not make newer lows in March like the S&P 500 or Dow Industrials did. But as time progressed, many believed the rally would fade, that the move was simply a bear market rally. The individual volume bars showed a decline, leading some analysts to believe that there was not sufficient participation due to light volume. However, let's examine Figure 7.23. Notice the

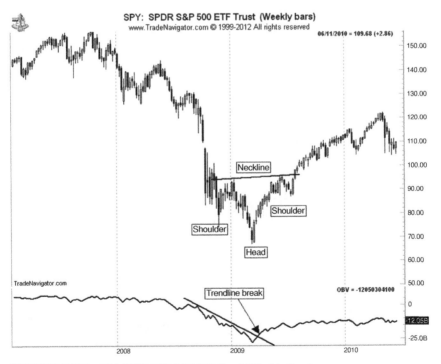

FIGURE 7.23 SPY: SPDR S&P 500 ETF Trust (Weekly Bars)
www.TradeNavigator.com © 1999–2012. All rights reserved.

trend-line break that occurred with the OBV indicator. Also, as the year progressed, we had completed an inverted head-and-shoulders pattern by mid-July. The formation was even complete with the shoulder-head-shoulder symmetry, but this time, the market formed a rising slope in the neckline.

As I mentioned, the divergence between the SPY and the Nasdaq 100 was formed in March 2009. As the SPY was declining, making a newer low that formed the head, the Nasdaq 100, as shown in Figure 7.24, was forming a double bottom. More accurately, we had what we call a W-bottom formation. As the March low was completed, the OBV indicator had also broken out above its downtrend line. One element that is missing in this chart or this discussion is acknowledgment that when they were creating the lows on March 6, 2009, these two markets were also at or near the respective Person's Monthly Pivot support. However, we will save that topic for Chapter 10. The point here is that if you see a bullish chart pattern, check similar or related markets to see if there are corresponding bullish or bearish setup patterns. This may give you a higher degree of confidence in order to establish positions. Know what is shown here; as the market was making these lows, the media were focused on how bearish the markets were and how bad the economy was at

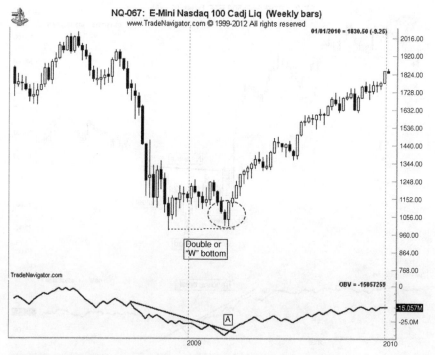

FIGURE 7.24 NQ-067: E-mini Nasdaq 100 Cadj Liq. (Weekly bars)
www.TradeNavigator.com © 1999–2012. All rights reserved.

that time. If you listened and followed the media back then, you couldn't help but be scared away from buying stocks. That was the furthest thing from the truth, as history has now shown. Perhaps some part of an investor's thinking applied a common sense approach, such as looking at buying SBUX under $9 and a host of other bargains as just that—buying a bargain. As it turns out, that was a rewarding thought process. However, as more and more buyers entered the market as a whole, these indicators and patterns reflected that same opinion and not the headline media reports. The point is, if and when we have another flash crash or catastrophic market event—and most likely, we will—these tools will help you to form an educated and concrete trading decision.

M tops

As for top or bearish patterns we sometimes do not form an LCD or head-and-shoulders formation. What we might encounter are what are considered M tops and take the form shown in the graph in Figure 7.25.

This is also referred to as a 1-2-3 top pattern, double tops with a lower right side. In any event, these are very reliable and have a high frequency of developing at major peaks. Basically, we see these patterns develop after a prolonged uptrend, and they take shape over a period of time. It is during these pauses or consolidation phases that many traders actually get caught up and get "whipsawed." They sell the break thinking that the absolute top is in, and then the market rallies back up and they reverse and go long at the top. The idea is to enter a long when a market makes a price correction or retracement, and thus the term *buy the break* makes sense. But when do we know just when to buy the break or identify that the uptrend has ended? I have an observation that answers the question of how to know when a bullish trends ends.

My answer is: when the bullish tendencies cease to exist. So let's examine what constitutes a bullish trend.

- Higher highs.
- Higher lows.
- Closes greater than opens.
- Closes closer to the high of the range.
- Closes greater than prior closes.
- Closes greater than past or prior highs.

FIGURE 7.25 M Top

Typically, the first sign that an uptrend is ending is when we have a lower close below a past or prior low.

In the creation of an M top pattern, since we normally see tops taking longer to form than bottoms, it is crucial in my trading to be a bit speedier to identify a top.

If you are long or are looking to sell, there is no arguing the fact that the closer you are to the initial peak, the better the sell. If you are establishing a short position, this gives an advantage of a low-risk trade. As an aggressive trader, once the middle or low point of the M formation is made—as the market rallies back up to test the highs—selling that rally with stops above the initial high at point A offers a unique low-risk profile. Unfortunately, it also comes with a low probability. Many times, markets can—and do—take out the highs, hitting the buy stops above that price point.

A well-planned and conservative approach would be to wait until the market closes below that low point. Study Figure 7.26, which is a weekly chart on Diamond Offshore Drilling (DO). One of the interesting aspects of this company is that, being in the Oil and Gas drilling sector, it falls in a seasonal strong buying time frame from February into August.

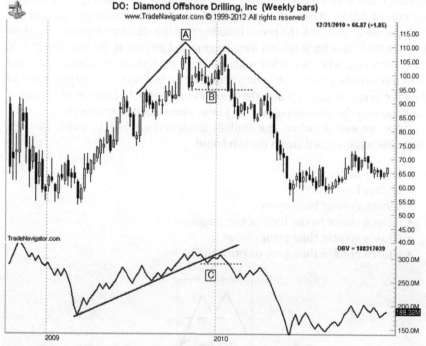

FIGURE 7.26   DO: Diamond Offshore Drilling, Inc. (Weekly Bars)

Notice that the market posted a secondary high for the week ending January 15, 2010. By the week ending January 29, the closing price was below the M low, as shown at point B on the chart. In addition, the OBV indicator broke down below its up trend, signaling that selling pressure was increasing.

A conservative play would be to sell short this stock once prices closed below the low at point B, and then initially place the buy-stop to limit losses above the secondary high. You might also notice that the high was made by a doji, and the next week, an LCD pattern developed. So the initial high was made with an LCD pattern, and the pattern later completed with an M top formation; this led to the company's stock price being cut in half in just about five months.

W Bottoms

As the saying goes, tops take longer to form than bottoms, and many times we see what is termed a V bottom or a spike low. I am sure there is no need for any further description of what a V bottom looks like. Typically, the lows are put in place on high volume; as we have mentioned, longs throw in the towel and simply capitulate. Along those lines, we do tend to see W bottom formations as the bearish trend ends. My definition of a bearish trend is not just a downtrend in price; I also look at these 6 conditions to help determine the condition or health of the downtrend:

- Lower highs
- Lower lows
- Closes less than the opens
- Closes closer to the low of the range
- Closes less than prior closes
- Closes below past or prior lows

When these conditions cease to exist, then that is when we look for a consolidation or examine further evidence that might tip us off to a bullish price reversal.

Just as in the opposite of the uptrend observations, the downtrend ceases to exist when one or more of these conditions changes. The first and most important is when we see a close above past or prior highs—after all, isn't that one of the main conditions of an HCD? The next is when we start to see the close greater than the open. In most downtrends, the close is below the open. This book being black and white shows downtrends consisting of black candles. Most charting packages will show a negative or lower-close-than-open candle as red.

When we start to form a bottom, when the W formation develops, it will represent a similar pattern, as shown in Figure 7.27. The key here is whether you want to be aggressive or conservative.

After the market has had an extended move to the downside, the first low will form on relatively higher volume reflective of an exhaustion bottom. Then a small bounce occurs and the stock price begins to consolidate. The next low typically should not take out the initial low thus forming a higher right side low.

1. After the secondary low forms when the market crosses and closes above the peak in the W point, that is when conservative traders can enter a long position with stops initially below the secondary low.

2. Enter a position with your full size position, anticipating that price will continue in the direction of the new trend. Remember, the larger the pattern or the longer the time period it takes to form, the greater the move you can expect to follow.

3. Exit half the position with the 100 percent of risk rule, and adjust stops as the price action dictates with this in mind. Exit the trade on the open of the session after the first lower closing low, especially when the price projection has been satisfied or price is at or near a key pivot number.

Now that we have the rules in place, examine the weekly chart in Figure 7.28. This is the financial ETF XLF. The market cratered, for a lack of a better description, in October 2011, then rallied sharply by early November, and the secondary low was posted by three week later. An aggressive trade could have been buying near point C on the charts with stops below the low in October. This would have been the more profitable and less risky trade setup; however, there wasn't much in the way of determining technicals to support that view.

The conservative trader would have bought on confirmation of the closing breakout above point B with stops under the low at point C. Now, as the rules above define up- and downtrends, if you are long on that breakout, you can see that every week since December 16 has closed above the prior week's low. Granted, there have been lower closes than opens, but

FIGURE 7.27 W Bottom

FIGURE 7.28 XLF: Financial Select Sector SPDR F (Weekly Bars)
www.TradeNavigator.com © 1999–2012. All rights reserved.

not one single week has the close been below the prior week's low. This shows the new found bull trend is still intact. You would be liquidating half the position at a 100 percent gain from your stop and so far the trend is your friend on the remaining balance of positions.

If you went with the aggressive long play, once the W bottom formation completes, you can anticipate that since the pattern took time to form and complete, the expected move can last a bit longer as well.

Commodity Channel Index (CCI)

The CCI was introduced in 1980 by Donald Lambert and was designed to detect beginning and ending market trends. The CCI is derived by measuring the average daily price distance from a moving average of average daily prices based on the math formula using the sum of the high, the low, and the close, then divided by three, otherwise known as the pivot point value. There are many people using a modified version of this indicator, but it is basically a zero line trigger. This means that when the value is under the zero line and then once the CCI reading crosses positive a buy signal is generated and the opposite is true for sell signals.

Examine Figure 7.29, a daily chart on Microsoft (MSFT), which—along with the technology space—enjoyed a health gain from December 2011 through April 2012. The CCI indicator is on the lower quadrant. There are a few nuances associated with this indicator, such as a "zero line" test, as shown at point B on the chart. Typically, if one is looking for a breakdown in prices, the CCI line will hit the zero line, but not close two consecutive days below that zero line; this means that prices rejected the lows and can now trade higher. The zero line retest is a great technique to be aware of, because when the indicator does not cross above or below the zero line, it can help detect false breakouts or breakdowns of consolidations in the prices. One of the drawbacks of this indicator is that it is not effective for the less experienced technician to use as an overbought or oversold oscillator. The value extremes can peak at over +300 or –300 reading, and prices can continue to trend. This can give a false sense of a market condition that is overbought when in fact the market is making healthy stairstep advances. As you can see

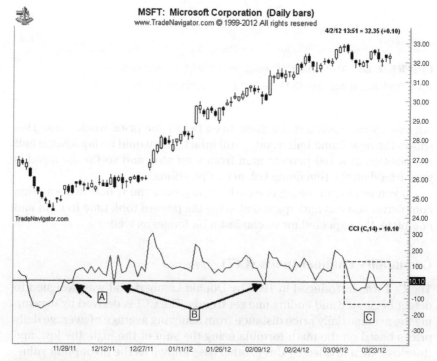

FIGURE 7.29   MSFT: Microsoft Corporation (Daily Bars)

at point C on the chart, the indicator is experiencing a whipsaw phase, as the price action is trending sideways. The indicator does work well with zero line crosses and zero line rejects, but as I have pointed out in this book so far, there is no single tool that holds the answer to all our trading and investing needs. The CCI is no exception to that rule either.

Moving Average Convergence-Divergence (MACD)

MACD is an indicator that shows when a short-term moving average crosses over a longer-term moving average. Gerald Appel developed this indicator as we know it today, and he developed it for the purpose of stock trading. It is now widely used for short-term trading signals in stocks, futures, and Forex markets, as well as for swing and position traders. It is composed of three exponential moving averages. The initial inputs for the calculations were a 9-period, a 12-period, and a 26-period. The idea behind this indicator is to calculate a value, which is the difference between the two exponential moving averages, which then compares that to the 9-period exponential moving average. What we get is a moving average crossover feature and a zero line oscillator, and those help us to identify overbought and oversold market conditions. Some general points to help you understand how to use this indicator include:

1. When the fast line crosses above the slow line, a buy signal is generated. The opposite is true for sell signals.
2. MACD also has a zero base line component, called the histogram, which is created by subtracting the slower signal line from the MACD line. If the MACD line is above the zero line, prices are usually trending higher. The opposite is true if MACD is declining below the zero line.
3. MACD is a lagging indicator that is based off of moving averages. We want to look for the zero line crossovers to identify market changes and help confirm trade entries or trigger action to exit a position.

Figure 7.30 shows a weekly chart on Symantec Corp. (SYMC) with the MACD indicator in the lower quadrant. As the overall stock market began to pick up value in the beginning of January, this company also began to break out above its declining trend line. The moving averages indicated a positive crossover, and the true intermediate trend change occurred as the moving average components crossed back above the zero line. Some look for this moving average crossover feature to coincide within the histogram component as confirmation to trade from the long side. The opposite is true for confirmed sell signals. As you can see, this line-up occurred as indicated at point A on the chart.

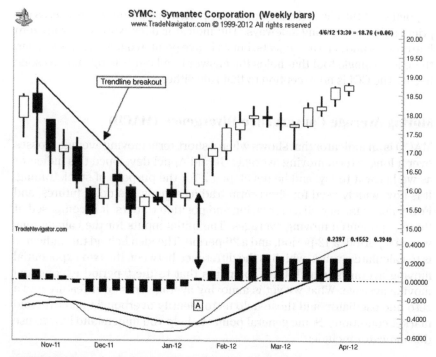

FIGURE 7.30   SYMC: Symantec Corporation (Weekly Bars)
www.TradeNavigator.com © 1999–2012. All rights reserved.

However, many times the moving average will be well above the zero line, but you will see the short-term moving average cross over the longer-term moving average as the histogram component crosses back over the zero line. This is also a solid buy signal setup.

Stochastics

Stochastics, a range-based oscillator, is also considered a momentum oscillator. George C. Lane is credited with creating the formula. The indicator is a popular technical tool used to help determine whether a market is overbought, meaning prices have advanced too far too soon and due for a downside correction, or oversold, meaning prices have declined too far too soon and due for an upside correction. It is based on a mathematical formula that is computed to compare the settlement price of a specific time period to the price range of a specific number of past periods.

The method works on the premise that in a bull or uptrending market, prices will tend to make higher highs and the settlement price, or close, will usually tend to be in the upper end of that time periods trading range, or at least closer to the high. When the momentum starts to fade, the settlement prices will start to push away from the upper boundaries of the range and the stochastics indicator will show that the bullish momentum is starting to change. The exact opposite is true for bearish or downtrending markets.

There are two lines that are referred to as %K and %D. These are plotted on a horizontal axis for a given time period, and the vertical axis is plotted on a scale from 0 percent to 100 percent. The %K line is the faster of the two lines and will change direction because the %D line is a moving average of %K. The unique feature of the stochastics reading is the moving average crossover feature. The *general* guidelines reflect the thought that readings over 80 percent indicate that a market condition is overbought and ripe for a downside correction and a reading under 20 percent signals the market is oversold and ripe for a bounce. While that certainly is the general guideline that most traders understand, there are certainly better ways to read the indicator to look for better trade signals. For example, when using stochastics as a confirming tool, these rules will help to make better trading triggers for buy and sell signals.

- When the readings are above 80 percent, and %K crosses below the %D line and *both* lines close back down below the 80 percent line, a hook sell signal is generated.
- When the readings are below 20 percent, once %K crosses above %D and once *both* lines close back up above the 20 percent level, a hook buy signal is generated.

Figure 7.31 shows a weekly chart on one of my favorite tech stocks, Akamai Technologies (AKAM). As the chart shows, we not only have the setting illustrating 80 percent overbought and 20 percent oversold, but I have illustrated the fact that there are two patterns that stochastics is generous in supplying: bearish divergence patterns, as shown at point A, and bullish convergence patterns, as point C shows. Due to the nature of the formula, which measures the close as it relates to the highest high or lowest low in the past 14 periods as I have my fast stochastics settings, these divergence and convergence patterns are more pronounced than they are with the OBV indicator.

While prices were making higher highs—as shown at point 1—at the same time the OBV indicator was making newer highs—since it is in synch with the price movement—, the stochastic indicator was warning us of a "weak" high by forming what is termed a bearish divergence pattern, wherein prices make newer highs and simultaneously the indicator makes a corresponding lower high. Then, as the price starts to carve out a low as shown at point 2 the stochastics indicator clearly shows the bullish convergence, as point C shows, while the OBV indicator trends in gear with prices making

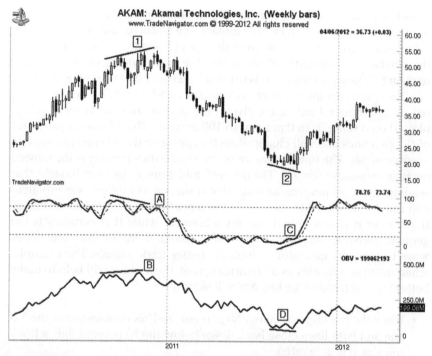

FIGURE 7.31 AKAM: Akamai Technologies, Inc. (Weekly Bars)
www.TradeNavigator.com © 1999–2012. All rights reserved.

a lower low, as shown at point D. It is necessary to reveal or compare an "apple to an apple" between which indicators do what. That way, you will be better armed with not just what to expect from each indicator but what you might miss by simply using one indicator. Or if prices have been declining and make a quick sharp low but not a substantially lower value, then I am looking to see if that break was on heavy or light volume and if we perhaps created a bullish convergence reading in the stochastic indicator.

I found that the more indicators I used, the less productive I became in my trading. That is not to say I do not check various indicators at specific crossroads or potential turning points in the markets. If we are nearing a seasonal peak in prices after a lengthy run-up, I am checking and have up on my screens the various tools that will alert me to a directional trend change. Another time where I will use the indicators is after a long trend develops with a substantial change in price and we see a bearish chart formation like the LCD pattern form; then I like to use the stochastics indicator to see if the highs were created on a bearish divergence pattern. Examine Figure 7.32, which is a daily chart on Nike (NKE). As you can see,

FIGURE 7.32 NKE: Nike, Inc. (Daily Bars)

a textbook LCD formation appeared, and using the stochastics indicator confirmed that the high was in fact established on a bearish divergence pattern. This helped confirm an interim top was in place.

These are a few of the examples of when, why, and how I like to use these technical tools to confirm price action. These are what I consider to be the best momentum indicators and oscillators.

CONCLUSION: INDICATOR 101

There is no holy grail of indicators. Some work better than others under various market conditions. More times than not, the three indicators we discussed—stochastics, MACD, and CCI—will all generate a buy signal within a few bars of each other. As the weekly chart on lululemon athletica (LULU) shows in Figure 7.33, I have a simple resistance trend-line breakout in price confirmed with a %K and %D crossover in stochastics lined up as point A shows. CCI on the lower quadrant lines up with a zero line cross

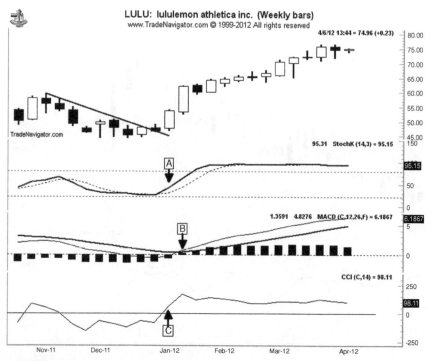

FIGURE 7.33 LULU: lululemon athletica inc. (Weekly Bars)
www.TradeNavigator.com © 1999–2012. All rights reserved.

over trigger simultaneously, as point C indicates. The MACD indicator triggers both a moving average component and histogram trigger one bar after both the stochastics and CCI. Since the MACD is a lengthier moving average setting, it is less sensitive to price changes, which means it can take more time to trigger, and as this example shows, it can confirm a bottom and/or a top later than you would want. However, due to this timing factor, it is less likely to give false signals. Let's give it respect, as it is a great trend confirmation tool, as well as an overall trigger mechanism.

Stochastics is great for uncovering bullish convergence bottoms and bearish divergence tops. However, it can give a false sense of trend exhaustion, as the markets can remain either overbought or oversold for long periods of time. Therefore, you cannot and should not rely on one or two indicators. You want to combine a few noncorrelated yet confirming indicators in your decision-making process. In this last section, I simply wanted to point out how and why I use these indicators and when I don't. Hopefully, this chapter shed light on some of the most reliable patterns and formations that help me select and filter out trades.

CHAPTER 8

Scanning for Profits

The pure technician does not focus on news or fundamentals. The purist believes that the charts and technical studies represent the opinions of the market as a whole, which includes the fundamentalist. Those who are "in-the-know"—you know, the folks who may be buying ahead of earnings; a technician, for example—may uncover a hint of their positions or buying pressure, which may show up in the form of a positive reading either from volume or price action. In the beginning of trend phase, momentum changes can be subtle and hard to detect by just looking at names of companies and stock symbols and their closing prices as is listed on most data sources, including brokerage platforms or print media such as *Investor's Business Daily* or the *Wall Street Journal*.

With over 7,000 stocks listed on various exchanges, between the news media, industry trade reports, direct mail pieces, Internet, blog sites, friends, or family members touting a great stock to buy, how do you make an informed decision? Stocks that are launched on their initial public offerings (IPOs) can at times post highs that day only to trend lower for several weeks or months. Chapter 2 can give you an idea of what sectors make typical highs and lows, but as you know, it's no guarantee it will work every time. In fact, nothing presented so far will give you a guaranteed profit. At best, what we have provided are methods to give you an edge and to help prepare you for a trading opportunity, so how do we select a stock to buy or sell on any given day or week?

As of the writing of this book in early 2012, you most likely will have had an opportunity to work with computers and the Internet for a few years (decades for some of you), so that's what we will cover in this chapter: learning to take advantage of the power of computers and software programs to scan for trading setups.

SCANNING THE UNIVERSE

Scanning the universe of stocks is just like mining for opportunities. I was going to avoid the cheesy cliché of saying digging or mining for gold, but that's essentially what we are attempting to do.

Scans can be complicated by more costly software or charting services, or we can simplify the methods and use less expensive measures, which might take more time, but are worth the effort. I will discuss several methods and explain what I have created which is available to the general public. I do not want this to come off as a self-serving promotional section in the book, I am letting you be aware of what products and services are available as well as where and how to create your own criteria and checklist for scans.

Many traders, educators, and system developers use scan criteria built on moving averages or oscillators, and then back-test and optimize the appropriate settings that adjust to the best results from a historic performance perspective. This is known or referred to as curve fitting. Changing the time component on the moving averages or the set of parameters on an indicator to make the system appear more profitable on one market during a set period of time might make that system seem more robust than reality. Good systems or scan criteria comes from constructing a concept with a set of variables and then testing several markets in a set of sample time periods and in various time frames like intraday such as a 60-minute time frame and then an end-of-day test. Do this with various products from noncorrelated individual stocks and exchange-traded funds (ETFs) and stock indexes. This is how you develop a robust system and scan criteria so that when a signal is generated, you can have confidence that the signal has merit. Then you need to apply your risk parameter and position sizing model. In essence, figure out how many shares or positions you will commit to each signal. Now let's look at ways to scan for trades, the tools and software that I use, and what else is available.

TRADE NAVIGATOR

Throughout this book, I have used Trade Navigator, also known as Genesis software; it has a scanning feature, which I have programmed in my own library of scanning criteria. All these can be used on intraday, end-of-day, end-of-week, on stocks sectors, indexes, commodities, and currencies. They have the Person's Triggers scans both for buy and sell signals, my high-close doji (HCD) and low-close doji (LCD) scans.

Then we have set up a scan for stocks above and below the 50-day weighted moving average (WMA), which is used to spot-check sectors that are entering or ending seasonally strong periods for buying/selling opportunities. Also, this is used to gauge the overall health of stock indexes such as the Standard & Poor's (S&P) 500 just as one would use a contrarian indicator. If there is a large percentage of stocks—say, 67 percent of the index—significantly over their respective 50-day moving average—say, greater than 20 percent—then we are on guard for a market correction, as this gives a significant overbought reading. Another way of using this is to identify individual stock-buying opportunities as an added filter. For example, a strong reading of stocks under their 50-day moving averages may give a more selective buying opportunity.

I would scan for a stock under the 50-day moving average that formed an HCD formation. It would be an added bonus if this setup occurred when the stock is in a sector that is in a strong seasonal time period. Figure 8.1 shows the scan selected for all stocks under their 50-period WMA. As the list shows, on March 20, 2012, there were 2,784 symbols populated with this criterion. It would be virtually impossible to go through this number of symbols each night without further filters.

FIGURE 8.1 Below 50 Stocks

HIGH- AND LOW-CLOSE DOJI SCANS

One can optimize or look to see which length of a moving average would work best to define "uptrend" and "downtrend" for the LCD and HCD. For example, if the market is above the 14-period simple moving average (SMA) and an LCD forms, this triggers a sell signal. If the market is below the 14-period SMA and an HCD forms, this triggers a buy signal.

With computer software programs and analytical charting software like Genesis, one can automatically search for the best-optimized relationship between these factors. So instead of doing a manual back-test on 500 individual stocks trying to see which time frame—for example, a 7-, 8-, 9-, 10-,11-,12-, 13-, or 14-day SMA—works best, the computer will help optimize the best setting based on the highest or best-performing results based on the history and market you run the test on.

Figure 8.2 shows a chart based on a scan criterion for an HCD. As discussed in the preceding chapter, what defines the rules that we need the market to trade under a moving average? Here, the scan was created with

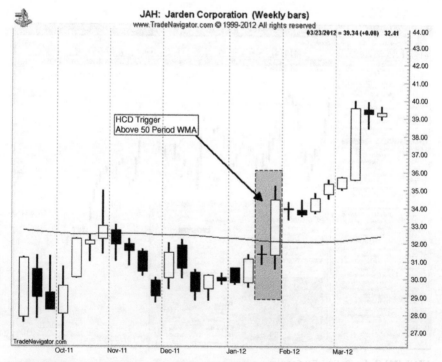

JAH: Jarden Corporation (Weekly bars)

03/23/2012 = 39.34 (+0.08) 32.41

HCD Trigger
Above 50 Period WMA

FIGURE 8.2 JAH: Jarden Corporation (Weekly Bars)

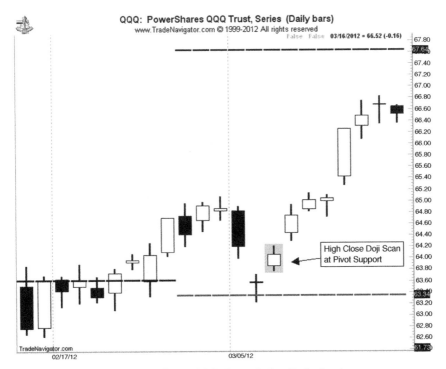

FIGURE 8.3 QQQ: PowerShares QQQ Trust, Series (Daily Bars)
www.TradeNavigator.com © 1999–2012. All rights reserved.

a 10-week moving average, which acts as a 50-day moving average. So, if we want to scan for trades that generate an HCD signal, the question now becomes: Does the doji form under the moving average, or does the high-close trigger need to be beneath the moving average as well?

I am of the opinion that the trigger can be above the moving average, as this helps to indicate a more solid breakout and buying opportunity.

Another scan is an HCD at or near (near is defined as current bar trading within a percentage rather than a price or tick value) a monthly support level. Figure 8.3 shows a scan result where the parameters were met, using the technology ETF QQQ.

Last and certainly not least, we have created the scans for LCDs, as Figure 8.4 demonstrates on Dean Foods (DF), with the trend being defined as the doji above the 10-week moving average. Now all we need to do is determine your position size—the amount of shares or contracts you want to sell—based on the risk factor if you wanted to take a short stock trade. Next, we determine that the stop loss needs to be placed above the highest high of the past four bars, or the high of the doji, as shown at point A on the chart.

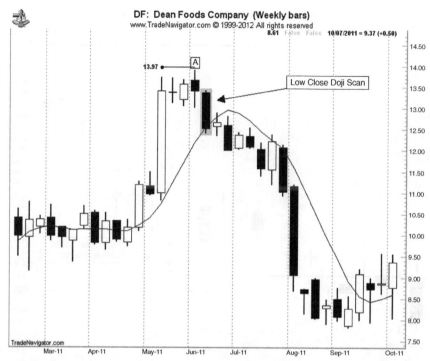

FIGURE 8.4 DF: Dean Foods Company (Weekly Bars)
www.TradeNavigator.com © 1999–2012. All rights reserved.

Remember, to successfully catch LCDs combining the moving average scans, it can take up to three time periods to create the trigger. As prices move, so does the moving average; therefore, we can see the trigger develop under or at the moving average value. Granted, these are all technically-driven buy and sell signals, but that is what using computer scans is all about. The computer does not understand fundamental or emotional analysis, such as "I bought it because it couldn't go much lower," or "I had to get short because it's never been this high before." Trust me when I tell you that markets can and do go much higher and lower than we feel. If you don't believe me, just look at Priceline (PCLN), Apple (AAPL), and a host of other companies that made incredible runs in late 2011 and early 2012.

DAILY SCAN SIGNALS

Using the Person's Triggers, we can scan for weekly and daily buy and sell signals on any targeted market sector. The task to choose which stock has the best setup from the search results would be an enormous event; therefore, I break down the scans by indexes, such as the S&P 500, and then I have them broken down by sector. So when I run a daily scan, I can see how many total stocks generated a buy or sell signal, and then I can break it down to see which sectors populated the most signals. On March 20, 2012, 87 stocks in the S&P 500—almost one-sixth of the 500 components—generated a daily sell signal. Of those stocks, 12 were isolated in the Energy sector, accounting for 14 percent of the total sell signals in the index for that day. My interest is typically piqued when over 10 percent of the total stocks scanned are concentrated in one sector that has sell signals. In cases like this, we need to investigate if the overall energy sector as represented by the XLE declined significantly or if crude oil prices declined. If not, then the scan warrants further monitoring over the next session or two to see if a sector-wide sell-off is in the works. As it turns out, on this date, we did start to see weakness in the crude oil market, so the scans did alert us to an impending sector-wide decline.

Figure 8.5 shows the stocks that generated a sell signal. Now the task of mining for a trading opportunity becomes less tedious. Now we can

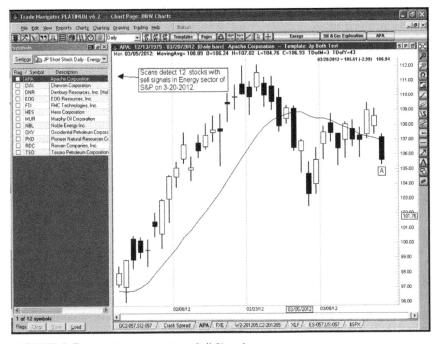

FIGURE 8.5   Stocks Generating a Sell Signal

apply other filters to strengthen our convictions, like the price declining below the 50-day WMA and a dreadful-looking chart pattern consisting of a failed rally and then the breakdown as shown at point A on the chart. Here is classic shorting opportunity in which I apply certain rules. Buy rules are the opposite.

Sell Rules
- Sell on the next open no less than one-half of 1 percent (0.5 percent) of the closing price.
- Place stops one-half of 1 percent (0.5 percent) above the highest high of the past four bars.
- The first profit objective on a 50 percent scale out is 100 percent of the initial risk.
- Adjust stops on balance of positions at breakeven after a profit target of 100 percent of the risk has been made.

Let's discuss the rules a bit. First of all, if you want to automate the rules into an automated trading system, the reason we need to talk in percentage terms rather than point or tick terms, is that you might want to cross over to the futures side of trading.

There, most markets have various tick and decimal variables. For example, grains trade in quarter-point ticks, while Treasury bonds (US or ZB) and notes (TY or ZN) trade in fractions, such as thirty-seconds. The E-mini Dow (YM) has no decimal points. By using percentage terms, the rules are robust to accommodate any market. As for the entry rule, you want to enter the trade as close as possible to the price of the trigger—which was generated by the closing price—so as not to increase risk and skew the trade results. That is why we have a rule in place to execute entry orders of no less than one quarter of 1 percent (0.25 percent) for sell orders. This will protect against a larger lower gap open; for example, your order would not be filled if the opening was lower than 105.73 from a close of 106.

I have a discretionary rule adjustment: If the last known price is distinctly further away from the close that triggered the sell signal, then I will enter a partial position and not the full lot amount. High-frequency traders (HFTs) also use this type of position management as price deviates too far from the ideal price point of entry. If the market pulls back closer to the ideal entry level, then you can add to the position size and place the stop size accordingly. Now all you need to do is manage the inventory part or execution of the position size of the trade by combining orders on the stops, rather than managing the risk price level since that is already established. You can also use the preopen outcry session to place entry orders. In addition, if the price is sharply lower, I will utilize a moving average like the Person's Pivot Study (PPS) on TD Ameritrade's thinkorswim platform,

Trade Navigator or TradeStation. If you are using other platforms to trade or do your analytical work, try a 7- or 10-period SMA, gauge the distance of the close, and subtract 25 percent of that distance to enter a full position size at that value. I refer to this as the 75 percent snap-back rule of order placement. As for the risk factor on a 106 dollar stock, if the highest high was 109.50, then the stop would be placed at 110.48; therefore, you initially have a one-to-one risk-reward ratio.

Since we are not fortunetellers, we cannot detect how far the market can decline, but it is necessary to take money off the table, especially if the trade performs within a short period of time. Discretion is useful to a degree in setups like this, since logic might dictate that buyers would place their sell stops under the last swing low. So a short-seller's profit objective would be around 102, just under that level. If you are an options trader, buying an at- or in-the-money put option would give you an initial profit target. Here is where a scan will help you select quality trade ideas. As Figure 8.6 shows, the market fell out of bed, declining closer to 100, a $6 move in two days. There is one other technical tool that we have not yet covered that

FIGURE 8.6 APA: Apache Corporation (Daily Bars)
www.TradeNavigator.com © 1999–2012. All rights reserved.

will help you target a support (low) or resistance (high) price level. That is the use of pivot point calculations. You may already know about these or even know my indicator, Person's Pivots. If not, we will cover these in detail, including some of the time frames I will for the first time release publicly in this book, in the coming chapters. If you turn your attention to point A on the chart, the dark horizontal dashed line is the Person's Filtered predicted monthly support target. I wish every trade worked out this perfectly, but as we say, if the trade has merit, you will be rewarded. The scans and the criteria that generate the sell signals are designed from a momentum indicator. If we scan for a sell signal, our next step is to see where our stop goes, and the next step after that is to determine the likelihood that the one-to-one risk-to-reward profit objective can be reached. The monthly pivot support target helped give confirmation that if the market did move lower, there was a probability that the stock price might reach that level. Using this tool helps give you a solid idea with pinpoint accuracy of the price level to take a profit. In this trade, the support level was 100.22, and the exact low was 100.27.The market tested this support for two days, allowing one to satisfactorily exit the allotted position.

TRADESTATION

TradeStation has many pre-laid-out features within both its scanning and radar packages. Figure 8.7 shows the layout I have programmed in my library for three buy scans and three sell scans.

Here are the criteria; the sell scans are the same criteria reversed.

- A daily momentum buy signal when the weekly time frame is in a buy mode.
- A daily momentum buy signal when the price is near the pivot point down to the pivot support level.
- Any daily momentum buy signal.

When I am scanning for a buy signal my preference is to buy a stock in a seasonally strong sector when the daily signal is lined up with the weekly signal. In other words, the lower time frame is in sync with the higher time frame. In Figure 8.7, the scans gave a buy signal based on the close of business back on March 23 for a total of 41 stocks. Now, if you do not know the names or the sector the stocks are in, you can quickly look these up. The Person's scans are on the left; the symbols and description of the stock and the volume is in the next column. I then have the daily chart with the on-balance volume (OBV) indicator in the upper quadrant and the weekly

FIGURE 8.7 TradeStation Buy Signal

© TradeStation Technologies, Inc. All rights reserved.

chart with the same indicator in the lower quadrant. The stock that struck my interest was International Game Technologies (IGT) in the Casino and Gaming sector. Typically, this sector has a strong seasonal tendency to rally in the second quarter as Vegas fills up for March Madness and college spring breaks. Conference traffic typically picks up from March into the May time period. The weekly charts look healthy, the volume indicator broke out above a downtrend, and the daily OBV Indicator is rising with prices. Now I will do a bit more investigating to see where the targeted support and resistance levels are. This way, I can get a better idea of the risks, where I need to place my stops, and what I can target my profit objective to be. I do this by looking at the pivot levels. After that, I can then look at the size of my position or how many shares I want to place the order for, based on my equity.

To do this, we have built the RadarScreen in TradeStation—a top-down sector-to-stock table that lists the sectors and the top stocks in those sectors. As you can see in Figure 8.8 at the top of the graph, we listed the Technology sector starting with Apple, Google, Akamai Technologies, the ETF XLK, IBM, Hewlett Packard, Oracle, Microsoft, Verizon, Cisco, and

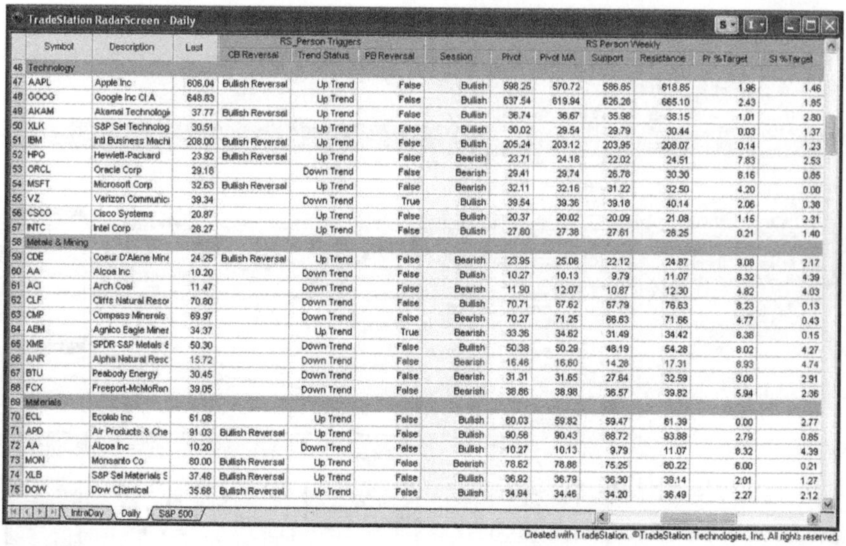

TradeStation RadarScreen - Daily

Symbol	Description	Last	RS_Person Triggers			Session	Pivot	Pivot MA	RS Person Weekly		Pr %Target	Sl %Target
			CB Reversal	Trend Status	PB Reversal				Support	Resistance		
46	Technology											
47 AAPL	Apple Inc	606.04	Bullish Reversal	Up Trend	False	Bullish	598.25	570.72	586.85	618.85	1.96	1.46
48 GOOG	Google Inc Cl A	648.83		Up Trend	False	Bullish	637.54	619.94	626.26	665.10	2.43	1.85
49 AKAM	Akamai Technolog	37.77	Bullish Reversal	Up Trend	False	Bullish	36.74	36.67	35.98	38.15	1.01	2.80
50 XLK	S&P Sel Technolog	30.51		Up Trend	False	Bullish	30.02	29.54	29.79	30.44	0.03	1.37
51 IBM	Intl Business Machi	208.00	Bullish Reversal	Up Trend	False	Bullish	205.24	203.12	203.95	208.07	0.14	1.23
52 HPQ	Hewlett-Packard	23.92	Bullish Reversal	Up Trend	False	Bearish	23.71	24.18	22.02	24.51	7.83	2.53
53 ORCL	Oracle Corp	29.18		Down Trend	False	Bearish	29.41	29.74	26.78	30.30	8.16	0.85
54 MSFT	Microsoft Corp	32.63	Bullish Reversal	Up Trend	False	Bearish	32.11	32.16	31.22	32.50	4.20	0.00
55 VZ	Verizon Communic	39.34		Down Trend	True	Bullish	39.54	39.36	39.18	40.14	2.06	0.38
56 CSCO	Cisco Systems	20.87		Up Trend	False	Bullish	20.37	20.02	20.09	21.08	1.15	2.31
57 INTC	Intel Corp	28.27		Up Trend	False	Bullish	27.80	27.38	27.61	28.25	0.21	1.40
58	Metals & Mining											
59 CDE	Coeur D'Alene Min	24.25	Bullish Reversal	Up Trend	False	Bearish	23.95	25.08	22.12	24.87	9.08	2.17
60 AA	Alcoa Inc	10.20		Down Trend	False	Bullish	10.27	10.13	9.79	11.07	8.32	4.39
61 ACI	Arch Coal	11.47		Down Trend	False	Bearish	11.90	12.07	10.87	12.30	4.82	4.03
62 CLF	Cliffs Natural Reso	70.80		Down Trend	False	Bullish	70.71	67.62	67.79	76.83	8.23	0.13
63 CMP	Compass Minerals	69.97		Down Trend	False	Bearish	70.27	71.25	66.63	71.66	4.77	0.43
64 AEM	Agnico Eagle Mine	34.37		Up Trend	True	Bearish	33.36	34.62	31.49	34.42	8.38	0.15
65 XME	SPDR S&P Metals &	50.30		Down Trend	False	Bullish	50.38	50.29	48.19	54.28	8.02	4.27
66 ANR	Alpha Natural Reso	15.72		Down Trend	False	Bearish	16.46	16.80	14.28	17.31	8.93	4.74
67 BTU	Peabody Energy	30.45		Down Trend	False	Bearish	31.31	31.65	27.64	32.59	9.08	2.91
68 FCX	Freeport-McMoRan	39.05		Down Trend	False	Bearish	38.86	38.98	36.57	39.82	5.94	2.36
69	Materials											
70 ECL	Ecolab Inc	61.08		Up Trend	False	Bullish	60.03	59.82	59.47	61.39	0.00	2.77
71 APD	Air Products & Che	91.03	Bullish Reversal	Up Trend	False	Bullish	90.56	90.43	88.72	93.88	2.79	0.85
72 AA	Alcoa Inc	10.20		Down Trend	False	Bullish	10.27	10.13	9.79	11.07	8.32	4.39
73 MON	Monsanto Co	80.00	Bullish Reversal	Up Trend	False	Bearish	78.62	78.88	75.25	80.22	6.00	0.21
74 XLB	S&P Sel Materials S	37.48	Bullish Reversal	Up Trend	False	Bullish	36.92	36.79	36.30	38.14	2.01	1.27
75 DOW	Dow Chemical	35.68	Bullish Reversal	Up Trend	False	Bullish	34.94	34.46	34.20	36.49	2.27	2.12

IntraDay \ Daily \ S&P 500

Created with TradeStation. ©TradeStation Technologies, Inc. All rights reserved.

FIGURE 8.8 TradeStation RadarScreen—Daily
© TradeStation Technologies, Inc. All rights reserved.

Intel. Then to the right we have the last trade price, and then the next column has a text version of the scanner. CB Reversal stands for "current bar reversal"; then it lists whether it's a bullish or bearish reversal. This signals that there was a buy signal generated in the current time frame. Then we have the trend status; if the stock has been in an uptrend, that will appear in the trend status. Here's the best part, and something most investors do not do. This targets the percentage of profit and the percentage of loss to the stop-loss target based on the pivot point support and resistance levels. The reason this is helpful is twofold: (1) I know if the market breaks support I can immediately see what the loss amount is, and (2) I can then look to establish my position size according to the risk parameter.

When using TradeStation RadarScreen, another major benefit is that you can immediately see what stocks generated a new buy signal and how many of the top stocks in a particular sector generated buy signals. If I see only one or two stocks in a fresh buy mode, it does not warn me of a sector-wide broad-based buying spree. However, if we see the majority of stocks in the sector, as well as related sectors, this alerts me to the fact that we might be seeing more capital being committed to this sector. That significantly motivates me to hone in on this area for a long stock purchase. Additional filtering with the aid of pivot support targets and the OBV study helps me to determine which stock to buy, where to place my stop, and what the initial profit expectations can be in a specific time frame. To clarify, if I am in a weekly pivot time period, then I am looking for the trade to manifest by week's end. If I am looking at the monthly pivot levels and trend, then I am looking for the trade to materialize by month's end. In Figure 8.9, I have broken down the financial sectors by ETFs with their respective components: the XLK, then the Regional Bank sector ETF KBE and the stocks in that sector, and finally the capital markets ETF KCE. You might notice some redundancy, as some stocks in the financial sector are the same as in capital markets, such as Morgan Stanley (MS) and the Chicago Mercantile Exchange (CME), which are both listed in the FXE and the KCE. If you examine the column listed as CB Reversal, you will see the majority of stocks in this space generated a buy signal and are in a bullish trend, as indicated in the column titled "Session."

With this layout, you can immediately see what sectors are bullish or bearish. If there is a concentration of stocks in that sector that are bullish, you therefore know that a sector is not up based on just a few stocks with higher capitalized weighting, but rather an equal weighting shows more stocks are bullish than bearish. I also have a spreadsheet in front of me that shows the last trade price and where each stock is in relation to its targeted support and resistance levels. Finally, with this layout you also have a percentage of the current price in relationship to a profit-and-loss target level.

You may be aware, but if you are not, TD Ameritrade's TOS platform has Person's Pivots and PPS built into the platform under Licensed Studies. The

TradeStation RadarScreen - Daily

Symbol	Description	Last	CB Reversal	Trend Status	PB Reversal	Session	Pivot	Pivot MA	Support	Resistance	Pr %Target	SI %Target
Financial												
MS	Morgan Stanley	20.99	Bullish Reversal	Up Trend	False	Bullish	20.11	19.10	19.52	21.50	1.56	5.27
BAC	Bank of America C	9.88	Bullish Reversal	Up Trend	False	Bullish	9.78	8.97	9.46	10.48	5.54	1.53
JPM	JPMorgan Chase &	45.90		Up Trend	False	Bullish	45.01	42.92	44.35	46.47	0.85	2.58
USB	U.S. Bancorp	31.96	Bullish Reversal	Up Trend	False	Bullish	31.62	30.82	31.06	32.83	2.24	1.55
WFC	Wells Fargo	34.34	Bullish Reversal	Up Trend	False	Bullish	33.75	32.59	33.01	35.01	1.80	1.90
C	Citigroup Inc	37.42		Up Trend	False	Bullish	37.36	36.55	36.32	39.22	4.78	0.19
XLF	S&P Sel Financial S	15.98	Bullish Reversal	Up Trend	False	Bullish	15.72	15.29	15.47	16.22	1.50	1.65
BK	Bank Of New York	24.53	Bullish Reversal	Up Trend	False	Bullish	24.07	23.31	23.44	25.21	2.52	2.16
GS	Goldman Sachs Gr	128.30		Up Trend	False	Bullish	125.41	121.18	122.96	131.07	2.34	2.12
AXP	American Express	58.93		Up Trend	False	Bullish	57.07	55.10	56.59	58.21	0.00	2.79
TRV	The Travelers Com	59.20	Bullish Reversal	Up Trend	False	Bullish	58.57	58.27	57.58	60.18	2.26	0.46
Regional Bank												
BOH	Bank Of Hawaii	48.08	Bullish Reversal	Up Trend	False	Bullish	47.84	47.10	47.02	49.45	2.70	0.65
SIVB	SVB Financial Grou	67.44	Bullish Reversal	Up Trend	False	Bullish	65.95	64.06	64.68	68.86	2.11	2.26
CVBF	CVB Financial	11.85		Up Trend	False	Bullish	11.53	11.12	11.09	12.48	5.32	2.78
FMER	Firstmerit Corp	17.19	Bullish Reversal	Up Trend	False	Bullish	16.95	16.68	16.40	17.96	4.48	1.42
FULT	Fulton Financial	10.59	Bullish Reversal	Up Trend	False	Bullish	10.51	10.22	10.22	11.03	4.15	0.76
EWBC	East West Bancorp	23.68		Down Trend	False	Bullish	23.54	23.04	22.89	24.72	4.39	0.59
FNB	FNB Corp (FL)	12.34	Bullish Reversal	Up Trend	False	Bullish	12.23	12.03	11.96	12.72	3.08	0.90
MBFI	Mb Financial	21.85	Bullish Reversal	Up Trend	False	Bullish	21.48	20.81	20.70	22.74	5.03	0.79
KRE	SPDR S&P Regiona	28.90	Bullish Reversal	Up Trend	False	Bullish	28.60	27.89	27.84	29.96	3.85	0.67
SBNY	Signature Bank	65.15	Bullish Reversal	Up Trend	False	Bullish	63.77	62.73	61.56	67.75	4.28	1.88
HBHC	Hancock Holding	36.47	Bullish Reversal	Up Trend	False	Bullish	35.63	35.04	34.77	37.21	2.37	2.02
Capital Markets												
MS	Morgan Stanley	20.99	Bullish Reversal	Up Trend	False	Bullish	20.11	19.10	19.52	21.50	1.56	5.27
BEN	Franklin Resources	124.82	Bullish Reversal	Up Trend	False	Bullish	123.54	122.00	121.09	127.65	1.99	1.31
LM	Legg Mason Inc	29.16	Bullish Reversal	Up Trend	False	Bullish	28.87	28.17	28.15	29.68	1.54	1.95
CME	CME Group Inc	297.70		Up Trend	False	Bullish	295.53	286.16	286.45	314.16	5.53	0.73
JEF	Jefferies Group	19.45	Bullish Reversal	Up Trend	False	Bullish	19.13	18.21	18.44	20.88	6.32	1.67

IntraDay / Daily / S&P 500

Created with TradeStation. ©TradeStation Technologies, Inc. All rights reserved.

FIGURE 8.9 TradeStation RadarScreen—Daily

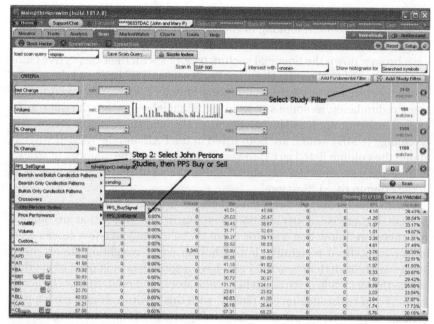

FIGURE 8.10 Thinkorswim Platform
© TD Ameritrade IP Company, Inc.

PPS indicator is the bullish and bearish momentum study. In late 2011, TD Ameritrade made available the PPS Indicator as a scan feature. This is, of course, free to their clients. You can access this by clicking on the tab at the top of the platform labeled "Scan." On the upper right-hand side, click where it reads "Add Study Filter," as shown in Figure 8.10. A drop-down widow will open. Expand this, and you will see John Person's Studies. A separate window will open, offering you to select PPS, Buy Signal and PPS, or Sell Signal. Now all you need to do is select the market product or sector you wish to run the scan on and select the time period you wish to run the scans on, such as intraday like 15-, 30-, or 60-minute signals for day and swing traders to end-of-day buy or sell signals for swing and position trading.

You can select Indexes such as the S&P 500, the Nasdaq, or the Dow Jones. You can also choose other markets, including—but not limited to— Forex, other futures markets, and predetermined selections, from anything between stocks in the top 10 percent gainer or volume either up or down, to a sizzle index of hot stocks, and even double- and triple-leveraged ETFs.

Once the list is populated, within one click, you can set up a chart and then apply the layers of confirming technical tools such as Person's Pivots or the OBV indicator to plot out the risk-reward parameters for entering a

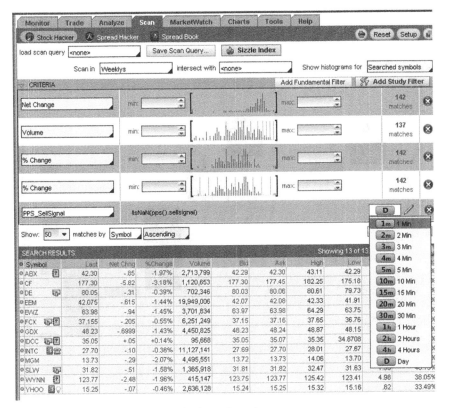

FIGURE 8.11   Scan Run on End-of-Day Signals
© TD Ameritrade IP Company, Inc.

trade. Depending on what you find or what you are searching for, you may have started looking at buy signals for stocks within sectors that are in a seasonally strong period. Conversely, if you scan for stocks using the PPS Sell Signals, then you may look to line these up in sectors that are ending their seasonally strong time periods or are entering their respective annual peaks.

One sector I like to run a scan on to look for trading signals is stocks that have weekly options. There is a big attraction to these stocks, and as such, there tend to be more swing trading opportunities. Examine Figure 8.11. This scan was run on the end-of-day signals for the trading session ending on March 29.

What is interesting is that we got a mix of stocks and ETFs by using the scan on stocks that have weekly options. Knowing what we learned from the chapter on seasonality, you may recall or refer to the graph on precious metals, namely, gold. Typically, this sector peaks out in price in February.

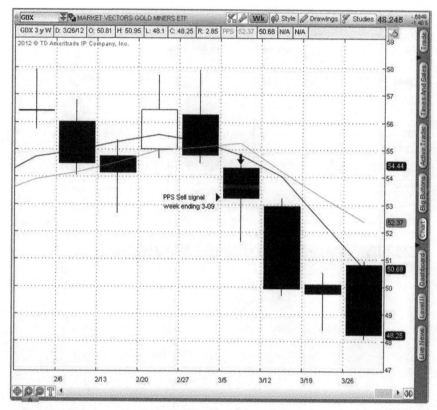

FIGURE 8.12   Weekly Chart on GDX
© TD Ameritrade IP Company, Inc.

Now notice the symbol (GDX) that popped up on our daily scan in
Figure 8.11. This is Market Vectors Gold Miners ETF. Here is a seasonal
trade situation where a sector typically peaks out in February and the
bearish trend extends into the June to July time frame. Now let's examine
Figure 8.12, where we have a weekly chart on GDX. We have discussed that
it helps to take shorter-term time frame signals when the higher-degree
time fame is in the same trend mode. Notice that a PPS sell signal was
generated on the week ending March 9. This suggests that the GDX is in
a weekly sell mode and is in sync with its typical seasonal bearish trend.

In Figure 8.13 we have the daily graph that was generated once we picked
up on the GDX in the daily TOS scan featuring PPS sell signals. Seriously, if
we focus on seasonal trends and then watch for weekly and daily market
signals to line up, then you should have a higher probability to see a favorable
outcome on that trade. I am not saying that by using these scans, every trade

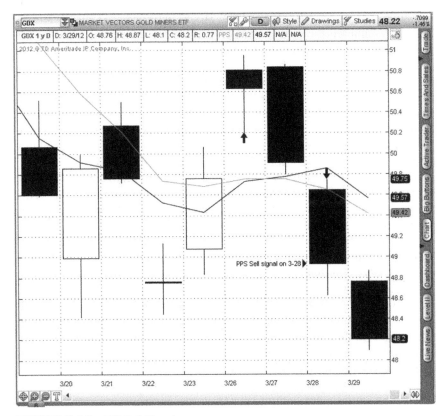

FIGURE 8.13 PPS Sell Signals
© TD Ameritrade IP Company, Inc.

will be a winner, but your odds will increase that the trade may have a favorable outcome. The length of time holding the position and the degree of a move that was already under way are factors in determining the profitability.

In order to determine if the market has already reached near an oversold condition or if there is more room to the downside to enter a short position, we will use one more layer of market analysis such as the Person's Pivots. This we will cover in the next chapter. Here, we showing what tools are available to you and how they can be effective in searching for trade ideas.

If you are trading with a company that does not offer the scanning feature or you are just looking to see how this will work for you, before investing in other software programs like Trade Navigator or TradeStation, which may incur further expenses, I might suggest a free scanning service through StockCharts.com.

Founded by Chip Anderson, in 2002, StockCharts acquired MurphyMorris, owned by John Murphy and Greg Morris. There are several predefined scans you can run. Unfortunately, they do not have the PPS indicators, but you can run scans on various indicators, including volume studies. From the home page, select "Free Charts," and then on the right-hand side about halfway down the page, select "Predefined Stock Scans" and you will see the list of available scans, which you are able to run on several different market sectors. You can focus on just Bullish Technical Indicators and/or Bearish Technical Indicators.

I would suggest to start with running scans using the Strong Volume Gainers for both the New York Stock Exchange (NYSE) and Nasdaq. Once I have the scan, I first filter out those stocks that have substantial liquidity. In order to keep the number of scan results from being excessive, all Predefined Scans look for stocks that traded an average of at least 40,000 shares per day over the past 20 days.

The definition StockCharts.com uses for strong volume gainers is: Volume is four times greater than the 20-day SMA and is above prior day's close. I like to add this filter: stock that triggered a buy signal with volume over 400,000 shares.

As you can see in Figure 8.14, the columns list the stock name, symbol, the exchange the stock is listed under, and the industry group the stock falls under. On the far right it lists the volume. To the left of the symbol, you will notice three boxes, which you can click to see either a single chart, a daily and weekly chart, or a point-and-figure (P&F) chart.

The first thing I suggest you do once the list of stocks populates is to look at the sector seasonality to see if we are entering or nearing the end

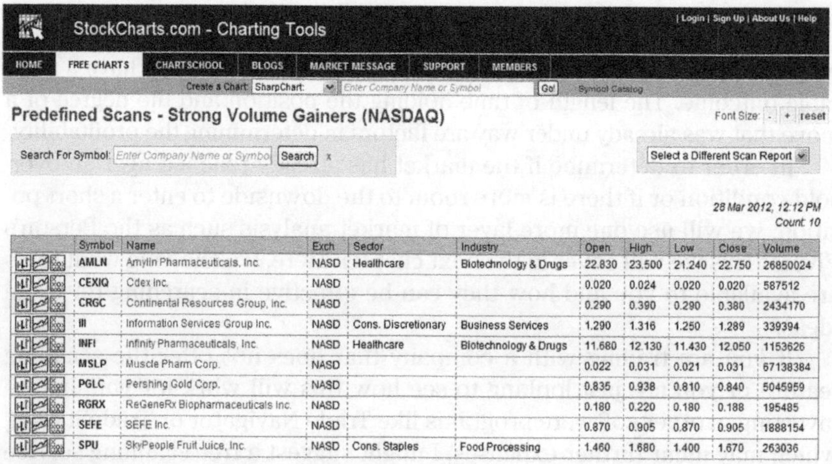

Predefined Scans - Strong Volume Gainers (NASDAQ)

28 Mar 2012, 12:12 PM
Count: 10

	Symbol	Name	Exch	Sector	Industry	Open	High	Low	Close	Volume
	AMLN	Amylin Pharmaceuticals, Inc.	NASD	Healthcare	Biotechnology & Drugs	22.830	23.500	21.240	22.750	26850024
	CEXIQ	Cdex Inc.	NASD			0.020	0.024	0.020	0.020	587512
	CRGC	Continental Resources Group, Inc.	NASD			0.290	0.390	0.290	0.380	2434170
	III	Information Services Group Inc.	NASD	Cons. Discretionary	Business Services	1.290	1.316	1.250	1.289	339394
	INFI	Infinity Pharmaceuticals, Inc.	NASD	Healthcare	Biotechnology & Drugs	11.680	12.130	11.430	12.050	1153626
	MSLP	Muscle Pharm Corp.	NASD			0.022	0.031	0.021	0.031	67138384
	PGLC	Pershing Gold Corp.	NASD			0.835	0.938	0.810	0.840	5045959
	RGRX	ReGeneRx Biopharmaceuticals Inc.	NASD			0.180	0.220	0.180	0.188	195485
	SEFE	SEFE Inc	NASD			0.870	0.905	0.870	0.905	1888154
	SPU	SkyPeople Fruit Juice, Inc.	NASD	Cons. Staples	Food Processing	1.460	1.680	1.400	1.670	263036

FIGURE 8.14 StockCharts.com Charting Tools

of a seasonal bullish or bearish time frame. For example, when this screen shot of the scan results was printed out, it was March 29, 2012. In Chapter 2, if you examine the Health Care sector as represented by the XLV, you will see it has a strong tendency to see price gains from the third week of March into early May. There are two stocks in this list that are in the health care sector, AMLN and INFI. Both meet the volume and seasonality filter criteria, so in order to see where a market might go, it's best to take a look at where it is and where it's been. Therefore, when you are using StockCharts. com, select the gallery view to take a quick reading of the weekly chart. When doing this you want to look at the chart pattern and also identify a previous high or the next level of strong weekly resistance. This level is then compared with the current price to determine the potential upside for a new long position. This is important because even if the stock and volume look very positive, if it is too close to the next level of major resistance or if it has already made a substantial move, the stock then becomes less attractive. In this case, I will still keep the stock on my radar for a few weeks in case it corrects so I can buy on a dip.

One of the other reasons to examine a higher-degree time frame is to identify swing low on the weekly chart that could be used to identify a good stop level. If a stock is already in a strong uptrend and is well away from support, then I will often go on to the next stock, since the risk on new positions in the initial stock is likely going to be too high.

Once I find a stock that has sufficient upside potential and a reasonable stop level, I look at the OBV. You can plot the OBV indicator on StockCharts.com, and it is important to see that the OBV is in gear or in sync with prices.

By now you should know that means if prices are moving higher, the OBV indicator should also be making higher highs. It is also important that the OBV is either in an uptrend or has completed a base formation.

I also look at the relationship of the daily chart and the weekly charts with the corresponding on balance volume indicator to see if both time frames are in a bullish mode. I have mentioned Tom Aspray's name, as he is also an avid user of the OBV indicator. One of the techniques he uses is to apply a 21-period WMA over the indicator itself. If the OBV indicator is above the moving average, then he has confirmation that the indicator is reflecting positive buying pressure. Let's now put the steps outlined above to work. Examine Figure 8.15, which is a weekly chart on the first stock in that daily scan, Amylin Pharmaceuticals (AMLN). While it is considered part of the Health Care sector, it is in the subsector of Biotechnology. As you can see, the scan produced a winner, unfortunately well after the fact. However, notice the OBV breakout above the 21 WMA as shown at point A on the chart. In addition, six weeks earlier an HCD triggered, as the shaded

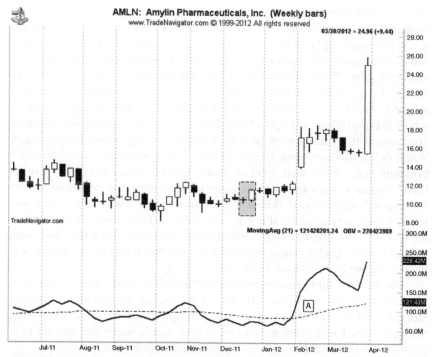

FIGURE 8.15 AMLN: Amylin Pharmaceuticals, Inc. (Weekly Bars)
www.TradeNavigator.com © 1999–2012. All rights reserved.

box shows. So at least we can from see the patterns and theory, using the OBV has merit. The stock has soared from under $10 to over $25 per share in less than 10 weeks, but the risk is more than I would like, considering the stops would need to be placed under 414.00 or under the low of the marubozu candles low. This is an example of when I will put this stock on my radar or set an alert on my trading platform to warn me when the price pulls back. Using the information from Chapter 7, the midpoint of the marubozu candle at 20.00 will be the price level where I will reevaluate that stock if the market corrects back down to it.

Now let's look at the next stock that came up on the scan: Infinity Pharmaceuticals (INFI). This is also a stock in the subsector listed under Biotechnology. As you can see, the weekly chart in Figure 8.16 reveals that this company has also undergone a significant price appreciation. Notice that this stock also formed an HCD pattern on the week ending February 24, as shown at point A on the chart. One week later, the OBV indicator crossed above the 21 WMA, giving a strong confirmation of buying pressure. Once again, I am going to need a pullback as the risk profile is out of my

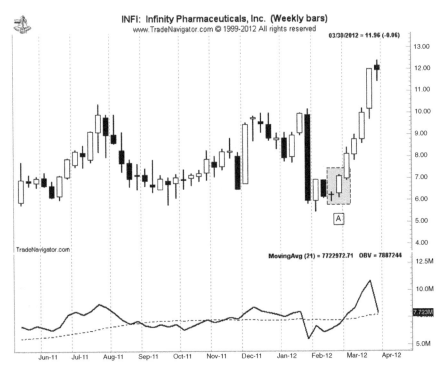

INFI: Infinity Pharmaceuticals, Inc. (Weekly bars)

03/30/2012 = 11.96 (-0.06)

MovingAvg (21) = 7722972.71   OBV = 7887244

FIGURE 8.16   INFI: Infinity Pharmaceuticals, Inc. (Weekly Bars)

parameters. Normally, one will start thinking, "What a waste of time—everything has already moved." The good news is that if I start to see several stocks making big moves, then I will start to dig around for other stocks in that sector, and more importantly, on top of scanning for high-volume movers, I also scan for HCDs! The neat thing is that we can and we do have scans set up in Trade Navigator just for that reason. High- and low-close dojis are one of my most reliable setups. Typically, they generate a lower risk high-probability trade and earlier than any volume or moving average scan.

There are over 100 companies in this industry sector, so now it's my job to continue to dig for stocks with more than 400,000 daily volume and positive OBV readings, and hopefully find some with an HCD pattern.

As we narrowed our search here, we found that using the process outlined above produced two candidates. The first, as shown in Figure 8.17, is Human Genome Sciences (HGSI). This chart is a daily graph that shows we have a breakout of the OBV indicators above its 21 WMA, as shown at point B on the chart. A daily HCD pattern was created at the close of business on March 20, 2012, which is in the shaded area marked point A on the chart.

FIGURE 8.17 HGSI: Human Genome Sciences, Inc. (Daily Bars)
www.TradeNavigator.com © 1999–2012. All rights reserved.

According to our rules, we would be buying at 8.24 or no higher than 8.28 (0.005 percent entry rule). Once the market closes, you can place the buy order in the preopen session as a limit order at 8.28 or better, then, once filled, place your stops no more than 0.005 percent below the low of the doji or the lowest low of the last four time periods. This would place the stop under the doji low. The first scale out for a short-term trader would be 100 percent of the risk factor, and in this setup, would be $0.60 or a first profit target at $8.88.

On a daily chart, this looks like a solid trading plan. The seasonal trend shows that this sector moves up from mid-March into early May, the OBV indicator is breaking out about the 21 WMA, and we have a high-probability candle chart pattern with the HCD formation. Finally, we have a reasonable risk factor of $0.60, which is just over 7 percent of the entry price at $8.28. The next course of action is to see how many shares you want to buy in your portfolio.

Now let's examine the weekly chart in Figure 8.18 to see if the higher-degree time frame looks as impressive. We do have an HCD formation

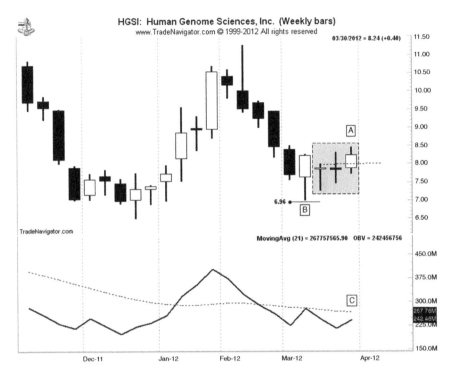

FIGURE 8.18 HGSI: Human Genome Sciences, Inc. (Weekly Bars)

in the weekly chart, as point A in the shaded area suggests; however, the OBV indicator has not broken out of its 21 WMA, as shown at point C on the chart. If you take the trade based on the merits of the daily chart information, the seasonal analysis, and the weekly HCD, the higher-degree time frame or weekly chart suggests that you buy at 8.28, with stops under 6.96—which is under the low—as shown at point B on the chart. Typically, if I enter a trade on the lower-degree time frame such as the daily chart, I should see positive improvement in the weekly technical picture within one or two weeks. In this case, I am buying this stock at the 8.28 with the risk factor outlined in the daily chart pattern.

Now let's examine a competitive stock in the same industry sector. Figure 8.19 shows a daily chart in Gilead Sciences (GILD). Notice that we have a textbook HCD pattern, as shown in the shaded area marked point A on the charts. The OBV indicator is trading above the 21 WMA, marked as point B on the chart, showing there is positive buying pressure. To enter this trade using the rules outlined earlier, the HCD pattern formed with the closing price on March 29, 2012, at 47.77, which means we would place a

FIGURE 8.19   GILD: Gilead Services, Inc. (Daily Bars)
www.TradeNavigator.com © 1999–2012. All rights reserved.

limit order to buy 0.005 percent higher as an "or better" limit order at 48.01. If the stock opens or trades lower than that price, we will be filled on a long position. As you can see, on the next trading session, March 30, 2012, the market opened higher, but the low was 47.93, thus triggering our long entry. The stop was placed 0.005 percent below the low of the doji or the lowest low of the last four bars. In this example, the lowest low was on March 26, 2012, at 46.68, so the stop price was at 46.44. We had an immediate winner with prices closing at 48.86, but not enough to take a partial position off and certainly not enough to adjust the stop. We will cover stops and position sizing techniques in the Chapter in section on trade management.

Now let's examine the weekly chart, as shown in Figure 8.20. While we do not have a weekly HCD, we do have a breakout on the closing price from a five-week sideways channel, as shown at point A on the chart. If you are not using the technical information drawn from the daily chart to place the entry and stop-loss levels, then using the weekly chart, you would be looking for a pullback of half the distance of the real body or the midpoint of the open–close relationship to place the buy order. Since the

FIGURE 8.20   GILD: Gilead Services, Inc. (Weekly Bars)

www.TradeNavigator.com © 1999–2012. All rights reserved.

market opened the week ending March 30, 2012 at 47.00 and closed at 48.86, the midpoint was 47.93. The stop would go 0.05 percent below the lowest low of the past four bars. That level was 44.77 for the week ending March 2, 2012. So the stop would be placed at 44.54. That equates to a $3.39 risk or a little over a 7.5 percent loss on the purchase price. Now we ask ourselves if the market can rally at least $3.39 in the life span of its seasonal strength time frame. Considering it will be seven weeks until May that the price was at an annual high at 56.50 during the week ending February 10, my answer is yes.

CONCLUSION

Scanning for stock trading opportunities really helps filter out better choices. When you apply seasonal analysis combined with the technical tools—such as the OBV indictor integrated with the 21 WMA—and then layered

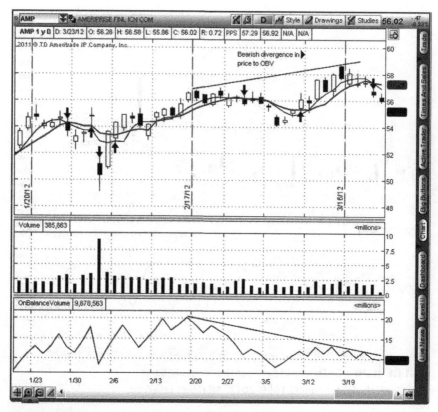

FIGURE 8.21 Daily Chart on Ameriprise Financial (AMP)
© TD Ameritrade IP Company, Inc.

with the trading patterns that have the specific entry and exit rules. It certainly should help you formulate better trades with defined risk. There is one other concept I would like you to keep in mind: If you have a hunch or suspect that a stock or market sector is a buy because it is too cheap or oversold, or perhaps too expensive and therefore a sell because you believe the market is overbought, run a scan and check to see what the seasonality of that sector is and if there are several other stocks within that group that may show the same technical elements to support your beliefs. The point is that you should use the tools within these pages to support your beliefs. Take a look at Figure 8.21; this is a daily chart on Ameriprise Financial (AMP), using a chart from TD Ameritrade's TOS platform. Notice that the PPS indicator generated a bearish momentum signal. Looking at the volume bars, it was hard to develop a strong opinion one way or the other. However, the OBV indicator certainly demonstrated a significant bearish divergence pattern between prices and the indicator itself. As we were editing the book in mid-May 2012, just two months later this stock had declined to a low of 46.15 per share.

Hopefully, you now see how specific indicators when used together can aid in determining higher-quality setups. Next thing you need to do is simply learn how your computer and trading software can do the heavy lifting for you by taking the time to learn how to use the scanning features. Then run just remember to actually run the scans.

As a follow-up to Human Genome Sciences, Inc. (HGSI), examine Figure 8.22, which is a weekly chart showing the market nearly hit our stop under 6.96, as shown at point A. The actual low was 7.01. The method for the combined order entry and stop placement using the daily and weekly time frame combinations will also aid you in mastering more profitable trades. Some may consider this outright lucky. I will not argue that point either, but I must say, combining the seasonal analysis with the rule-based set-ups using the reversal pattern trigger such as the HCD adds a tremendous element to better trades. The reality here is that GlaxoSmithKline (GSK)

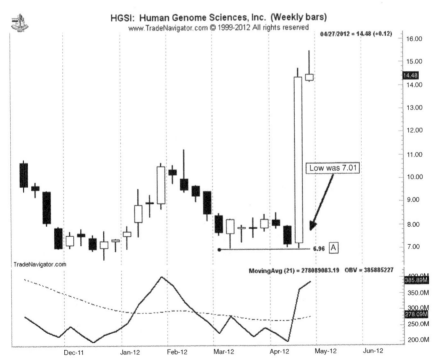

FIGURE 8.22 HGSI: Human Genome Sciences, Inc. (Weekly Bars)
www.TradeNavigator.com © 1999–2012. All rights reserved.

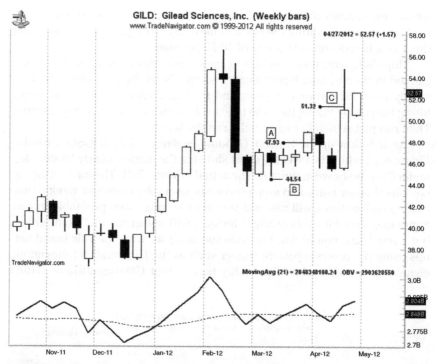

FIGURE 8.23 GILD: Gilead Sciences, Inc. (Weekly Bars)
www.TradeNavigator.com © 1999–2012. All rights reserved.

made a buyout offer to acquire the company and the stock more than doubled. I had no knowledge of this when writing the book, and the book was sent to the publisher for editing before this news hit. The selection of this trade was made purely on the foundation of the principles set in these chapters.

As a follow-up in regards to the projected profit objective, study the weekly chart on Gilead Sciences shown in Figure 8.23. The entry was $47.93, as shown at point A, with a stop-loss order placed at 44.54, as indicated at point B. The initial risk was $3.39, or a little over a 7.5 percent loss on the purchase price. The initial profit or reward target was set at a one-to-one level or $3.39 for the life span of its seasonal strength time frame. As the chart shows, the trade was profitable within two weeks or time periods on a weekly chart from the time the trade was entered. Granted, we did take a little heat on the trade, but even as prices moved close to our stop-loss level, notice that the OBV indicator showed a higher low. This observation is important, as many times markets show price weakness, but it is not accompanied by strong volume. Again, this was another setup discovered by using a scanning feature incorporated with the use of seasonal analysis triggered by an HCD confirmed with a bullish OBV pattern as well.

When you apply rules such as mandatory profit taking on partial positions, it is only a matter of time before you will see enhanced performance in your results. We have covered some exciting techniques, and as we get into the Person's Pivots, as well as risk management—including a calculation for determining lot sizing and trail stop methods—I know you will be eager to use these methods immediately. Quite frankly, I hope you find the value in this methodology as I have. Again, there is no holy grail of trading indicators, but combining these methods has helped reduce my losing trades and the losses in those losing trades. As I stated before, if the trade has merit, then you will be rewarded.

CHAPTER 9

Pivot Point Analysis

S o far, we have covered methods for determining trend direction using seasonal studies, the power of contrarian data using the Commodity Futures Trading Commission's Commitment of Traders (COT) report, and confirming tools and techniques such as comparative relative strength using trend-line analysis and moving averages. In addition, we covered how to view the overall health of the market with advance-decline (AD) work and volume analysis using the on-balance volume (OBV) indicator. We covered trading patterns with rules for entering and placing stops, as well as indicators and oscillators to help reveal markets hidden strengths like bullish convergence and weaknesses like bearish divergence.

I have discussed several research systems that can be used to scan for trading opportunities; Trade Navigator, TradeStation, and Thinkorswim by TD Ameritrade (yes, it is a coincidence that these platforms and trading companies all start with the letter T). I also showed a free Internet service using StockCharts.com. Here is another fact: Futures traders have been using my momentum indicator and Person's Pivots on the Open E-Cry (OEC) trading platform, and they are available with Ninja Trader. In the future, we may include these with E-Signal, Bloomberg, and Meta Stock, as there have been many requests to add these into those platforms. The reason my indicators have been so popular is that they have been instrumental in helping traders identify opportunities; the method is simple and easy to learn. In fact, this is the basis for my Person's Pivot Indicator.

As a result, I felt it was important to devote a chapter to my favorite technical tool, pivot point analysis. This is the tool that will uncover the price levels at which to enter orders and, most importantly, help filter out better trade setups from lowering the risk parameter and setting the profit targets.

I remember just under eight years ago this was one of the least used predictive indicators by the masses. Today, I see a majority of marketing on the secrets of pivots and the powerful predictive qualities this tool possesses. Quite frankly, I absolutely agree, as I have been using this tool for nearly 30 years.

I consider this tool to be a predictive indicator, as it gives traders a futuristic look at what the next time period's potential high and or low might be. Simply put, point analysis gives projected support and resistance target levels. This is a tool that many traders either misuse or do not understand entirely. Hopefully, after reading this chapter, you will be better informed on the nuances of using this powerful tool.

First of all, pivot analysis can be used to help confirm the market trend or condition, whether that is bullish, bearish, or neutral. The integrated formulas can then project under those assumptions what the next time period's range or support or resistance levels might be.

This is extremely helpful to determine support levels in which to buy when bullish, especially on pullbacks, and selling opportunities against predetermined resistance levels in bearish market conditions. Moreover, traders can use longer-term pivot point targets to project the price level at which a potential trend reversal could occur.

Think about this for a moment: As a trader, what more do you want than to stay with the trend but also have a clearer profit objective? Pivot analysis can help traders achieve both of these goals. This section will describe in full detail the mathematical calculations and the rationale behind the psychological impact that drives traders to make decisions around these levels.

The amazing aspect of this technical tool is that it is very diverse. It works for short- and long-term trend traders, and the analysis can be applied for stock, exchange-traded funds (ETFs), futures, and especially the foreign currency markets.

Granted, each investment vehicle has its own nuances, such as trading session hours, time periods in which volume flows change, contract sizes, and decimal point placement, so it's important that you know how to correctly apply the mathematic calculation for each market in order to get the right pivot point levels.

First, let's go over the foundation of the methodology of pivot point analysis. This will then allow you to apply it to the specific markets of interest that you are trading.

The power in using pivot analysis is that the strategy works in all markets that have established ranges based on significant volume or a large group of collective participants. After all, the current market price equals the collective action of buyers and sellers. Pivot point analysis is a robust, time-tested, and, best of all, testifiable form of market analysis. This means that you can back-test to see the accuracy of this trader's tool's predictive analysis. The really unbelievable aspect of pivots is who uses them. In fact, many traders feel compelled not to learn about them because they seem complicated. I will dispel that myth.

In my first book, *The Complete Guide to Technical Trading Tactics* (John Wiley & Sons, 2004), I illustrated many trading methods that one can apply using pivot point analysis with candlesticks patterns, including the power of multiple time frames, or what is known as confluence of various target levels. This chapter will highlight those techniques, as well as explain how to filter out and narrow the field of the respective support and resistance numbers and divulge various formulas that are popular today.

Pivot point is a mathematical formula designed to determine the potential range expansion based on a previous time period's data, which include the high, the low, and the close or settlement price, the basis for which is the formula $(H + L + C) / 3$. One reason why I believe in using these variables from a given time period's range is that they reflect all market participants' collective perception of value for that time period.

I want to quote the legendary trader Jesse Livermore, who made this observation nearly 70 years ago, and it rings as true today as it did then: "The patterns the traders and technicians observe are simply the reflections of human emotional behavior."

The range, which is the high and low of a given time period, accurately reflects all market participants' exuberant bullishness and pessimistic bearishness for that trading session, whether it is a day, week, or month. This is what forms "patterns" Jesse Livermore was talking about. Let me interject by adding that Jesse Livermore looked at opens, highs, lows, and closing prices, not candle or bar charts, so some of the price patterns that he was looking for were, for example, on strong bullish days closes closer to highs of the session and the reverse on bearish days, closes closer to the lows. These price patterns helped him make trade decisions to add or exit positions.

The high and low of a given period is certainly important, as it mirrors human emotional behavior. Think of it this way: The high is a reference point for those who bought out of greed thinking they are missing an opportunity. They certainly won't forget how much they lost and how the market reacted as it declined from that level. The opposite is true for those who sold the low of a given session out of fear they would lose more by staying in a long trade; they certainly will respect that price point the next time the market trades back at that level, too.

So the high and low are important reference points of interest. With that said, pivot point analysis incorporates the three most important elements—the high, the low, and, of course, the close of a given trading session. The most common formula is:

- Pivot point is the high, low, and close added and divided by 3.

$$P = (H + L + C) / 3$$

- Resistance 2 (R2) is the pivot point number plus the high and minus the low.

$$R2 = P + H - L$$

- Resistance 1 (R1) is the pivot point number times 2 minus the low.

$$R1 = (P \times 2) - L$$

- Support 1(S1) is the pivot point number times 2 minus the high.

$$S1 = (P \times 2) - H$$

- Support 2 (S2) is the pivot point number minus the high plus the low.

$$S2 = P - H + L$$

Some analysts are adding a third level to their pivot calculations to help target extreme price swings on what has occurred on occasion, such as a price shock resulting from a news-driven event. Currency markets tend to experience a double dose of price shocks, as they are exposed to foreign economic developments as well as U.S. economic developments that pertain to a specific country's currency. This tends to make wide trading ranges. Therefore, a third level of projected support and resistance was calculated.

$$Resistance\ 3 = H + 2 \times (Pivot - Low)$$

$$Support\ 3 = L - 2 \times (High - Pivot)$$

There are other variations, which include adding the opening range, which in this case, would involve simply taking the open, high, low, and close and dividing by 4 to derive the actual pivot point.

$$P = (O, H, L, C) / 4$$

There is one more variation that takes into consideration gap situations, which occur frequently in individual stock transactions, especially when calculating from one time frame to another.

We take the high, the low, and the close, then wait for the next time period's open, and then combine those values to get the typical price or pivot point:

$$Old\ High + Old\ Low + Old\ Close + Next\ Open / 4$$

Let's go over these together and see what these numbers mean and how price action reacts with these projected target levels. Here is how the numbers would break down by order what typically occurs and how the market behaves. Keep in mind, this is a general description and we will learn what to look for at these price points to spot reversals in order to make money and reduce risk.

I believe in looking at the progressively-higher time period's price support or resistance projections. For example, from the daily numbers, I would look at the weekly figures, and then from the weekly numbers I would look at the monthly numbers.

The data from the longer-term time frame are usually the most important or significant. Furthermore, it is rare that the daily numbers will trade beyond the extreme R2 or S2 numbers, but when market conditions do exceed those projections, it is generally in a strong trending condition. In this case, we have methods to follow the market's flow, and we will cover this in more detail in the next few paragraphs.

Here is a quick description of what I would describe as a general guideline of what the various support and resistance levels mean and how to trade with them.

Resistance level 3. An extreme bullish market condition generally created by news-driven price shocks. This is where a market is at an overbought condition and may offer a day trader a quick reversal scalp trade.

Resistance level 2. A bullish market price objective or target high number for a trading session. It generally establishes the high of a given time period. The market often sees significant resistance at this price level and will provide an exit target for long positions.

Resistance level 1. A mild bullish to bearish projected high target number. In low volume or light volatility sessions, or consolidating trading periods, this often acts as the high of a given session. In a bearish market condition, prices will try to come close to this level, but most times will fail.

Pivot point. The focal price level or the mean, which is derived from the collective market data from the prior session's high low and close. It is the strongest of the support and resistance numbers. Prices normally trade above or below this area before breaking in one direction or the other. As a general guideline, if the market opens above the primary pivot, be a buyer on dips. If the market opens below this level, look to sell rallies.

Support level 1. A mild bearish to bullish projected low target number in light-volume or low-volatility sessions, or in consolidating trading periods. Prices tend to reverse at or near this level in bullish market conditions, but most times fall short of hitting this number.

Support level 2. A bearish market price objective or targeted low number. The market often sees significant support at or near this level in a bearish market condition and is a likely target level to cover shorts.

Support level 3. In an extremely bearish market condition, this level will act as the projected target low or support area. A price decline to this level is generally created by news-driven price shock. This is where a market is at an oversold condition and may offer a day trader a quick reversal scalp trade.

Daily, weekly, and monthly time frames can and should be utilized as well. There are three various parameters that I have experimented with, of which two are available on TD Ameritrade's thinkorswim (TOS) platform with the Person's Pivots. One is combining or averaging two days of price data, and the other is using a monthly options expirations calendar based on the third week of the month. This has been very effective in determining the potential four-week range between option expiration dates in various markets such as stock indexes, stock, or ETFs like the SPDRS (SPY) or QQQs.

STOCK TRADER'S TIME FRAME

Now, I would like to reveal publicly for the first time the one time frame I have used for well over a decade that may help in your longer-term outlooks. This is a quarterly time period. This outlook should help stock traders gain insights over not only the trend condition but also the potential price range for a specific instrument over the three-month period or, more importantly, a quarter.

Here is the list of time frames that traders can incorporate into their analysis.

- Daily
- Two-day average
- Weekly
- Monthly
- Option expiration
- Quarterly

The chart in Figure 9.1 shows the price range on the Select SPDR (SPY) using Person's Pivots monthly option expiration cycle. Since this book is

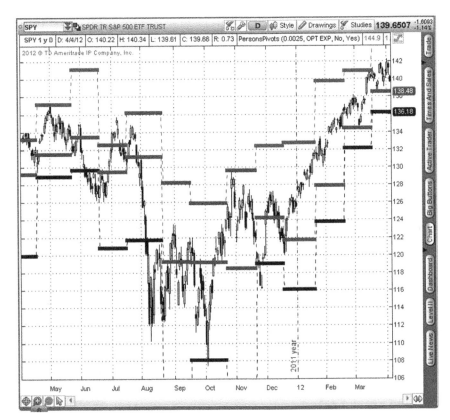

FIGURE 9.1   SPDR TR S&P 500 ETF Trust
© TD Ameritrade IP Company, Inc.

printed in black and white, we used gray scale to distinguish the different pivot levels and candlestick. You can customize all trading platforms to any color you want to help identify the indicators. As the chart shows, the projected resistance level is a gray horizontal line, the targeted support level is black, and the light gray color is the actual pivot point.

Since you now have the choice of using a calendar month time frame as well as using the option expiration dates as shown, I would like to take a small sample using the SPY the IWM and a highly active stock and share with you the results. Unlike regular pivot point analysis, Person's Pivots filters out whether the market condition is in a bullish mode, and if so, it projects out for the next time period a higher resistance level (R2) and a higher support level (S1) with the actual pivot point as the midpoint. When the market condition is determined to be in a bearish mode, Person's Pivots project out a lower resistance level (R1) and a lower support target (S2), with the pivot point in between those levels.

As you can see, the projected low was almost spot-on in October 2011. Needless to say, the options expiration has been fairly accurate in forecasting both the market trend (bullish or bearish) and the respective price range for that time frame.

This is not to say that the monthly pivot points are invalid; there are times when the monthly pivot analysis works. The main feature in the Person's Pivots is the trend identification feature. The chart in Figure 9.2 is a sampling from the same data using the SPY during that same time period; however, we are using the calendar month pivots. As you can see, in bearish times the pivots adjust for projecting lower resistance and lower support levels, and when it detects a bullish reversal, see how the resistance and support targets are consecutively raised with higher highs and higher lows.

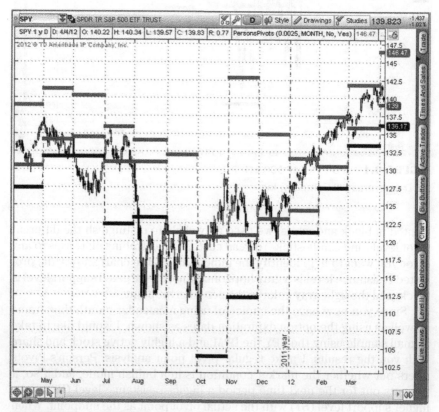

FIGURE 9.2   SPDR TR S&P 500 ETF Trust
© TD Ameritrade IP Company, Inc.

I would like to emphasize that the Person's Pivots options expiration setting on TD Ameritrade's TOS platform works well with most high-volume stocks, ETFs, and the various stock indexes such as the Russell 2000, as shown in Figure 9.3 represented by the (IWM). As you will see, just as in Figure 9.1, the October low was predicted almost perfectly using the Russell 2000, as it was in identifying the low in the SPY. Two different indexes confirmed their support held. This is why we like to use the options expiration pivots for longer-term price targets.

Comparing an apple to an apple, so to speak, in Figure 9.4 we have the IWM with the calendar month pivot calculations, just as in Figure 9.2 in the SPY; here the monthly support numbers were off in the IWM. This goes to show why you should look at the two monthly time periods, as one may give a better indication of the high or low being in place.

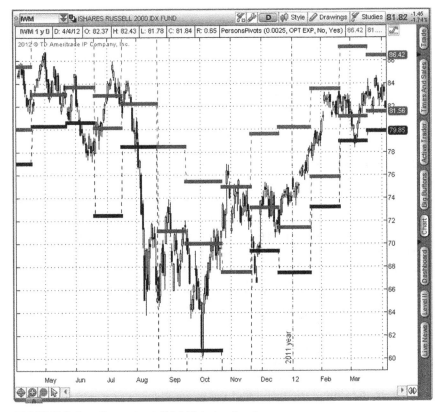

FIGURE 9.3   iShares Russell 2000 Index Fund
© TD Ameritrade IP Company, Inc.

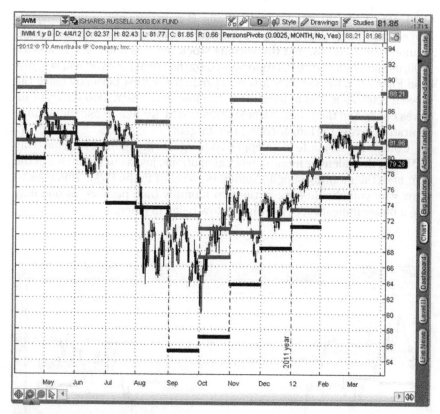

FIGURE 9.4   3 iShares Russell 2000 Index Fund
© TD Ameritrade IP Company, Inc.

Now let's examine one of the most active stocks as far as daily volume and option volume—Apple (AAPL). The monthly options expiration so far in 2011 and early 2012 was pretty accurate in predicting the market trend and targeting the potential price levels of support and resistance.

In fact, I believe the monthly options expiration pivots have done a bit better in filtering the predicted highs and lows than the calendar month, as shown in Figure 9.6.

Now what about the less active stocks? Let's examine Figure 9.7, where we have, as I mentioned before, one of my favorite tech names, Akamai Technologies (AKAM). Here, we used the Person's calendar monthly pivots to help determine the trend and the respective support and resistance levels. Keep in mind that these may look like they were drawn in after the fact, but the pivot support and resistance levels are drawn in advance of

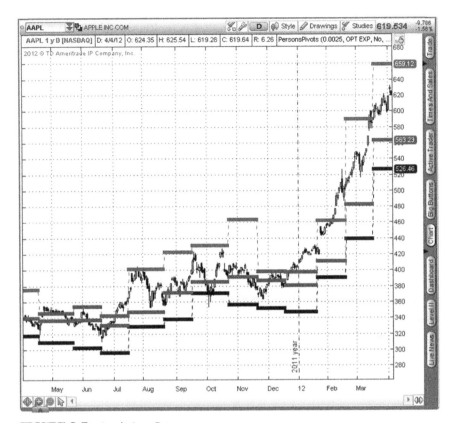

FIGURE 9.5 Apple Inc. Com
© TD Ameritrade IP Company, Inc.

the month based on the high–low close data from the prior month's trading session.

Now that we have compared a calendar month to the options expiration calendar month, which is the third week of the month, let's review the importance and the reasons why I use the quarterly pivots levels.

- We only need to calculate these once every three months.
- Equities tend to trend with quarterly earnings and gross domestic product expectations.

Examine Figure 9.8, which is a weekly chart on Starbucks (SBUX), my favorite coffee company and second favorite Nasdaq stock to trade. Notice the ability of the Person's Pivots to adjust in bearish conditions the lower projected resistance and support levels as occurred in 2006, as seen

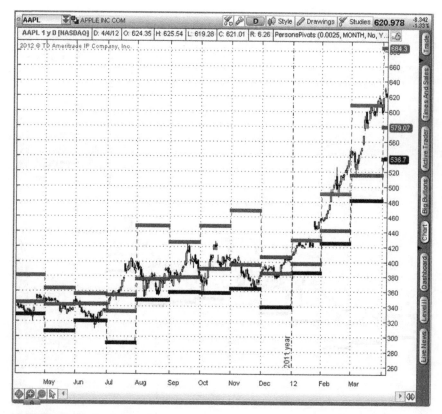

FIGURE 9.6   Apple Inc. Com
© TD Ameritrade IP Company, Inc.

at point A on the chart. As the market starts to bottom in March 2009, the
quarterly pivots adjust to the reversal by projecting higher resistance and
higher support levels, as indicated at point B. These are the changes I look
for to spot and confirm trend reversals. When we apply the volume and cumulative relative strength tools as added confirmation, we can trade with a
specific price model that gives a level of where we will take a profit and a
level at which, if we are wrong, the support targets will be broken. A great
example here is at point C, where the price corrected but did not violate or
break the quarterly predicted support level. In fact, as the overall market
succumbed to a correction in October, SBUX did hold the fourth-quarter
predicted support level as well, as seen at point D on the chart.

In Figure 9.9, I zoomed in to the more recent quarters, and as you can
see, the trends prediction is maintained, as are the support and resistance
levels.

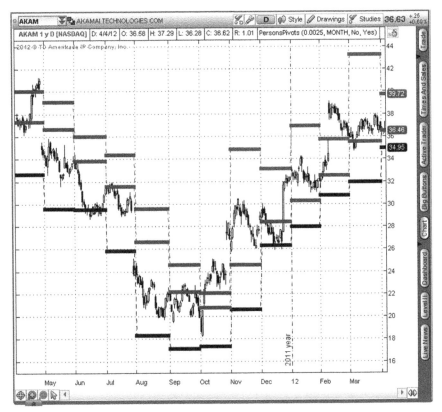

FIGURE 9.7 Akamai Technologies Com
© TD Ameritrade IP Company, Inc.

Overall, the quarterly pivots are a great tool not only for confirming the trend, but also for examining what the potential low and high of a time frame might be within that condition. In fact, they also have helped in uncovering major reversals, as was the case in March 2009, as the chart in Figure 9.10 shows, as the lows in the QQQ held right at the quarterly support level. This is one indicator that helps provide us several trading opportunities, as I mentioned in Chapter 7.

Now let's discuss the Person's Pivot Study (PPS) indicator, which is overlaid onto the prices. This is a proprietary moving average study that helps identify changes in bearish and bullish momentum. When a dark arrow appears pointing up, a buy signal is generated; when a dark arrow appears pointing down, a sell signal is initiated. This is extremely helpful in identifying turns in prices, especially when the market is at a Person's Pivot targeted resistance or support level.

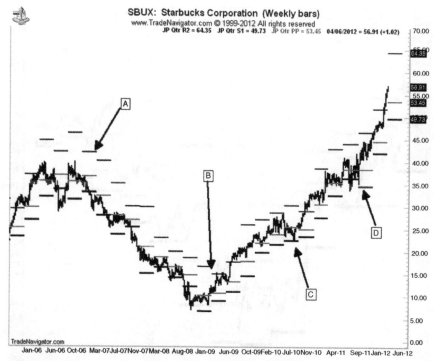

FIGURE 9.8 SBUX: Starbucks Corporation (Weekly Bars)
www.TradeNavigator.com © 1999–2012. All rights reserved.

To understand how price moves within the pivots, let's begin by breaking down the time frames from longer term to shorter term. As traders, we should begin with a quarterly and then monthly time frame. Here is how I utilize it in my research. There are approximately 22 business days, or about four weeks, in a month. Every month there will be an established range—a high and a low. There are typically five trading days in a week. Now consider that in one day of one week in one month, a high and a low will be made. It is likely that this high and low may be made in a minute or within one hour of a given day of a given week of that month. That is why longer-term time frames such as monthly or weekly analysis should be included in your market analysis.

Again, unlike regular pivot point analysis, Person's Pivots filter out whether the market condition is in a bullish mode, and if so, they project out for the next time period a higher resistance level (R2) and a higher support level (S1), with the actual pivot point as the midpoint. When the market

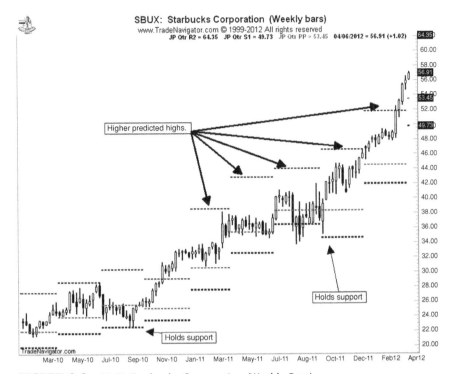

FIGURE 9.9 SBUX: Starbucks Corporation (Weekly Bars)
www.TradeNavigator.com © 1999–2012. All rights reserved.

condition is calculated to be in a bearish mode, Person's Pivots project out a lower resistance level (R1) and a lower support target (S2), with the pivot point in between those levels. When we combine the use of the PPS indicator when the market is in a bullish mode (R2 up to S1), when an up arrow develops, it helps traders to identify higher probability buying opportunities.

The reverse is true when prices roll over and turn bearish from a bullish uptrend. Due to the 1- and 3-period pivot moving average component, the Person's Pivot indicator changes quickly and adapts to the market conditions when the market starts to head lower. This is the filtering mechanism that gives us the predicted highs and lows. When the market turns bearish, the support and resistance levels are projected out to give a lower high and lower low than the previous time period (R1 to S2). Armed with that information, when we combine the use of my PPS indicator, it helps traders to identify higher-probability selling opportunities when an arrow appears pointing down.

FIGURE 9.10 QQQ: PowerShares QQQ Trust, Series (Weekly Bars)
www.TradeNavigator.com © 1999–2012. All rights reserved.

PERSON'S PIVOTS CALCULATIONS

I believe in keeping things simple, and that less is better. I use the numbers and the filtering method to help me select either the high or the low of a given trading session, and sometimes this works to project both the high and the low with amazing accuracy. Therefore, it is important not to be burdened with information overload. Remember:

- Pivot point calculations help determine when to enter/exit positions.
- They help act as a leading price indicator.
- Pivot points are used to project support and resistance or actual highs and lows of trading sessions.
- They help confirm other technical methods.
- Daily, weekly, and monthly time frames can and should be used.

Remember that pivot point analysis relies on prices from specific time frames in determining futuristic support and resistance levels. Therefore, the analysis or calculations from the prior day or time frame will not be applicable, in most cases, two, three, or four days or time periods later.

So, at the end of whatever time frame you are analyzing, it is important that you recalculate your figures. Most trading platforms and charting packages calculate these levels for you automatically; however, if these applications do not calculate weekly, monthly, or option expiration time frames, then you can do this on your own. One easy way is to visit www. Personsplanet.com. Under the tab "Trading Tools," you will see the label for the free pivot point calculator, with more articles and tips I have written on how to use this specific technical tool.

An example of the importance of integrating longer-term pivot point analysis with the shorter term is, if in a given trading day, the market goes through my daily target numbers, the weekly and even monthly numbers are what give me an indicator for the next major target levels of support and resistance.

I use the actual pivot point for many things. For example, it is important to understand that it can be used as an actual trading number in determining the high or low of a given time period, especially in strong bull or bear market trend conditions. In an extremely bullish trend condition, the pivot point can become the target low for that trading session. We see this in a number of examples, even in the charts used in this chapter; carefully examine the price action in the next few graphs.

The pivot point number represents the true value or typical price of a prior session. In theory, how it can work is simple: In an uptrending market, if the market gaps higher above the pivot point, then retraces back to the pivot point, this is perceived as a typical or true value and will attract buyers. Until that pivot point is broken by prices trading below that level, traders will step in and buy the pullback. Ever heard the phrase, "If bullish, buy breaks"? Well using the pivot as a price level to buy helps traders define at what price a break might occur.

The opposite is true in an extremely bearish market condition. The pivot point will act as the target high for the session. If a news-driven event causes the market to gap lower, traders will then access the news, and once prices come back up to test the pivot point, if the market fails to break that level and trade higher, sellers will take action and start pressing the market lower again.

By focusing on just a few select numbers and learning how to filter out excess information, I eliminate the analysis paralysis from information overload.

Technically speaking, in a bearish market, the highs should be lower and the lows should be lower than in the preceding time frame. If they are, then to help me filter out unnecessary information or excessive support and resistance numbers on my charts, I use the actual pivot point up to the

R1 number for resistance, and then I target the S2 for the potential low or for that time period's trading range.

As you can see in Figure 9.11, if I determine that the market is bearish and I understand the relationship of the geometric distance of the resistance and support targets, I can eliminate the R2 number, since in a bearish environment we should see a lower high. If I am looking for a lower low, then I can eliminate the S1 support number as well, and now I have reduced the field to just three numbers.

Once again, I am not using the numbers to place orders ahead of time (even though you could); I am using the numbers as a guide. These numbers work so well and often act as a self-fulfilling prophecy because so many institutions and professional traders do use them. Many have different size positions; some traders may not wait for the exact number to hit and may start scaling out of positions (as I do). With this method, you can use these numbers as exit areas on your trades. Now let's incorporate this tool using seasonal analysis. If we look at a market or sector that enters a bearish time frame we can look for signals using the PPS indicator on TD Ameritrade's TOS platform. Remember, we have the metals markets that enter a weak period in February. As such, examine Figure 9.12. The Person's Pivots options expirations setting targeted a lower high and lower low reading in addition the PPS indicator flashed a sell signal for the week ending March 9.

This is a great combination of trading tools to use to determine confirmation that in fact there was selling pressure in this sector.

Since the GDX is the ETF for mining stocks, we can start to look at individual stocks to see what the technical picture is for each of them. Look at Figure 9.13, which is a weekly chart on Newmont Mining Corporation (NEM). The PPS indicator had flashed a sell signal all the way back in November. In this chart, I am also using the option expiration Person's

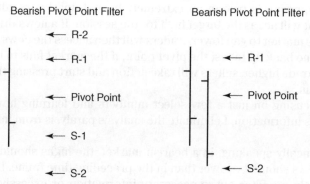

FIGURE 9.11   Bearish Pivot Point Filter

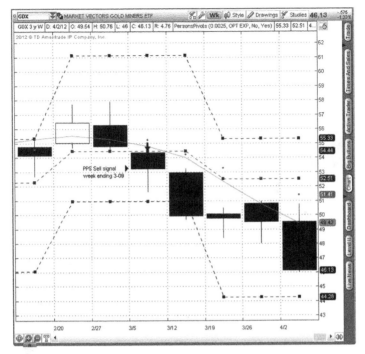

FIGURE 9.12 Market Vectors Gold Miners ETF
© TD Ameritrade IP Company, Inc.

Pivots that show bearish conditions with lower resistance and support levels. As far as confirming that the sector is in a weak seasonal period, the PPS indicator and the Person's Pivots did an excellent job in that regard. This goes to show you, year after year in a sector that enters its seasonally weak period, you should check to see if the indicators confirm that outlook. If you were long this stock, I would imagine that you would have exited sooner rather than later, and if you were looking to take short positions, the timing element of these tools would have been instrumental in helping confirm that a bearish trend was intact.

Now let's zoom in on a daily chart for this same stock. Figure 9.14 shows how to use multiple time frame analysis in your trading. Since the seasonal trend suggests weakness in this sector, as the ETF GDX is in a sell mode, we also checked to see what an individual stock's technical picture was, and obviously the Person's Pivots were indicating a bearish outlook. So if a market has already begun the descent, how do you get in on a trade?

The one technique that works for all markets, whether bullish or bearish, is to drop down to the next time frame. That is why we are looking at

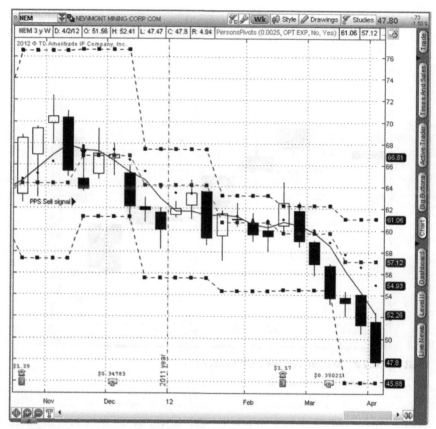

FIGURE 9.13 Newmont Mining Corp.
© TD Ameritrade IP Company, Inc.

the daily charts, and as they show, we had a significant decline forming a bearish engulfing or close marubozu candle on February 29. In addition, the PPS indicator flashed a sell signal. The Person's Pivots were pointing to a lower low and lower high. So at this point, we can either make the decision to stay away from this stock altogether or decide on a short position, at the least a bearish options strategy. With the options expiration pivots, you can see it had targeted a low in March for 54.50; based on the close from when the sell signal was generated at 59.43, this left approximately a 10 percent price decline into expiration—a potentially realistic achievement that came to fruition. In fact, this market continued to give into the April expiration as well. For the options strategist, this is a perfect example of when you would want to "roll" out or down your position. When a market is in a strong trend and the technicals point to lower prices, adjust your position accordingly.

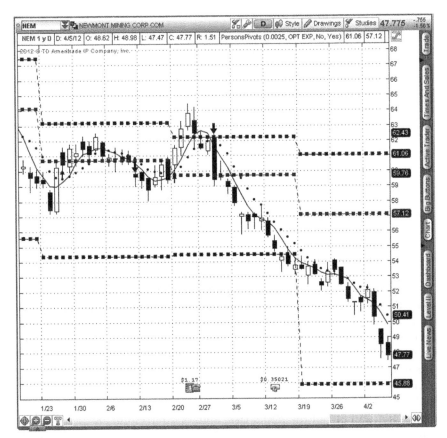

FIGURE 9.14 Newmont Mining Corp.
© TD Ameritrade IP Company, Inc.

As Figure 9.15 depicts, in a bullish market environment, by definition, you may agree that the highs should be higher and the lows should be higher than the preceding time period. When I have determined that we are in a bullish trend, I target the S1 up to the pivot point for the low of the session and the R2 for targeting the high, and that will give me an idea of what the potential trading range will be.

Now let's examine stocks that lined up in a bullish technical formation with the Person's Pivot analysis and see if it confirms that they are following along with their seasonal bullish trend. Here, we are looking at some drug stocks in early January, as this sector continues to show strength into the May time period. Several stocks popped up on our scans. One was Abbott Labs (ABT), as shown in Figure 9.16 in a weekly chart. The PPS indicator popped into a buy for the week ending February 17, and the Person's

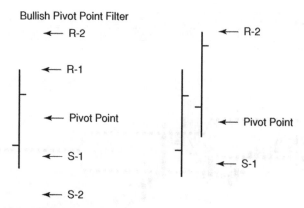

FIGURE 9.15 Bullish Pivot Point Filter

option expiration pivots continued to reflect a bullish technical bias by projecting higher resistance and support levels.

One more stock in that space was Baxter International (BAX), as the weekly chart shows in Figure 9.17.What makes this an interesting case study is the fact that, not only is it a stock in a seasonally strong time period—the Person's Pivots reflect a bullish bias as well, with the higher resistance and support projections—but you will see the PPS fired off a buy signal in conjunction with a high-close doji (HCD) formation. If you were trading from the rulebook, you would have been buying on the next open with stops under the lowest low of the past four bars. The first profit objective would be 1,005 of the initial risk, and, of course, the balance of positions would have at least been traded with a trailing stop method, which we will cover in the next chapter, but the pivot resistance level would have given you a great target to exit the trade.

What About When a Market Is Extremely Bullish or Bearish?

This a great question, as markets can and do just so happen to blast through the projected target numbers. In this situation, I then use the next time periods to give me the next reliable price objective. That is where the significance of the weekly, monthly, and quarterly numbers comes into play.

Take, for example, the quarterly chart on BAX in Figure 9.18, using the quarterly Person's Pivot levels. In this chart example, I am using my indicators on Trade Navigator from Genesis Financial.

Notice that when the market was in a bearish trend in the fourth quarter of 2011, the actual target levels were projecting out a lower resistance

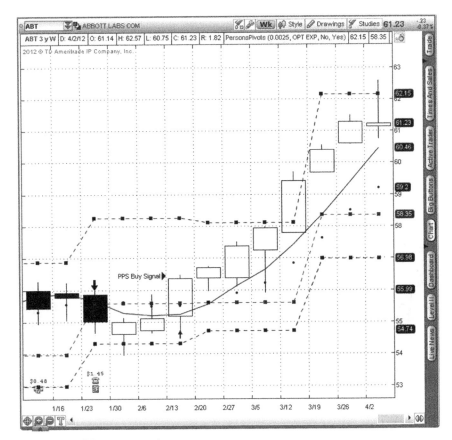

FIGURE 9.16 Abbott Labs

© TD Ameritrade IP Company, Inc.

target and a lower support target level. Then, as the market reversed in a bullish trend, you can see how the quarterly Person's Pivots started to project out a higher resistance target and higher support target level. This, in essence, gives traders in advance not only what the market condition is but also under that condition what the potential high and low for each month might be or what the range might be expected. Add to the fact that we had an HCD the week ending January 13; these levels may have helped keep you in a trade a bit longer knowing what the potential high for the quarter might be.

Not only can pivot point analysis help keep you on the right side of a trending market condition, the support and resistance target levels also help navigate price extremes, allowing you to set entry and exit orders according to the market price direction.

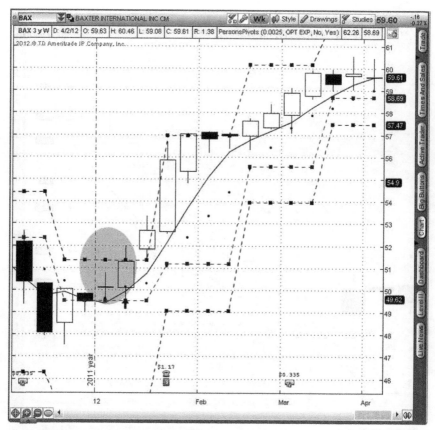

FIGURE 9.17   Baxter International Inc.
© TD Ameritrade IP Company, Inc.

The Person's Pivot Point filtering method works well in all time frames in most major markets where there are consistent price changes. That is why it works in most asset classes, such as actively traded ETFs and individual stocks. Commodity traders have been using this tool for decades, as are foreign currency traders. The latter are two areas or asset classes that equity traders have the ability to participate in without opening commodity accounts, thanks in part to ETFs and exchange-traded notes (ETNs).

In addition to using the futures markets to gather data to discover the historic seasonal trend of a commodity or currency, you can also then apply the tools from the consensus study such as the COT data, as well as applying the pivot point analysis to uncover hidden support and resistance levels. With this information, then, all that is needed is to relate the underlying commodity to an ETF or a leveraged ETF.

FIGURE 9.18 BAX: Baxter International Inc. (Weekly Bars)
www.TradeNavigator.com © 1999–2012. All rights reserved.

As an example, let's examine the next graph in Figure 9.19, using Trade Navigator, which is a weekly price chart on live cattle futures with a monthly pivot analysis overlaid on the candle charts. I know you are reading this to gain better knowledge for trading stocks, but keep reading through these next few sentences. As you can see, the pivot levels recalibrated every month helping to confirm the bullish market condition until April by displaying higher highs and higher lows, and it did so with almost pinpoint accuracy. But notice that in March a low-close doji (LCD) formed, as indicated at point A on the chart, signaling that a top was in place. The stochastics indicator, as covered in Chapter 7, flashed a sell signal as the %K and %D lines crossed under the 80 percent line, as indicated at point B. In addition, the selling pressure was confirmed by a trend-line break in the OBV indicator, as shown at point C, again another tool we covered in Chapter 6. But, most importantly, the seasonal trend indicator revealed that typically beef prices begin to decline on or about the week ending March 9, which can last into late May, as indicated at point D. Moreover, this is a trade that is covered in the *Commodity Trader's Almanac 2012* (page 28).

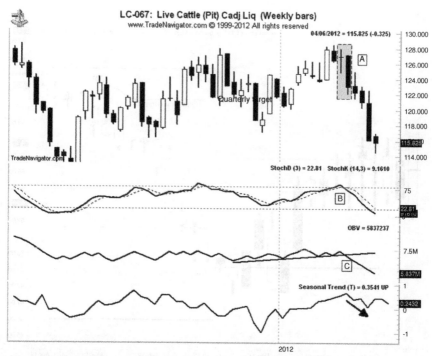

FIGURE 9.19   LC-067: Live Cattle (Pit) Cadj Liq. (Weekly Bars)
www.TradeNavigator.com © 1999–2012. All rights reserved.

So what does this have to do with trading stocks or ETFs? Simple. There is an ETF for almost all commodities. As a trader and investor, it is your responsibility to seek out the best low-risk, high-probability trade that you can profit in. Throughout this book, you may have been wondering why I have been identifying both buying and selling strategies, and I have stated that many of you may also be looking for opportunities to apply option strategies. Here is a perfect example of a market that gave a textbook selling opportunity, in addition to the fact the monthly Person's Pivots indicated the market was entering the month of April on a bearish note with a lower projected potential profit target.

There is a livestock ETF from iPath with the aptly-titled symbol COW, as shown in Figure 9.20.

As of April 2012, the option volume and open interest is extremely light, but there are several points I want to make. Using the futures markets, you can identify better trading opportunities, since the vast majority of ETFs are too new to comb through historic data to derive seasonal trend analysis. Next, since most ETFs are not as actively traded, you might not

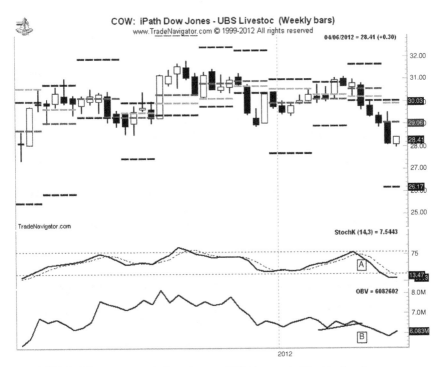

FIGURE 9.20 COW: iPath Dow Jones - UBS Livestock (Weekly Bars)
www.TradeNavigator.com © 1999–2012. All rights reserved.

see the daily candle formations develop like they will in the underlying futures markets. As you examine Figure 9.19, note that the monthly pivots did correctly identify a change in trend from bullish to bearish; however, it did not generate an LCD as the futures markets did. The stochastics would not have triggered a sell setup from a scan, as %K and %D did not trade above the 80 percent line and then cross back under that threshold to trigger a sell, as shown at point A on the chart. The OBV indicator did confirm selling pressure by closing below the minor support trend line, as shown at point B, but realistically the trend was down even back in 2011. The moral of the story here is that using Person's Pivots on the underlying futures and foreign currency market may give you cleaner and clearer trading signals that you can then apply a strategy in the ETFs or ETNs or with a highly-correlated stock to the underlying commodity. You can use this technique for the metals, such as copper, gold, and silver. You can apply this analysis to the financials, such as the 30-year Treasury bond futures using the TLT, or the inverse ETF, the TBT. Of course, we have the foreign currencies such as the euro with its ETF FXE and the Japanese yen with the FXY. As this

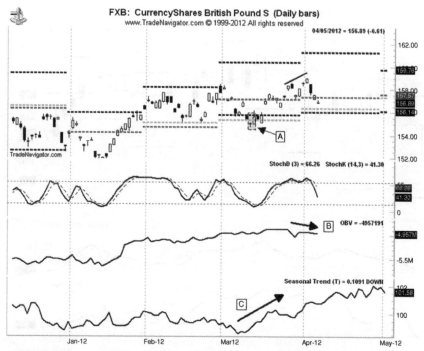

FIGURE 9.21   FXB: CurrencyShares British Pounds S (Daily Bars)
www.TradeNavigator.com © 1999–2012. All rights reserved.

book was nearing completion, the British pound (FXB) entered a seasonal buy near the predicted monthly support; as Figure 9.21 shows, the buy signal was triggered with an HCD, as shown at point A on the chart. As point B shows, the seasonal trend is up at this time of the year.

This was another featured trade from the *Commodity Trader's Almanac 2012* (page 36). One of the interesting elements of this trade that the OBV did help confirm the buying pressure; however, as the market moved up close to the predicted resistance target, the indicator also demonstrated a bearish divergence pattern alert to lighten the position and adjust stop orders. As you can see, an LCD formation occurred, helping to confirm that a potential intermediate-term top was in place. As a stock trader, you can utilize these ETFs based on the seasonal trends built in by the underlying futures markets, and using the longer-term pivot support and resistance target levels scan for high-quality setup signals such as these HCD and LCD formations.

Using seasonal analysis can really help to identify potential trends of stocks and individuals stocks, but using the power of computers and software programs to scan for reliable patterns is a significant achievement for trading in the new millennium. Specifically, running a daily scan of an HCD near a monthly support in a sector that is in a seasonally strong time period can produce great results. Just remember that not every trade will be a winner and not every year will produce the same results or performance. That is why traders need to monitor their positions. With that said, look at Figure 9.22, as point A on the chart shows an HCD formed right at the predicted monthly Person's Pivot support. The stochastics indicator gave a bullish convergence pattern, as point B shows, the OBV indicator at that time gave a trendline break, confirming that buying pressure was evident, and as the seasonal trend indicator shows at point D, Agilent Technologies was indeed in a seasonally strong time period. If every trade we entered appeared to be this easy, life would be even that much better, but I am here to tell you that not all trades are created equally, meaning we don't have the power of foretelling the future as to how much money we will make and how high the market will go once we get into a long position. But, thanks to the trading rules for the HCD, we do have slight control over the entry price, where our stop is to be placed, and our first or partial profit target. The rest of our job is to manage the trade and raise the stops on the balance of positions, as we will

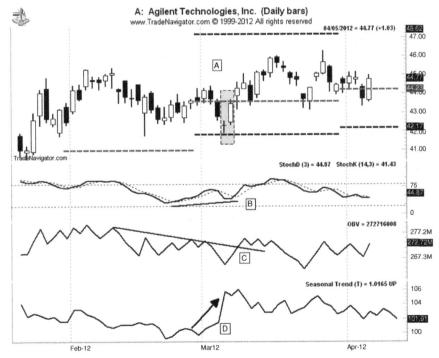

FIGURE 9.22 A: Agilent Technologies, Inc. (Daily Bars)
www.TradeNavigator.com © 1999–2012. All rights reserved.

cover in the next chapter. From what we have covered so far, the fact that this stock gave a buy setup at monthly support and allowed for a nice profit in a short period of time makes a strong argument for following the steps and technical indicators illustrated throughout this book. These steps make for a good checklist, or at the very least, provide the indicators with which you can construct a chart template on your trading platform.

FIBONACCI COMBINED WITH PIVOT POINTS

Fibonacci analysis has gained significant popularity among novice traders and mainstream investors. Thanks to the computer, most trading platforms come equipped with a Fibonacci study tool. I can't give an exact statistic, but in my experience, there have been a significant number of times where a support or resistance level that is determined by pivot analysis also coincides with a Fibonacci retracement number. For this reason, I have depended more on the pivot analysis throughout the decades. One specific reason is that pivot analysis defines a support or resistance level in a specific time period, as I have discussed in this chapter. However, it would not be fair to not discuss the validity and usefulness of Fibonacci numbers.

Most traders are familiar with the common Fibonacci correction levels, also referred to as retracements. These are calculated when a market makes a move from a low to a high—the price will have a tendency to pull back, retrace, or correct. The percentage of the pullback can be 38.2 percent, 5.0 percent, 61.8 percent, 78.6 percent, and at times, even 100 percent. When looking for bullish setups, it makes sense to target buying opportunities, especially on pullbacks when the market is in an uptrend. This is when we will use a Fibonacci tool to identify the percentage figure and look for that as a potential support to enter a long position.

As I mentioned, these numbers coincide with pivot levels; examine Figure 9.23, which shows a 15-minute intraday chart from TD Ameritrade's TOS platform reflecting three days of data for the S&P 500 futures contract. Overlaid on the chart is the PPS momentum indicator with the daily Person's Pivots combined with a Fibonacci retracement tool. As we draw a Fibonacci line from the low at point A on the chart and extend it to the high at point B, you will see the horizontal lines drawn, which represent the percentage of the price correction of the distance of the A–B line. In this example, notice that the 0.618 percent retracement coincided near the daily pivot support at point C. This is a great example of one of many coincidences that Fibonacci retracement levels have with pivot analysis.

Many books have been written on the subject, including my last book, *Forex Conquered* (John Wiley & Sons, 2007). Fibonacci For those

FIGURE 9.23 E-mini S&P 500 Index Futures
© TD Ameritrade IP Company, Inc.

interested in learning more on Fibonacci, this book has a chapter devoted to the subject. I would highly recommend it, as it also covers the relationship of Fibonacci to the Elliott wave principle.

SUMMARY

Pivot point analysis certainly is a worthwhile trading tool. Once again, there is no holy grail of indicators, but combining noncorrelated technical tools, and Fibonacci levels in particular, can help you better map out your trades and will certainly give you an edge in the markets, especially when one is looking to trade both with a trend and when looking for clues as to when or at what price level the trend may end. If you are interested in furthering your education on the use of pivot point analysis, including how to construct a trading methodology using a pivot point moving average, please feel free to visit my website at www.nationalfutures.com, where we have more articles and a free pivot point calculator. You will find this under the "Trading Tools" section tab.

CHAPTER 10

Putting It All Together

Position Sizing, Trade Entry Techniques, Risk Management, Trailing Stops, and Trade Management

I have been asked many times in the past a very simple question, to which I usually respond, "I need more information." To most this is a very poor answer. The question I'm asked is: "How much money do I need to make?" and usually it's something along the lines of $100,000 dollars or some crazy number like $1 million per year. The truth is, it really does depend on how much money you start with, whether you are leveraging your trades using margin, or power playing a directional move in the markets with bankrolling a deep out-of-the-money option position. The latter is akin to playing a high-limit slot machine; if you time everything right, the return can be incredible.

The reality is, to become successful in trading stocks and exchange-traded funds (ETFs) takes time, money, and a bit of work. The techniques and tools discussed in this book are excellent analysis tools that will help you uncover value, from both an under and over perspective.

As I stated before, it takes time and money to become a successful trader and investor, and time is a relative word. Ten or more years ago, investors were trained to use the "buy-and-hold" approach. As we have discovered in the past 12 years, a buy-and-hold strategy has only worked for a few companies. A few that come to mind are Ralph Lauren (RL), Apple (AAPL), International Business Machines (IBM), Priceline (PCLN), Chipotle Mexican Grill (CMG), Starbucks (SBUX), and perhaps 20 or so more. One point I like to make is that many mutual funds stopped or liquidated many of their positions in these companies and failed to put theory into practice as a buy-and-hold core holding in some of these issues.

Due to changes in regulation and improved technology, retail investors have a higher degree of transparency of information and faster speed with which it is delivered. I believe this combination has also increased the frequency of trading habits. Investors are now better educated not only about what they trade, but also how they trade it. No longer do we look at just stocks, but also ETFs, options strategies, and a combination of them all.

One issue I question is that now that many investors have figured out that they should be more active in their trading, they will now longer be interested in a buy-and-hold philosophy. So let's compromise and say it is important to apply a buy-and-hold philosophy when the business cycle dictates when we are entering in an expanding economic environment. I will be looking for conformation that the U.S. economy is in a period of expansion when we start to see employment numbers improve and a rise in the financials and transportations, and confirmed by further gains in the technology sector. As the economy improves, we will see a gradual increase in bond yields.

I believe this 12-year-plus bear market, —as measured by a stagnant performance of the overall stock indexes,—will be a thing of the past by 2015.

That means we will want to participate more as buy-and-holders of solid companies. If we begin to adopt a trader's mind-set, then what may happen is you enter a long position at an under- or fair-valued price level, and as you begin to make profits, you may exit this trade prematurely. However, you also do not want to hang on for every last penny and be slaughtered like a pig as greed takes over. Using the technical data to help guide you to overall market direction, using the seasonal analysis to discover the price trends of stocks and industry sectors, and using the tools to help determine value levels such as the Person's Pivots will improve your game. So how long do we hang on to a trade? How will we know when a trend will continue or end? The tools in this book will help, but I believe it is trade management skills that will help you over the long haul. We touched on scaling out of half of positions when we meet 100 percent of the initial stop-loss amount, we covered why the Person's Pivots can also be used as a profit target combined with momentum loss triggers such as a lower closing low, but there are other tactics, and most importantly, other areas we have not covered, such as:

- How should you decide how many positions or shares to put on per trade?
- How will you enter this trade? Will you enter at any price just to get in or look for a pullback? And what is the method to determine a sizeable pullback?
- How, when, and where should you adjust a trailing stop?

All trading and investment decisions should be dictated by a series of criteria and then backed by sound risk management that includes the use of protective stops and responsible capital allocation.

Capital allocation is the one area that will help us to contain risk, increase profitability, and maximize that relationship over a long period of time by establishing a properly positioned trade.

There's an old saying that goes something like, "When you are right, you're only in a few, and when you're wrong, you're always loaded to the hilt." The phrase that states the key to success is to "manage your risks." While it is true, I believe one needs to also manage position sizing. Since we all know, or at least you now should be aware, that not every trade will be a winner, drawdowns will occur. To avoid financial ruin, proper position sizing on every trade is critical.

Tolerance of large losses tends to come from those who swing for the fences; they justify the incident with thoughts like "I'll get them back next time" or "It wasn't my fault."

CALCULATING POSITION SIZE

In the 2012 Masters golf tournament, the winner, Bubba Watson, had to go to a playoff with Louis Oosthuizen, who had become the fourth person in the tournament's history to post a double eagle. As they were going into the playoff, Bubba reportedly told his caddy, "We are going for it. It's do or die. To win this it's going to rely on my driver." That's the "all in" mentality, going for it, and yes, that's the way to win golf tournaments, taking big risks for big rewards. At the Masters, winning means bragging rights for life and a green jacket. But remember, when we are trading we don't receive green jackets; therefore, trading is about winning with controlled risks. One of the areas that is helpful is managing risks with stop-loss or dollar amounts through position sizing. We cannot ever guarantee what our losses will be with a stop due to adverse market moves when a trade is against us; all we can do is place the intended stop-loss amount. So how much of our trading capital should be devoted to a trade? We certainly don't want to underposition ourselves, and, obviously, we don't want to overly expose. So let's go over some parameters that I employ.

Let's assume you are trading with a $100,000 nonmargined account.

If you risk 2 percent (0.02) per trade, that's $2,000 per trade. This is not the line-in-the-sand figure, but it is a good starting point to determine position sizing.

If your stop-loss per share amount is under 10 percent of the value of the overall stock price and you are risking 2 percent of the total value of your account in a stock, how many shares should you purchase?

- Risk 2 percent per trade.
- Percentage of risk divided by stop-loss amount.
- Trade with 25 percent of initial capital per position.

Let's combine our techniques from the lessons learned in previous chapters and apply them to this trade as shown in Figure 10.1. Here we have Eli Lilly (LLY), a major pharmaceutical company. As the shaded area shows, a high-close doji pattern forms. Our rules state to enter on the close or the open of the next session.

- The HCD pattern completed on November 28.
- The high of the doji was 35.69, made on the 25th, Black Friday, the day after Thanksgiving. The closing price made on Monday the 28th was 36.27.
- Using our 8 percent entry rule, you would have placed an order to buy using a 36.56 limit buy order.
- The stop-loss in this trade was beneath the low of the doji, as it was the lowest low of the past four bars; we add a 0.005 percent price rule here, so if the low of the doji was 35.46, then your sell stop would be at 35.28.

FIGURE 10.1   LLY: Eli Lilly and Company (Daily Bars)

The risk, as we know now, would be between the entry price at 36.56 and the stop price at 35.28. That's a 3.5 percent risk of the stock value on entering the trade or $1.28 per share.

Risking a total amount of 2 percent of your trading capital, based on $100,000, the number of shares you should purchase would be 1,562 shares. That would represent more than 50 percent of your account, as the total investment would be $57,106.72 ($36.56 × 1,562). That's a large percentage of capital to devote to one trade, so if we apply the guideline using only 25 percent of total capital to one trade, then you are looking at a total of 781 shares.

The total dollar amount risk if there is no slippage would be just under $1,000 or 1 percent of the total account before commissions and fees.

The initial profit objective to scale out of half of a position is no less than 100 percent of the initial stop-loss amount. In this trade, the initial profit objective would be $1.28 or $37.84. The next step is to manage the trade on the balance of the position trailing the stops, which we will cover in the next few pages, as well as setting a profit target.

PROFIT TARGETS

Examine the next chart in Figure 10.2; one element of the analysis process I left out was applying the Person's Monthly Pivots to the price chart. Now you can see the doji was created on the predicted monthly support. Let's review when and how I apply Person's Monthly Pivots. First, I use them to help uncover a support level, which would be a setup; then, when we have a reason to enter a position such as an HCD pattern, this would be the trigger to initiate the trade. As the past time period concludes, new price projections are calculated; now we can use the new resistance targets as profit targets or the exit objective for our remaining positions.

So if you applied the position-sizing guidelines of a total of 781 shares at the initial entry of 36.56, and took half the position off at $37.84, for a $1.28 profit, that would equate to 390.5 shares (round up) or 391 shares on the first half for a gain of $499.84. The remaining balance is a net free trade.

The balance of positions, 390 shares if you used the monthly pivot target near 41.00, would net you a gain of $4.44 per share, for a gain of $1,731.60. Your total gain would be $2,231.44 (before commission and fees) on an initial investment of $28,553.36, just under 8 percent on investment, or a total of over 2 percent on your total trading capital. The total initial risk on this trade was $999.68, just under 1 percent of your total trading capital. So, as this trade worked out, you ended up with a two-to-one risk-reward

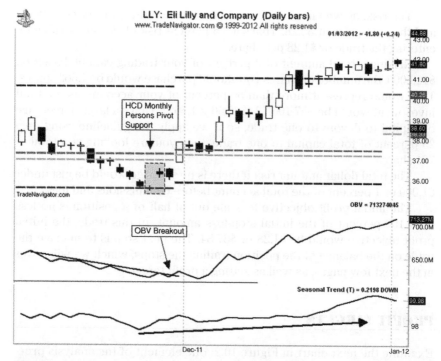

FIGURE 10.2 LLY: Eli Lilly and Company (Daily Bars)
www.TradeNavigator.com © 1999–2012. All rights reserved.

ratio. This trade took 12 trading sessions to complete. To many, this would seem like a swing trade. I believe a trade that can net 8 to 10 percent in fewer than 30 days without the use of leverage requires action to take a profit. Many traders struggle with that one concept, knowing when and how to take a profit. This methodology is designed to help gear you toward taking money from the markets and then move on to the next opportunity.

This is guideline is a starting plan, not a rule etched in stone. Some traders will ask why get out of half, others will ask why not add to the trade, and others still may ask why not trail the stop. These are all very valid questions and each have a valid point.

This formula is a guideline to help you understand position-sizing analysis. Many times, you will hear of all the stock-trading opportunities; as you and I know, it's all but impossible to take every trade and buy every stock. As such, we need some guidelines to manage proper sizing of our working capital. This formula works for those not wishing to trade on margin or using leverage. The trade parameters of the high-close (HCD) and low-close doji (LCD) near an important support and resistance level typically shows us immediate results. When we use this trigger mechanism with the half out rule, it takes risk out of the trade, allowing you to be more comfortable in the position, thus holding it longer—in this case, up to the next time period's monthly resistance target.

If you are wishing to trade using leverage, then apply a simple option strategy. Do not buy out-of-the-money options; instead, buy an in-the-money call option within one or two strike prices. A stock replacement option strategy is a great tactic for the HCD setup since we are looking for immediate results. This book is not designed to delve specifically into options; however, as you develop your trading skills and further your education on investing, this strategy will help you.

STOCK REPLACEMENT OPTION STRATEGY

Here are my guidelines when I am applying a stock replacement options strategy on a strong directional trade such as the HCD. An LCD setup uses the same rules except using put options. Stock replacement strategies use substantially less capital; they are a leverage position with defined risks, without borrowing costs, but have time restrictions (time decay, theta) and have no dividend participation.

- Buy in-the-money (ITM) calls greater than 45 days until expiration.
- There should be a delta of .50 percent or more.
- Risk half the time or half the premium paid or mental stops on HCD failure.

DAY TRADING POSITION SIZING

If you intend to trade stocks for more than a week, typically—unless you are really correct in your analysis with an immediate winner and exit the trade the same day, or if you enter a trade and then are stopped out within the same session—then you are day trading, but that was not your intention. I use the futures markets for day trading; many of my day-trading setups are similar to what we have covered in this book. However, one piece of advice I would like to share with you if you do intend to day trade, then try the futures markets and do not use less than 50 percent of the initial margin requirement. Some brokerage firms will only let you day trade or initiate a trade with 100 percent of the initial margin monies. Other companies will let you day trade the stock indexes like the E-mini S&Ps for under $1,000. I will share with you my thoughts on position sizing for day trading futures.

- Risk 15 percent per trade of the initial margin based on a 25,000 account.

As of April 10, 2012 the initial margin on the E-mini S&P 500 futures contract was $4,375. Using the preceding guideline, that would be approximately $650. If your stop is three full E-Mini S&P points, each point is $50, then use a $150 stop-loss; if you take $650, divide by $150 and you will round out to see that your lot size is four (4) contracts.

- Use 50 percent of the initial margin requirement per day trade, applying 40 percent of your trading capital.

When determining your lot or position size, on a $25,000 account using 40 percent of your trading capital would give you a result of $10,000. Using the rule of 50 percent of the margin requirement, if the margin requirement is $4,275, half of that is rounded out to $2,130, so a maximum lot size per day trade would be 4.69 positions. In this example, it is best to round down to four contracts.

One tactic that I have never attempted to is to add day trade positions. Typically, I am all-in on the entry, or at times I will scale in and use limit orders for a pullback, as I will show in the next few pages. Time is not on our side, as the game ends at the close of the day. That is why I do not add to positions when I am day trading; I am merely participating in a momentum play.

AVERAGE TRUE RANGE

How much can a market move on any given day? The average true range (ATR) provides insight into how much the market can move, based on past and current market data. The true range equals the greatest of the following:

- The difference between today's high and today's low.
- The difference between today's high and yesterday's close (if market gaps higher).
- The difference between today's low and yesterday's close (if market gaps lower).

The average true range is a moving average, generally 14 days of the true range. I like to narrow the field to a 10-day moving average. Since there are 5 trading days in a week, this keeps the data within the two most recent weeks of market action.

The importance of this information is that if the ATR for the E-Mini S&P is 15 points and the market has moved 18 points, then you should be carefully considering exiting the trade. Professional traders watch the ATR and begin covering or reversing positions when the market has reached the ATR for the day. You may miss part of the move, but on average, you will be much better off. Another reason we can use the ATR data is that, due to the leverage involved in the futures markets, it is important to be aware of each markets point move value in respect to the margin requirement. The ATR may help you understand the nature of a market's potential move. This may also aid you in being overexposed to leveraged positioning, which leads to excessive risk taking.

For example, as of April 10, 2012, live cattle has an initial margin requirement of $1,620 per contract. Every 100-point move represents a $400 dollar value. If live cattle moves from 114.00 up to 115.00, that is a $400 value move. If over the past 10 trading sessions the average daily trading range has been 194 points, which would be $776, that is about 47.5 percent of the initial margin requirement. The chart in Figure 10.3 shows the ATR 10-day simple moving average (SMA) calculation, which

FIGURE 10.3 LC2-201206: Live Cattle (Comb) June 2012 (Daily Bars)

reflects the recent trading range environment. With this type of volatility, one would want to reevaluate the lot size positioning formula. As we see volatility or daily price moves increase from the normal level, decrease your lot size to accommodate these swings.

Now let's compare the cattle market volatility—or percent of daily price range—to that of the E-Mini S&P. At the time this book was being written, the S&P futures contracts had a 17-point average daily range, as calculated by an ATR using a 10-day SMA. This would represent an $850 daily trading range value, which is just over 19 percent of the initial margin requirement. Examine Figure 10.4. As you can see at point A on the chart, in the middle of December, the 10-day ATR was at 30 points. We have had times in recent memory, such as August 2011, when the 10-day ATR spiked to 57 points, and in October 2008 we spiked to 96 points.

As you can see, market conditions change, and you need to adjust to these changes as an investor and a trader. Proper position sizing will make you money when you are correct in your analysis and will preserve your

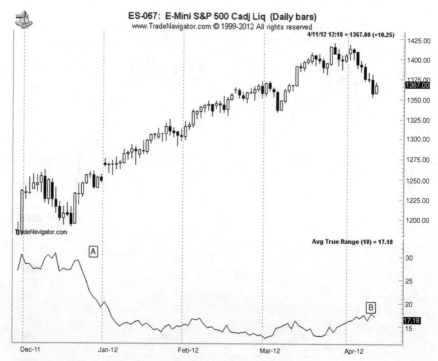

FIGURE 10.4   ES-067: E-Mini S&P 500 Cadj Liq. (Daily Bars)

capital when you are wrong. You are investing to win; trade the markets with an edge. Adding good position-sizing techniques when you put on a trade helps give you an additional edge.

TWICE BAKED

Correlated markets or being positioned in correlated markets can also get you into trouble. That is another reason why I like using the comparative relative strength (RS) charting technique. It helps to identify strong inversely correlated market relationships. Let's look at a scenario involving stocks and bonds. If you are long stocks in a seasonally strong period for equities and at the same time, short Treasury bonds when they are in a seasonally weak period, then you are essentially in the same trade twice. If the trade goes bad, you get burned on both trades, or twice baked.

Remember that traders can be in a long "the yield" component ETF for Treasury bonds, (the TBT), as bond prices have an inverted relationship with yield. When yield goes up, prices go down. Or, one can be short the pricing component ETF, (the TLT). In any case, if you are long stock index ETFs—such as the DIA, SPY, IWM, or QQQ,—or high-beta stocks that correlate well with the overall market and a bond position, even with a good risk-to-reward ratio, it is important to verify that the market you are trading is not overweighted with correlated positions, especially when using various ETFs and inverse-leveraged ETFs.

Here is why: If bad news—like a surprise negative employment number, or earnings reports on not one, but a few stocks in the financial sector—hit the market, we just might see stocks go down, resulting in a loss, and bonds go up, resulting in yet another loss, which in this case compounds the loss factor. Despite the fact that you adhered to a good percentage of risk per trade of investment capital, you are in virtually the same trade. That is valuable information: Be aware of market relationships as they relates to your overall position-size guidelines.

Another concept we need to discuss is along the lines used in gambling known as "pressing your bet." In the movie *Caddyshack*, one of the many famous lines was "Gambling is illegal at Bushwood, sir." Well, believe it or not, there is gambling on the golf course. If you ever bet playing golf, you know what it means when you hear "let's press the back nine." Or if you have played blackjack, you have heard "press your bets when you're winning and hold back when you are losing." To many, this does not make sense. Hand after hand of losing to the dealer makes people get angry and try to increase their bets on a losing streak. This is usually fatal.

Trading stocks is similar. If you have picked a stock using the steps in this book and start feeling a bit like a superhero and decide to step up your position size or press your bet, there is a time and place for that. There is also a time and place for lowering your position size in periods of drawdowns. Be aware; adverse market declines are usually unplanned occurrences. However, we do have coincidences with seasonal trends that typically connect with adverse moves. A recent example was the "flash crash" in May 2010. Typically, we have a stock market that peaks in May, thus the phrase "Sell in May and go away." Volume studies and other tools can help give hints to some of these events, as long as you know what to look for. Hopefully, the material in this book will be a tremendous service to you in your trading career.

ORDER ENTRY USING PPS

The Person's Pivot Study (PPS) that is on TD Ameritrade's platform is a bullish and bearish momentum indicator. There are two moving averages. For the record, the signals are not generated by the crossover of the averages; there are other proprietary criteria that generate the arrows. The moving averages are there to help confirm the trend. When the trend is bullish, the moving averages will act as support in relationship to the low of the candles. Examine Figure 10.5. This is the same stock in the same time frame as in Figure 10.2. The difference is that this is from TD Ameritrade's thinkorswim (TOS) platform using Person's Pivots with the PPS indicator overlaid onto the price chart. You can see that the HCD is still at the predicted pivot support, but the bullish arrow shows up two candles later. As you examine the price-to-moving-average relationship, see how this series of moving averages defines the uptrend and acts as support.

SNAP-BACK TECHNIQUE

One of my order entry tactics when using the PPS is if a buy signal is generated and the risks—or distance from entry to where my stop needs to be placed—is excessive, I will simply scale into 50 percent of the position at the best know price and then place a limit order to enter approximately 75 percent from the distance of the close to the last known value of the moving average. So, if the stock price closed at 37.90 and the moving average is at 37.10, the difference is $0.80. The 75 percent rule would be a value of $0.60 (75 percent of $0.80) subtracted from 37.90. Half of my position would be entered to buy at 37.90, and the balance would be placed on a

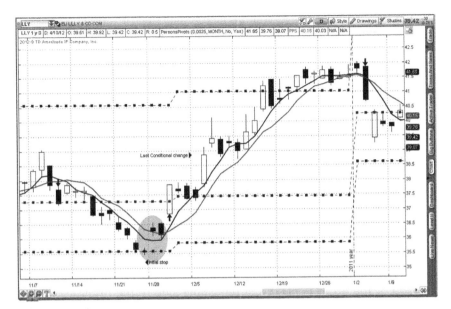

FIGURE 10.5 Eli Lilly and Company
© TD Ameritrade IP Company, Inc.

limit order at 37.30. This way, I would be in the trade in case it takes off so as not to miss the signal and trade setup. If the market pulls back, I have reduced my risk and lowered my average price. It's not the best price, but it would certainly be the best average price.

ORDER TYPES

Throughout the book, we have covered entering orders for getting into and out of the market, but I have not covered exactly how and why to do this. Typically, the most common types of orders to enter and exit a position are limit orders, market orders, and stop orders. Here is a quick rundown: For the veteran trader, I don't want to bore you with page-filler information, and for the beginner, you can download order types on almost any web site, but I will briefly explain how and when it's appropriate to use specific order types.

- *Market order.* A market order does not specify a price; it is executed at the best possible price available. A market order can keep the customer from "chasing" a market. When you place a market order to buy or go long a stock, you are simply meeting or hitting the asking price. When you are selling to liquidate or initiate a short position, a market order is simply hitting the bid.

- *Limit order.* The limit order is an order to buy or sell at a designated price. Limit orders to buy are placed below the current price, while limit orders to sell are placed above the current price. Even though you may see the market touch a limit price several times, this does not guarantee or earn the trader a fill at that price. In most instances, the market usually must trade through the limit price for you to get a fill. When you place a limit order to buy and the market trades down to that exact level and your order gets filled, you may get a little nervous, as this is an indication that the lows are not in. However, there have been times in recent history that, when placing a limit order to buy a pullback near a support (pivot level or moving average), we have had fills, which refutes this misconception.

- *One cancels the other (OCO).* This is a combination of two orders written on one order ticket. This instructs the platform that once one side of the order is filled, the remaining side of the order should be canceled. By placing both instructions on one order, rather than two separate orders, we eliminate the possibility of a double fill. This is a great order to use when setting the stop-loss and the profit objective on a trade. Most platforms allow for good until canceled (GTC) or open orders.

- *Stop orders.* Many traders focus so much of their time on entry methods that they fail to recognize the very important aspect of managing the trade once the entry is successful. Stop orders are very useful tools when placed at price points where you want to enter or exit a trade and assist you in maintaining the risk management guidelines you have established. Buy stop orders are designed to stop the loss on short trades and are placed above the current market price. Sell stop orders, on the other hand, are placed below the current market price and are designed to stop the loss on buy orders.

Stop orders can be used for three purposes: (1) to minimize a loss on a long or short position, (2) to protect a profit on an existing long or short position, or (3) to initiate a new long or short position.

- *Stop-limit orders.* A stop-limit order lists two prices and is an attempt to gain more control over the price at which your stop is filled. The first part of the order is written like the above stop order. The second part of the order specifies a limit price. This indicates that once your stop is triggered, you do not wish to be filled beyond the limit price.

Stop-limit orders should usually not be used when trying to exit a position.

- *Stop close only.* The stop price on a stop close only (SCO) will be triggered only if the market touches the stop during the close of trading. The disadvantage of this order is that a fast market in the last few minutes of trading may cause the order to be filled at an undesirable price. It can, however, protect the customer from having it filled during adverse price fluctuations during the course of the day. Some futures markets accept SCOs, but most do not, so we usually use a "mental" SCO. This means we do not place a physical stop order on the trading platform. We wait until the market closes and then exit using a market order or, in case of a fast-moving depth of market (DOM), by clicking on the asking price. This situation can happen in stocks, especially in the after-hours session during earnings season.

STOP SELECTION

There are four types of stops, but one can also use volatility and volume to reduce or increase positions, so these two variables could be considered your stop-loss criteria. Most traders, though, look at risking a set dollar amount first. I do not like this concept, as I prefer to give each trade the parameters needed. If the stop level is wide but the trade has been defined from a high probability setup based on price patterns, then I would rather reduce my position size and go with the price level stop method. Such is the case in the HCD setup. If we expect immediate results within one to three time periods—let's say five days—or periods transpire without a positive move, then I would apply a time element stop and exit the position. My favorite trailing stop method uses what I call the *condition change concept.* Here are the stop methods:

- *Monetary stop.* Maximum amount of money you are willing to lose.
- *Price-level stop.* Maximum price fluctuation you are willing to accept.
- *Time element stop.* Maximum time you will allow the trade to run.
- *Conditional change stop.* If the price pattern conditions change, then you will exit the trade.

The last conditional change concept is fairly simple. Once the market moves in the desired direction, for example, if I am long and prices rise, I like to trail or move my stop-loss order up until the price of the stock or trading instrument reaches the profit objective. Bullish conditions are defined by higher highs, and higher lows, but remember, I like to define the health of the bullish trend with closes greater than past or prior highs. That is the conditional trend change candle. So when a candle breaks out and closes above a past high, I like to place a stop-loss under that candle's low and the beneath both moving averages. This ensures I am protected and it keeps my stop from being hit prematurely. Remember, if the moving averages act as support, then we should not trade beneath them in a bullish market environment. Figure 10.6 points out a last conditional change candle; it is the tall white candle. As prices continue higher, I like to adjust the stops on the balance of positions left on, until the market has reached its price objective. So remember, when long and placing a sell stop for protection, it must be:

1. Beneath the low of a last conditional change candle.
2. Beneath the lows of both moving averages.

If you are using the last conditional change methodology when establishing a short position, simply apply the opposite approach:

1. The buy stop goes above the high of the last conditional change candle.
2. The buy stop is also above both moving averages.

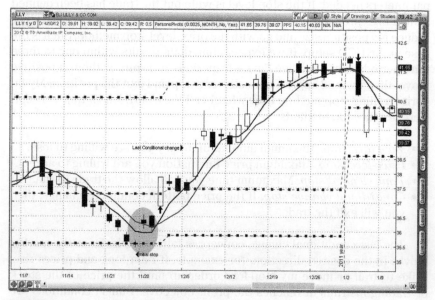

FIGURE 10.6   Eli Lilly and Company
© TD Ameritrade IP Company, Inc.

Trailing stops are designed to maintain a profitable trade while allowing the trader to let profits ride. Trailing stops are adapted to changes in market volatility. The last conditional change approach is my preferred method. It is important to try to maximize your trading results and stay in profitable trades as long as possible. Trailing stops are used in an attempt to lock in some of the paper profits that could accrue should the market move in the direction desired. Like an ordinary stop, the trailing stop is started at some initial value, but is then moved up (in a long trade) or down (in a short trade) as the market moves in your favor. Remember to always place a stop to try and limit losses, and once the trade is entered, adjust the stop as the trade matures. Remember, it is just as important where you get into a trade as it is where you get out.

THE EXIT

Many traders comment that they struggle with their exit strategies. Every trader is familiar with the saying, "Cut your losses and let your profits run." Amazingly, we do the opposite. By attempting to be conservative with our trades, we exit with a 1 or 2 percent gain, only to watch the market explode over time with a double or triple value move. Conversely, novice and even experienced traders will hold on to a losing position, waiting and hoping to get a better exit price or for the market to come back in their favor. Even the CEOs of major trading firms employ that mentality. One such incident comes to mind with MF Global. Talk about a career ender!

Incorporating an exit strategy and planning the strategy prior to entering the trade will assist the trader in not making premature exits and not over trading their account (not to mention holding onto losers). A successful trader must learn how to get out of a losing trade, place stops properly, and know when to take a profit. Successful traders lose. That is part of the business. The trader that masters the exit strategy in his or her trading system will find that the losers are small and the winners are large.

Part of a good exit strategy is learning the "scale out strategy." When a market makes a move and consolidates, the trader has three options: Get out of all positions, add to positions, or take off partial positions. I have discussed the partial exit strategy of 50 percent after reaching the initial risk factor, specifically for HCD and LCD setups.

In any trade, if the reason for your entry has changed, exit the trade. For example, if you entered a trade based on key support levels and the support fails, do not wait for your stop to get you out. Exit the trade immediately. This would apply in any trade situation, such as trend-line violations, reversal failure, or the timing element of the setup. If a pattern exists that typically the market should move in a prescribed time, take an HCD pattern or a wedge formation. Here we know that the typical setup is that prices do not trade beyond 70 to 80 percent of the distance to the apex. If prices trend sideways, this is not a typical wedge formation and you should not wait to get stopped out of the trade; simply exit the position and live for another trading day.

EXPECTATIONS

Without exception, new traders venture into trading with a mind-set of how much money they can make with their trading. They will have calculated their expected return on a daily, weekly, monthly, and yearly basis. These calculations, without fail, far exceed the amounts that are achieved by professional traders. In addition, these calculations rarely take into account that a new trader will need time to learn the basics of the markets, components of a trade strategy, development and testing of a trade strategy, building a business model, trading plan, and implementation strategy.

Realistic expectations will assist the trader by providing a framework on which to build their business of trading. Understand that there are many steps in the process and that assigning adequate time and resources to each of the steps will support the overall goal of becoming a successful trader and will alleviate unnecessary frustration.

DISCIPLINE

Self-control, mastery of self, willpower, hard work, and persistence all bring thoughts of discipline. What separates a disciplined trader from an undisciplined trader?

- Time for learning and development
- Process design and analysis
- Evaluation of systems
- Implementation
- Modification
- Maintenance

A disciplined trader has taken the time to learn about themselves and their business in order to build their trading business around their strengths and weaknesses. Once the process is completed, the disciplined trader has worked toward mastery and self-discipline required to implement, modify, track and maintain the system.

Below are some suggestions from our Trading Triggers classes that assist individuals in developing discipline for their trading:

Set the stage for success. Make certain you are exercising self-control in all areas of your life. If you have no discipline in the rest of your life, your trading business will reflect this lack of discipline.

Match your trading style to your lifestyle. If you have no desire to sit in front of the computer all day, then day trading is probably not the best choice for your trading style.

Build your business like a professional. Trading as a hobby is very expensive. Give yourself the time and capital to get set up properly.

Trade the right size for your risk tolerance and size of trading account. Overleveraging and overtrading increase stress and the risk of unrecoverable loss.

Don't lose sight of the bigger picture. Always knowing what is happening on the longer-term charts is a big key to not getting trapped in a big losing trade.

Set realistic goals and expectations. Setting goals and expectations that are not achievable sets a course of self destruction.

Practice, practice, practice. Then practice again. Trading will become second nature only after you have executed hundreds of trades. Reinforcement of positive behavior and results will decrease rogue trading behavior.

"I've missed more than 9,000 shots in my career. I've lost almost 300 games. Twenty-six times, I've been trusted to take the game winning shot and missed. I've failed over and over and over again in my life. And that is why I succeed."

—Michael Jordan

As a trader, you are the final decision maker for each individual trade and your trading business as a whole. Taking the time to educate yourself, building your skill sets, developing a trading plan, writing a business plan, and having reasonable expectations will provide you with the necessary tools to make your business a success.

All the best to you in all your trading endeavors.

John Person

About the Author

John Person is a 33-year veteran of the futures and options trading industry. He started on the floor of the Chicago Mercantile Exchange in 1979 and then had the privilege of working with George Lane, the innovator of the stochastic indicator. John has worked throughout the industry as an independent trader, broker, analyst and branch manager for one of Chicago's largest discount/full-service firms under the direct supervision of a former chairman of the Chicago Board of Trade.

John is the author of several top-rated trading courses and books, including *The Complete Guide to Technical Analysis for the Futures Markets, Candlestick and Pivot Point Trading Triggers, Forex Conquered: High Probability Systems*, and *Strategies for Active Traders*, and he is co-author of the *Commodity Trader's Almanac* series, all published by John Wiley and Sons. He was the first ever to introduce traders to a powerful combination of candlesticks and pivot point analysis.

In 1998, John developed his own proprietary trading system and began publishing *The Bottom-Line Financial and Futures Newsletter*, a monthly publication that incorporates fundamental developments, as well as technical analysis that includes the data from his trading system, his powerful Person's Pivots indicator, and his moving average methodology, which created the PPS indicator on TD Ameritrade's thinkorswim platform. In addition, John publishes "PA Stock Alerts," with daily and weekly stock trades and video analysis on select stocks and ETF's. The nation's most respected business journalists call on John for his market opinions, and he is widely quoted by CBS Market Watch, Reuters, Dow Jones, as well as having appeared regularly on CNBC, Bloomberg and Fox News. He is a sought-after speaker for many of the world's top professional organizations, such as the IFTA, ATAA and the MTA, as well as some of the country's top national investment conferences. John can be followed on Twitter at http://twitter.com/Personsplanet.

Index

Printed and bound by CPI Group (UK) Ltd, Croydon, CR0 4YY

16/04/2025

14658446-0004